Toward the Validation of Dynamic Psychotherapy

A Replication

Toward the Validation of Dynamic Psychotherapy

A Replication

D. H. Malan
Tavistock Clinic

PLENUM MEDICAL BOOK COMPANY · New York and London

Library of Congress Cataloging in Publication Data

Malan, David Huntingford.
  Toward the validation of dynamic psychotherapy.

  Bibliography: p.
  Includes index.
  1. Psychotherapy—Evaluation. 2. Psychotherapy—Cases, clinical reports, statistics. I. Title. [DNLM: 1. Psychotherapy. WM420 M237t]
RC480 M34   616.8'914   76-10182
ISBN 0-306-30896-7

Acknowledgments

This book consists of an examination of evidence provided by a large number of contributors.

The investigation of brief psychotherapy at the Tavistock Clinic was founded by Michael Balint in 1955, and the therapeutic work was carried out by a team including myself and the following other therapists: Enid Balint, J. L. Boreham, R. H. Gosling, J. J. M. Jacobs, Agnes Main, T. F. Main, M. Pines, E. H. Rayner, and J. L. Rowley.

The replication was designed and planned in collaboration with E. H. Rayner, who is co-author of chapters 3, 11, and 13; P. Dreyfus made independent judgments and is co-author of chapters 9 and 10; E. S. Heath, H. A. Bacal, and F. H. G. Balfour made independent judgments and are co-authors of chapter 3. Independent judgments were also made by R. Shepherd.

The work was supported by the David Matthew Fund of the London Institute of Psychoanalysis, and the Mental Health Research Fund; and the final preparation of the manuscript was supported by the Sigmund Sternberg Trust.

I have been advised throughout on statistical methods by Dr. A. R. Jonckheere of the Department of Psychology, University College, London.

A number of postgraduate students from Dr. Jonckheere's Department performed statistical calculations for me. Of these I should like to mention especially (in chronological order) Miss Esther Saraga, Mr. Richard Rawles, and Mr. Charles Owen.

Finally I should like to thank Mrs. Kathleen Sargent, who has been associated with this work from the beginning both as secretary and research assistant.

Contents

Contents

1

The Current Position of Research in Psychotherapy

More than ten years of research in any field, during which thousands of scientific papers are written, might be expected to yield many important definitive conclusions. At no time has this been true of psychotherapy, which of all subjects is one of the least amenable to scientific study. The overall result of the period leading up to 1963, when my previous book, *A Study of Brief Psychotherapy*, was published, had been little other than confusion. What of the period since then?

In 1973 I started to write the present chapter as a historical review of research in psychotherapy; but, eventually realizing how quickly such a review would become out of date, I published this as a separate article (Malan, 1973a). Here I shall discuss only some of the broadest trends.

These seem to have been largely negative and consist of the following:

1. The inability to demonstrate, from controlled studies, that psychotherapy brings about any greater improvement than life experience alone;

2. The lack of impact of research on clinical practice; and

3. The despair about research expressed by many leading workers in the field (see Bergin and Strupp, *Changing Frontiers*, 1972).

In my 1973 article I expressed some hope that these trends were beginning to be reversed, but I cannot say that the evidence—particularly insofar as dynamic psychotherapy was concerned—was very striking.

One of the strongest pieces of evidence seemed to lead to the extraordinary conclusion that dynamic psychotherapy had been more or less validated for psychosomatic conditions, and for nothing else. Luborsky, Singer, and Luborsky (1975) have since carried out an extremely careful review of controlled studies of all kinds of psychotherapy, which confirms on the one hand that certain conclusions do by now seem reasonably certain (including that for psychosomatic conditions); and on the other hand—considering the amount of work that has been done—that positive results are surprisingly meager.

Here I should add a fourth pessimistic trend, namely the growing view that therapeutic factors in most (or all) forms of psychotherapy are really nonspecific and have nothing to do with the specific elements in technique advocated by each school and supported by a mass of sophisticated theory. The chief advocate of this point of view has been Jerome Frank, and it was the main theme of his contributions reported in *Changing Frontiers*. Strupp (Bergin and Strupp, 1972, pp. 106 ff.) has passed through a phase in which he strongly held the same opinion, though in fact later experience with a controlled study of psychotherapy has now led him to return to a more optimistic view. However, before this happened, he wrote an article entitled "Toward a Reformulation of the Psychotherapeutic Influence" (1974), in which he forcefully suggested that the therapeutic factors in psychoanalysis itself do not consist of what analysts have always supposed—insight, the making of the unconscious conscious, or the corrective emotional experience resulting from the working through of the transference relationship and the discovery of its roots in childhood. Rather, these therapeutic factors consist of entirely nonspecific factors such as gaining a subtle control over the patient by the use of the fundamental rule, and modifying hitherto fixed neurotic patterns by identification or a kind of deconditioning. Strupp thus called in question much of the theoretical structure of psychoanalytic psychotherapy.

It is fascinating that some of the trends that were characteristic of traditional psychotherapies have now begun to show themselves in behavior therapy as well. The tendency in traditional psychotherapy has been from *clinical studies* suggesting powerful and specific therapeutic effects, toward *research studies* giving null results against controls and suggesting that any effective factors are nonspecific. The tendency in behavior therapy has been slightly different but the end result is similar: from clinical studies (Wolpe, 1958) suggesting powerful therapeutic effects; to *research studies on volunteers* confirming these therapeutic effects in comparison with either untreated controls or traditional psychotherapies (see Rachman, 1971 for a review); to *research studies on patients* giving a much less strikingly positive comparison with either untreated controls or traditional psychotherapy (for a review of the latter type of comparison, see Luborsky *et al.*, 1975). Moreover, there has been a tendency in behavior therapy also for nonspecific effects to appear to be unexpectedly powerful, e.g., the credibility of the treatment, or the demand on the patient to show an improvement, with the result that control treatments or what are intended to be pseudotreatments are sometimes unexpectedly effective. An example of such a study is that by Gelder, Bancroft, Gath, Johnston, Mathews, and Shaw (1973) in which desensitization and flooding were compared with a treatment that consisted essentially of free-associa-tion—without interpretation—to the anxiety-provoking stimulus. The result of this carefully designed study was essentially null, and the authors wrote: "The results suggest that current theories about the mechanisms underlying behavioral treatments are inadequate and in need of revision."

In fact, to an outside observer, it almost looks as if the main conclusion to come out of research on behavior therapy so far is that a patient will tend to improve if his anxiety is both aroused and reduced *in any situation that he strongly believes to be therapeutic*. Psychothera-pists may be forgiven if they experience some wry satisfaction.

Yet, at least behavior therapists are making a determined and realistic attempt to find the truth, and the next step is to go on to identify these nonspecific factors, which may not be so nonspecific as they appear to be at first sight. Unfortunately a similar statement cannot in general be made of psychotherapists. Here we find the same paralyz-ing weakness as has been there from the beginning, the split between researchers and clinicians. If we go on in the same way as before, there seems little evidence to suggest that the state of confusion that marks the field will be improved in ten years from now, or twenty, or any other figure one cares to name.

Both researchers and clinicians are in the position of a patient in a prolonged analysis, who needs a major interpretation to give him insight into his lifelong neurotic behavior patterns. It has been said, I think by Karen Horney, that a breakthrough in the therapy of some really refractory character problems can only come when the patient is finally brought to the realization that he *cannot go on like this*. It may well be true that both researchers and clinicians have by now reached this point, and just as in an analysis, the basic interpretations have been staring them in the face for years. To take researchers first, throughout their history they have suffered from a typically irrational form of thinking based on what Freud would call the primary process, which may be illustrated by the following true story: When, on a visit to the capital of Uganda many years ago, I asked a taxi driver to take me to Burton Street, triumphantly he deposited me at Speke Street. There was no relation between the two except that he knew the whereabouts of the one and not the other; by taking me to Speke Street he satisfied his need to take me *somewhere*. Translated, too many researchers have all along been studying meaningless and irrelevant variables, in order to measure *something*, because it is too difficult to isolate and measure meaningful and relevant ones.

This applies above all to outcome criteria. It should surely be clear by now that such measures as the Q-sort and MMPI are almost valueless unless they can be *interpreted*: A major increase in the self-ideal correlation can occur through defensive idealization; a major improvement in the MMPI profile, through the avoidance of a specific stress or the satisfaction of a neurotic need—in neither case is the change likely to be a desirable one. It is clear from Truax's opinions expressed in *Changing Frontiers* (see p. 324) that he must by now realize this. Unless outcome criteria can take account of the *meaning* of changes, and can consider the *patient and his environment as a whole*, they are only too likely to give false results.

The converse of this is illustrated by the Final Report of the Menninger Project (Kernberg, Burstein, Coyne, Appelbaum, Horwitz, and Voth, 1972). Here the outcome criteria fulfill the required conditions; and in the last paragraph we suddenly come across the following statement: "The clinical implications of the findings . . . have been or are being incorporated into the clinical practice of the Menninger Clinic" (p. 195). In other words, in contrast to Strupp's oft-repeated theme, research has immediately influenced clinical practice.

But this kind of statement is very exceptional, and the vast majority of clinicians still believe either that meaningful research in psychotherapy is impossible, or else that at best it can only lead to results that everyone knows already. This is emphatically not so. The contribution to knowledge that has been made by psychoanalysis, which is of course almost inestimable, conceals areas of ignorance perhaps almost as vast. The outpouring of wasted scientific papers by researchers is matched by a similar outpouring of generalizations from single cases, armchair theorizing, and ideological beliefs from clinicians. These have provided hypotheses enough for the next hundred years; but, with very few exceptions, no one bothers to set about testing them. Little further advance can come without the systematic study of larger samples by methods designed to exclude the fallacies inherent in drawing conclusions from clinical impression. Clinicians need researchers to design experiments for them. In turn, researchers need clinicians to ensure that the variables studied are relevant.

An example of what can be achieved by this kind of combined approach, without the necessity for any advanced statistics, was provided many years ago by the work of Bieber (1962) on male homosexuals treated by analysis. From this emerged two major findings, one of which had never been reached—though it had been approached—by clinical methods alone, while the other was in direct contradiction to clinical impression. The first was a predominant family pattern in homosexuals (the "close-binding intimate" mother and the detached-hostile father) leading at once to evidence about psychopathology; the second was the highly encouraging results of therapy. Yet, this has been followed by studies on different populations of homosexuals (e.g., Bene, 1965), in which the same family pattern has not been confirmed, suggesting at once that homosexuals who never come to analysis may differ from those who do. If a systematic study of this kind comes up against fallacies to do with sampling, how much more likely is clinical impression to do so?

Again, if clinical impression is inadequate in the area of psychopathology, how much more inadequate has it shown itself in the area of therapeutic results? As far as neurotic problems are concerned, no one really knows even *whether* psychoanalytic methods are effective, let alone which patients they are effective with or what elements in technique are responsible for their effectiveness. As an example, we regularly refer for analysis patients with severe disturbances that clearly go back to what Balint would call the Basic Fault. What chances have such patients of substantially benefiting from analysis or of being made worse? Which patients benefit and which are made worse? There is no information on which to begin to answer these questions. They can only be answered by systematic research, but the motivation for such an undertaking is almost entirely absent. One of the reasons, I am afraid, is that our methods are probably far less therapeutically effective, and far less widely effective, than we would like to believe. Over this issue there has been a degree of denial that can only be described as shameful, a mental mechanism of which we were supposed to have been cured by our training analyses. One of the results has been increasing isolation and defensiveness on the part of the psychoanalytic school, leading in turn to an impression of sterility and decline. In the questionnaire sent out by Bergin and Strupp (1972) to the researchers whom they interviewed, there occurs the question, "Is psychodynamic theory passé as *The New York Times* suggests it is?" In an article in the London *Evening Standard* (1973), the journalist Jeremy Campbell states that, in the United States, behavior therapy "has rushed into the vacuum of failure left by the collapse of Freudian psychology."

Freudian psychology has not collapsed in the United States or anywhere else, but it sometimes gives this impression because it can provide so little tangible evidence about the relevance of its theories or the effectiveness of its methods. A crucial result is that no one knows what contribution it can make to the over-riding medical problem in the world today, the mental health of humanity.

Thus, if researchers are suffering from "primary process" thinking, clinicians are suffering from thinking that is no less irrational. Here we come to the interpretation directed at clinicians: The undoubted difficulty of carrying out research on material of such subtlety and complexity is being used as a defense against anxiety, the anxiety of finding that cherished beliefs are incorrect or that therapeutic methods are ineffective. The isolation of clinicians from research is leading to a position as sterile as the isolation of research from clinicians.

There is nothing difficult about the solution. All that is needed is the principle on which the Menninger study is based, the *objective* handling by researchers of *subjective* judgments made by trained clinicians. As the following pages will show, the anxieties described above may turn out to be unfounded, the therapeutic methods may be found to be effective, and basic psychoanalytic principles may be confirmed.

2

Design of the Second Study of Brief Psychotherapy

My previous book, *A Study of Brief Psychotherapy* (1963), referred to in future by the initials *SBP*, was the result of working up the first twenty-one patients treated by a research team founded in 1955 by Michael Balint, whose aim was to examine from first principles the whole question of psychoanalytic brief psychotherapy.

While the results on the first twenty-one patients were being worked up, Balint's team continued to function and treated a further thirty-nine patients in all. These patients were thus available for a replication of the original study, for which we were given grants by the David Matthew Fund of the London Institute of Psychoanalysis and the Mental Health Research Fund, which we here gratefully acknowledge. Mr. Eric Rayner, one of the members of Balint's team, was my chief collaborator in this work.

AIMS OF THE STUDY

The aim was to replicate the previous study with longer follow-up and more rigorous scientific safeguards. The main results of this previous study had been as follows:

Clinical observations

1. That important and apparently permanent dynamic changes could follow brief psychotherapy (ten to forty sessions);

2. That these could occur in patients with relatively extensive and long-standing psychopathology; and

3. That the technique used could be thoroughly radical and involve all the main types of interpretation occurring in full-scale analysis, including interpretation of dreams and fantasies, analysis of resistance, interpretation of the transference, and the link between the transference and childhood.

Statistical findings

1. *Severity of pathology* (within wide limits) and *duration of complaints* did not appear to bear any relation to outcome; i.e., severe pathology and long duration were not contraindications in themselves.

2. The only selection criterion that appeared to be of any value was *motivation for insight,* especially if its fluctuations during the initial stages of therapy were taken into account. High or increasing motivation tended to correlate with favorable outcome, and low or decreasing motivation with unfavorable outcome.

3. Thorough interpretation of the transference seemed to play an important part in leading both (a) to favorable outcome, and (b) to an optimum relationship with the therapist after termination (as shown by the patient's behavior over follow-up).

4. Those therapies tended to be more successful in which (a) transference interpretation became important early; (b) the negative transference was interpreted; and (c) the patient's feelings about termination became an important issue.

5. Of all aspects of transference interpretation, the most important seemed to be the link between the transference and the relation to parents (the transference/parent or T/P link). The evidence was first examined by clinical judgment and was then confirmed by a content analysis of the case records, a quantitative measure of this kind of interpretation correlating significantly with the scores for outcome.

DESIGN OF THE REPLICATED STUDY OF BRIEF PSYCHOTHERAPY

The basic material for this study, as for the previous one, consisted of (1) full clinical notes dictated from memory by therapists and interviewers, and (2) abbreviated verbatim records of the workshop's discussions transcribed from a secretary's shorthand notes.

An important factor that had to be taken into account in the design was the inability of Rayner and myself to make blind judgments, owing to our heavy contamination by knowledge of what had happened to many of these patients. About a quarter of the patients had been treated by myself or Rayner; and he and I had also read material on all the other patients at the time when therapy was conducted, and had taken part in the discussions on them. A number of patients had already been followed up for a year or two after termination, and we were aware of this material also. The only sense in which we were not contaminated was (1) that we had forgotten most of the details of cases treated by others (some completely), the work having been conducted from three to six years before; and (2) most of the patients had now not been seen for several years, so that there was time for all kinds of further change to have occurred, of which we as yet could have no knowledge.

On the other hand, we were now joined by three more collaborators who could make independent judgments. These were, first, Drs. Howard Bacal and Sheldon Heath, and later Mr. Frederick Balfour, who replaced Dr. Heath when the latter returned to Canada. All were in psychoanalytic training and all were entirely uncontaminated by any previous knowledge of the clinical material. The question was how this advantage could best be used.

Any study of psychotherapy that is to be clinically useful must consist of a correlation of factors in the patients (*selection criteria*) and in therapy (*technique*) on the one hand with *outcome* on the other. In an ideal study, there should be three independent groups of judges, each assessing one of these sets of variables, uncontaminated by knowledge of the others. For tests of reliability, there must of course be at least two judges in each group, which makes six as a minimum requirement. At the time when the project was being planned we had only four judges in all, and we therefore had to make a choice of where lack of contamination was most important.

Of all the variables, *outcome* is both the most crucial and the most difficult to measure. As described in chapter 3, our method of measuring outcome involves matching the changes found at follow-up with criteria of dynamic improvement laid down in advance. The first requirement, therefore, is that the judges who formulate these criteria should be uncontaminated by knowledge (1) of follow-up and (2) of what happened in therapy. We therefore decided that the two uncontaminated judges (Bacal and Heath, Team 2) should be used to assess outcome and nothing else. The initial assessment material, consisting of initial interview, projection test, and first therapeutic session, was submitted to them. From this material, by consensus, they formulated (1) a simple dynamic hypothesis, and (2) criteria of an ideal outcome.

In the meantime Rayner and I (Team 1) agreed not to contaminate ourselves further by rereading anything concerning these patients that had been written after the first therapeutic session. We then, independently of Team 2, carried out the same operations as above. At the same

time we made judgments of the patient's motivation and its fluctuations during the initial assessment period.

Attempts were then made to follow the patients up. We succeeded
with thirty of the thirty-nine patients (77 percent). The follow-up
interviews were mostly conducted by the original therapists. This has
advantages and disadvantages. The main advantage is that the therapist is more likely both to be able to make deep contact with the patient
and to know significant areas in the patient's life that need exploring.
The disadvantage, of course, is that he may be expected to be biased in
his judgments of improvement; in fact, we had strong evidence that
this bias lay in the direction of *undervaluing* his therapeutic results (see
chap. 3 for details).

Where the therapist was not either Rayner or myself, he or she was
given a list of questions to which we needed answers. Rayner and I also
followed up some patients for whom we had not been the therapists.
Accounts of all these interviews were dictated from memory, in a few
cases with the help of tape recordings.

The follow-up material was then submitted to the four members of
the two teams. Each of the four independently gave a score for overall
outcome on a scale of 0 to 4 rising in half-points. The two teams then
met independently, and each formulated a detailed verbal consensus
assessment. In some cases the members of the uncontaminated Team 2
changed their individual scores after their conference together. Team 1
did not do this.

The two members of Team 1, still keeping themselves in ignorance
of the judgments of Team 2, were now allowed for the first time to
reread the accounts of therapy. According to the methods to be
described in chapter 11, each independently made a content analysis of
the therapist's interpretations. We were, of course, already partly contaminated by a knowledge of outcome, but since the content analysis
can be made relatively objective, this was not felt to be a serious
disadvantage.

Once we had completed this, we were allowed to become contaminated with the judgments of outcome by Team 2. The final score for
outcome was taken as the mean of the scores of the four judges.

Although I was now fully contaminated, I decided to make further
judgments of fluctuations in the patient's motivation during the next
five contacts with the clinic after the initial assessment period.

Subsequently we were fortunate in having the help of two further
entirely uncontaminated judges, also both in psychoanalytic training.
These were Dr. Peter Dreyfus and Mr. Ray Shepherd, who made
judgments of a number of selection criteria, using the initial interview

and projection test only; and Dreyfus went on to make judgments of two other variables, session by session, during the patient's first eight contacts with the clinic. These were (1) motivation, and (2) a new variable called *focality*, put forward in *SBP* as a possible selection criterion (see p. 213), which may be defined as the extent to which the therapist has a clear therapeutic plan and can make it the theme of his interpretations.

The clinical material will be presented with these hypotheses in mind, with special reference to those hypotheses that were confirmed, namely, the importance of motivation, focality, and the transference/parent link.

Before this, however, it is necessary to discuss two important issues: first, the outcome scale; and second, the mode of selection of the patients and hence the nature of the sample on which the whole study is based.

3

The Psychodynamic Assessment of Outcome

Written in Collaboration with E. H. Rayner, E. S. Heath, H. A. Bacal, and F. H. G. Balfour

As already mentioned (see chap. 1), two outstanding features of psychotherapy research have been, first, the lack of impact of research on clinical practice, and second, the despair about research expressed by many leading workers in the field. My own belief is that both these features are largely due to the failure to devise outcome criteria that do justice to the complexity of the human personality. Obviously, without valid outcome criteria, much of psychotherapy research is meaningless.

I have written extensively in other publications about the problem of assessing outcome on psychodynamic criteria (Malan, 1959, 1963; Malan, Bacal, Heath, and Balfour, 1968; Malan, Heath, Bacal, and Balfour, 1975; Malan, 1975) to which the reader is referred for further discussion. Here I shall summarize the principles of the method and go on to discuss its conversion into a rating scale.

DEFINING A PSYCHODYNAMIC HYPOTHESIS

In each patient we take the whole evidence provided by the initial assessment material (in the present work, this consisted of the psychiatric interview, projection test, and first therapeutic session), and first try to define a *basic neurotic conflict* that lies at the heart of the patient's difficulties. This is referred to as the *psychodynamic hypothesis*.

13

These hypotheses are kept relatively simple and are always carefully based on the available evidence. They avoid technical terms as far as possible, and employ only the simplest and most widely accepted aspects of psychodynamic theory. They serve several important and related functions, namely, to define by implication for each patient (1) a *specific kind of stress* to which he is vulnerable; (2) the main criterion of recovery, which must obviously consist of his ability to overcome his central difficulty, or to face his specific stress and to cope with it in a new way without developing symptoms; and (3) various ways in which he may *appear* to be recovered without actually being so, which mostly consist of *avoiding* his central difficulty or specific stress rather than facing it and overcoming it.

Having put forward the psychodynamic hypothesis, we then define *criteria of maximum improvement*, tailored for each patient, and—like the hypothesis—formulated before the patient is seen for follow-up. Theoretically, of course, a patient's improvement should be formulated in terms of "resolution" of his conflicts, which is the aim of all forms of psychoanalytic therapy. However, this is a concept that is difficult to define, let alone to measure, and it is therefore necessary to fall back on an operational definition based on behavior or feelings that can be observed or described. According to this definition, resolution is assumed to have taken place when "inappropriate" responses, which include especially the inappropriate reaction to specific stresses, do not merely disappear, but are replaced by other corresponding "appropriate" responses.

The final step consists of a comparison of the actual findings at follow-up with the criteria already laid down, and the giving of a global score.

Discussion of Dynamic Hypotheses and Criteria of Improvement. The following passage is adapted from our second paper on untreated patients (Malan *et al.*, 1975):

There are two main possible types of objection to our procedure, which come from opposite ends of the theoretical spectrum. The first, from the more strictly scientific and less dynamic approach, may suggest that the hypotheses are too subjective and contain too much unvalidated theory, and that the criteria are based on a series of value judgments that are not made explicit and can only be a matter of opinion. The second, from a more psychoanalytic approach, may suggest that the hypotheses are too superficial, often say nothing about certain causal factors, may ignore overdetermination, and may leave the inner mechanisms of some manifestations of the illness quite unexplained. Both objections are best answered by a description of how our procedure developed.

When we started we tried to make our hypotheses "deeper" and more psychoanalytic in an attempt to answer the second type of criticism. The result was absolutely clear, fully justifying the first type of criticism: The independent judges imposed their own theoretical bias on the material, often producing hypotheses that had little in common with one another. The policy that we then needed to adopt in reaching a consensus became equally clear: The amount of theory had to be reduced to the point at which agreement could be reached, and the final result was the *highest common factor* among all the hypotheses that had been made independently. In fact this process coincided exactly with the universal scientific principle of keeping the hypotheses as close as possible to the available evidence.

As far as the criteria are concerned, we accept unashamedly that they contain value judgments, which we believe cannot be avoided. This was discussed at some length in *SBP* (see pp. 49–50). We can only say in the end that since the evidence is published in detail any reader is free to formulate his own hypotheses and criteria, and with these as a basis to make his own judgments of improvement.

A Note on the Dynamic Hypotheses in the Present Series. An important question is whether two teams working independently, which was the situation in the present work, can reach similar hypotheses. Unfortunately, this cannot be fairly tested. The reason is that the accounts of interviews were written on special forms in which the interviewer was asked to put forward his own views about the patient's psychopathology. Thus, any judge was immediately able to base his hypothesis on that of the interviewer, and it is not surprising that on the whole the hypotheses made by the two teams should have borne a strong resemblance to one another.

It also needs to be said that the hypotheses given in the clinical material as presented here are those made by Team 1, Malan and Rayner. Being members of the workshop, we were often contaminated by knowledge of subsequent events. I do not believe this matters. We were very careful to base our hypotheses on the evidence available from the initial assessment material only. Moreover, we have demonstrated on two other and larger series (forty-five untreated patients, see Malan *et al.*, 1968, 1975; fifty-five group patients, see Malan, Balfour, Hood, and Shooter, 1976) that relevant hypotheses that make the assessment of follow-up meaningful can be made by judges who are entirely blind to subsequent events.

THE OUTCOME SCALE

In *SBP* the scale used (see p. 50) consisted of four points: 0, 1, 2, and 3. In the present work this scale has been extended and refined to include (a) a score of 4, (b) half-points, and (c) negative scores where the patient was judged to be "worse." As described in chapter 2, the final score was taken as the mean of four independent judgments. Since the minimum interval in the scale used by each judge was half a point, the minimum interval on the final scale was one half divided by four, or one eighth of a point (0.125).

It needs to be emphasized that patients are so diverse and so complicated that the scale has to be used in an essentially intuitive manner, in which the changes are fed into the computer of clinical judgment, are weighted and integrated, and finally emerge as a global judgment of "improvement" in the form of a single score. For this reason requests for schedules of the scoring system, which we fairly often receive, can only be met by a series of clinical examples. Nevertheless, our experience has been that psychoanalytically trained research workers have little difficulty in grasping the principles, and can achieve reasonable agreement after practice on no more than three or four cases.

Clinical Example. The system is best illustrated by a type of case that occurs quite frequently, namely a patient suffering from:

1. Symptoms;
2. Problems concerned with rivalry, hostility, or self-assertion, in relation to people of the same sex; and
3. Problems of full closeness and sexual satisfaction in relation to the opposite sex.

The best example in the brief therapy series is the Pesticide Chemist,[1] who suffered from:

1. Obsessional anxiety about work;
2. Inability to assert himself at work in such a way as to get his legitimate needs met; and
3. Emotional withdrawal from his wife, together with lack of sexual satisfaction on both sides.

The hypothesis made on the basis of the initial assessment material was approximately correct but was expressed less clearly than what emerged during therapy: namely, that (1) he felt resentful about having too much responsibility put on him; (2) he felt guilty about this resent-

---

[1] The clinical material is given in full in *The Frontier of Brief Psychotherapy* (Malan, 1976).

ment and afraid of expressing it; and therefore (3) defended himself by an exaggerated preoccupation with meeting the demands of others, a position that he could not maintain. The criteria for full resolution follow more or less automatically if the three main disturbances are replaced by the corresponding appropriate feelings and behavior.

We may now examine various hypothetical situations that might be found at follow-up, and the scores for them:

1. The only change observed is loss of *obsessional preoccupation*, but this has clearly been bought at the price of emotional disengagement from his work, and is accompanied by some loss of efficiency. This is a clear-cut false solution and scores 0.

2. The only change is *loss of obsessional preoccupation*, but there is apparently no disengagement or loss of efficiency. The mechanism of such a change would be obscure, but the result would definitely be something of value. This is a standard situation: loss of symptoms without other detectable changes. The score is 1.0 and no more, no matter what the severity of the original symptoms had been.

3. The patient is now found to be able to *demand his rights at work in a constructive and effective way, and his obsessional preoccupations have disappeared. There is no change in the relation with his wife.* This also is a standard situation: apparently genuine resolution of the problem with the same sex, accompanied by loss of symptoms, but no change in the problem with the opposite sex. Because of our emphasis on the importance of close relations with the opposite sex, this scores 2.0 and no more, leaving two whole points for further improvement in this latter problem.

4. This is the situation actually found at follow-up: *All the changes described in 3. had occurred, but in addition there was some limited improvement in the relation with his wife.* All four judges scored 2.5.

5. A score of 3.0 would be given for substantial resolution in the problem with his wife as well, but with some important reservations: 3.5 if there were few reservations; and 4.0 if there were hardly any.

Once more it must be emphasized that although many of the types of change described above represent standard situations found in practice, the changes do not necessarily occur in any clear-cut sequence; and the scale cannot under any circumstances be regarded as one in which half a point is awarded for such and such a change, one point for another, etc., and these points are summed to give a final score. The scale is intuitive and global and represents simply the number of points out of a maximum of 4 that a judge awards to the changes found, when these are weighted and compared with the criteria laid down beforehand.

As already stated, when the final score is the mean of four judgments, it rises in intervals of one eighth of a point, or 0.125. Comparison with verbal judgments of improvement suggests the following rough correspondences:

0–0.5	essentially unchanged
0.625–1.875	slightly to moderately improved
2.0–2.75	improved
2.875–3.375	much improved
3.5–4.0	recovered

A study of our actual cases suggests that any score below 2.0 is not really satisfactory, and thus therapies can be arbitrarily divided into "successful" (≥ 2.0) and "unsuccessful" (< 2.0).

Clinical Meaning of the Scale. The scale has *grown* out of the necessity for treating the outcome of psychotherapy statistically, and some of its properties need to be examined, together with the mental processes involved in arriving at a score.

Introspection suggests that a judge naturally makes his measurement from the end that is nearest, i.e., (1) toward the lower end of the scale, he mainly bases his score on *degree of improvement;* while (2) as he approaches the upper end, he is to a greater and greater extent influenced (in the opposite direction) by *residual disturbance.* This subtle alteration is reflected in the frequently used qualitative scale by a transition in the phrasing, from "much improved" to "recovered." Toward the lower end, therefore, the scale measures improvement, whereas toward the upper end it tends to measure mental health. Nevertheless, it is not a true mental health scale like the Health–Sickness Rating Scale used by the Menninger workers, in which there is room for differences in *initial* as well as final scores (Luborsky, 1962; Kernberg *et al.,* 1972). In our scale, as in the Menninger Absolute Global Change Scale, all patients start from zero, and the extent of possible change is encompassed by the same number of points, no matter what the severity of the initial pathology. This means, for instance, that possible improvements in the severe pathology of such patients as the Stationery Manufacturer and Dress Designer have to be compressed into the same range as those in the relatively mild pathology of the Almoner and Gibson Girl.[2] This disadvantage has to be accepted.[3]

---

[2] The clinical material on these patients is given in *The Frontier of Brief Psychotherapy* (Malan, 1976).

[3] An attempt, probably misguided, to compensate for this was made for the Stationery Manufacturer by one of the judges (DHM), by extending the scale to include a score of 5. In fact this probably just resulted in an overvaluation of outcome in this particular patient.

Although, therefore, scales of this kind contain less information than mental health scales, they have one important advantage: They avoid a statistical artifact that otherwise has to be eliminated by various sophisticated mathematical techniques, namely, that where there is room for more change due to severer initial disturbances, an inevitable statistical result is that the more severely ill patients tend to show greater improvement, and hence, apparently, a better prognosis, which contradicts clinical common sense. For a discussion of these issues in the Menninger study, see Kernberg *et al.* (1972, pp. 20–39, 35, and 249–50).

RELIABILITY

Although this is a subject that is not likely to arouse any great passions and may well be passed over by the reader who wishes to proceed to more interesting matters, it in fact contains a result of almost incalculable importance. This is that the inter-rater reliability for our judgments of outcome has always been satisfactory and most of the time has been strikingly high. In a sense this could be said to be the most important result presented in this book, because it points forward to the proper scientific study of all kinds of psychotherapy, whereas the present work is concerned only with a particular type of patient and a particular type of therapy. Since the opinion has always been widely accepted that such judgments are so subjective and unreliable as not to be worth attempting, this would be publishable in its own right even if the result of our whole study had been entirely null.

The two teams worked in slightly different ways. The contaminated Team 1 (DM and ER) never modified their independent scores after discussion; the blind Team 2 (HB and EH or FB) sometimes did so. Inter-rater reliability between the two members of Team 2 therefore has little meaning. Also, whereas Dr. Bacal, the first member of Team 2, remained throughout the study and scored all thirty patients, Dr. Heath left for Canada after scoring nine patients, and was then replaced by Mr. Balfour.

Counting the composite judge EH/FB as a single judge, this gives five meaningful inter-rater reliabilities. These varied from $r = +0.67$ to $r = +0.82$ with a mean of $r = +0.76$. Perhaps more important, the reliability between the mean of the contaminated Team 1 and that of the blind Team 2 was $r = +0.83$. Comparison of the actual scores on the individual patients (Mean Team 1/Mean Team 2) showed the following:

1. For twenty-one patients (70 percent) the difference was half a point or less.

2. For two patients the difference was more than half a point and less than one point.

3. For five patients the difference was one point.

4. For two patients the difference was more than one point (1.125 and 1.5 respectively).

We can now add to these reliabilities those obtained in our long-term follow-up study of patients who had had group treatment at the Tavistock Clinic (Malan *et al.*, 1976). In this study, also with four independent judges, two of whom were the same as in the present study, inter-rater reliability varied from $r = +0.73$ to $r = +0.83$ with a mean of $r = +0.80$; and the blind/contaminated reliability (usually based on the mean of two judgments in each case) was $+0.89$ ($N = 52$). Thus, the satisfactory agreement obtained in the present study has been not merely repeated but increased.

The generally high values for the inter-rater reliability go some way toward justifying the statistical studies described in *SBP*. These were based on my own single-handed judgments, which now have been shown in two other series to agree to a considerable extent with those of five independent judges. (My own inter-rater reliabilities with these judges have varied from $r = +0.70$ to $r = +0.82$, mean $r = +0.78$.)

Here I should add the following important notes:

1. For eight of the thirty patients, one or other member of Team 1 (DM or ER) was the therapist. One might suppose that these judges would have an unconscious interest in scoring their own patients more highly. In fact, in only two cases was the score given by the therapist higher than the mean given by the other three judges, in one it was equal, and in the other five it was lower. Whatever this means it is at least good public relations!

2. It needs to be asked whether the scores are in accord with clinical judgment. My short answer to this question is yes; and moreover, where clinical judgment suggests the possibility of reconsidering a score in a particular situation, the result almost always is a strengthening of the correlations described in the later part of this book.

3. In some cases we have follow-ups later than those on which the scores are based. Again, in almost all cases, the result is to strengthen the correlations. The most important example of this is the Contralto. At the time of assessing her follow-up, she was still continuing her analysis, and improvements seemed to be minimal. Because the initial stages of her therapy were highly dynamic, she stands out as a glaring exception in several of the important correlations, making a considerable negative contribution. However, she has since completed her analysis with apparently major benefit, and if her probable new score of 3.0 to

3.5 were introduced, this would strengthen the correlations and eliminate her anomalous position altogether. The same applies, though to a much smaller extent, to the most anomalous patient of all, the Dress Designer, who has shown certain improvements since the follow-up on which her score is based.

These considerations can only strengthen one's belief in the clinical meaning of the conclusions reached.

Finally, it is worth comparing our reliabilities with those obtained in the Menninger study. Their outcome measure most relevant to ours is the scale of Global Change (see Kernberg *et al.*, 1972, p. 219), which was rated by two judges using the method of paired comparisons in overlapping batches of twelve patients, and which contained a maximum of twenty-two points that could be awarded by each judge to each patient. They obtained an average rank order reliability of $\rho = +0.93$ at termination and $\rho = +0.74$ at follow-up. Thus, our reliabilities and theirs appear to be of much the same order of magnitude.

When I met Dr. Kernberg at the meeting of the Society for Psychotherapy Research in Philadelphia in 1973, he said that he regarded the problem of measuring outcome on psychodynamic criteria as essentially solved, and I could only agree with him.

4

Criteria for Rejection and the Nature of the Sample

This is an important chapter for two main reasons. First, it gives a detailed account of the criteria that we used for judging that patients were *unsuitable* for our kind of brief psychotherapy, which from a clinical point of view is as important a subject as the criteria used for judging them to be suitable. Here it needs to be said that since in general we did not take such patients on, our rejection criteria have not been properly tested out and are based essentially on clinical common sense. Second, this chapter defines the characteristics of the sample of patients whom we did take on, a preliminary step that is essential to creating a situation in which statistical analysis can become meaningful.

Although much of our own selection procedure was not fully thought out at the time, the following retrospective analysis shows that it was in fact based on clear-cut principles.

Patients were brought for discussion to the workshop at two main stages. The first was the *referral stage*, before the patient was seen, when the information available would consist of an application form and/or a report from a referring agency. At this stage certain types of patient were never considered. The following list of excluding factors is taken from the work of H. P. Hildebrand, who has introduced it into the screening process for patients applying to the London Clinic of Psychoanalysis:

> Serious suicidal attempts
> Drug addiction
> Convinced homosexuality

Long-term hospitalization
More than one course of E.C.T.
Chronic alcoholism
Incapacitating chronic obsessional symptoms
Incapacitating chronic phobic symptoms
Gross destructive or self-destructive acting out

On the other hand, certain positive criteria were used at this stage, which were thought to constitute a *prima facie* case for brief therapy. The underlying principle here was the search for a *discernible simplicity* that, it was hoped, would lead to the possibility of discovering a focus. By a focus is meant, as always, a unifying theme that can be made the basis of interpretations.

This simplicity might mean (1) simplicity of complaints (though we were quite aware that it was naïve to suppose this necessarily implied simplicity of pathology); (2) apparent simplicity of current issues in the patient's life; or (3) the appearance of symptoms in relation to some definite precipitating event. These three often came together in the form of a *current or recent crisis,* which in fact was present in a high proportion both of patients finally accepted and of those accepted for interview and then rejected. This might or might not imply *recent onset,* and it does not introduce as much bias into the sample as might be supposed, since there must always be some reason why a patient seeks treatment at one particular point in time rather than any other.

The second stage at which the patient might be brought for discussion was the *interview stage.* This happened when a member of the workshop, on the lookout for suitable patients, felt that he had found a *prima facie* case in a patient already seen in routine consultation. Here the *prima facie* case might include the factors mentioned above, but in addition it could now be based more firmly on the knowledge of the pathology, the degree of contact and response to interpretation, and the interviewer's ability to think of a possible focus. If accepted at this stage, the patient would go on to *projection test.*

Once the full initial assessment, consisting of interview and projection test, had been completed, the members of the workshop were in a position to project themselves into the future and to undertake an imaginary therapy. It must be emphasized (1) that this can only be done with extensive experience of what actually happens in analytically oriented psychotherapy; and (2) that since our experience was mainly with long-term methods, it was much easier to forecast what would happen in those patients who would need long-term therapy, i.e., easier in those whom we rejected than those whom we accepted.

An analysis of patients interviewed, brought up for discussion, and rejected, shows that the negative criteria that we used can be formulated quite specifically. They consist essentially of various aspects of *inability to find a feasible focus*, which may mean either (1) inability to see any focus or unifying theme for interpretations at all; or (2), with emphasis on the word "feasible," that a unifying theme can be seen but will involve certain specific dangers if an attempt is made to use it in brief therapy. These dangers are summarized in Table 1.

In the companion to the present book, *The Frontier of Brief Psychotherapy* (Malan, 1976), I have described nineteen rejected patients in some detail, to which the reader is referred.

It must be emphasized once more that our predictions of failure of brief therapy were never directly tested. Yet, a partial test by implication can come from a study of what happened in those patients whom we accepted and treated: In none of these did nothing of importance happen; in none was contact never made or only made after months of apparently fruitless work; only one patient was worse at follow-up, while all of the others were at least slightly improved; in only one of those followed up had there been a suicidal attempt. (Mr. Upton); only two patients (Mr. Upton and the Dress Designer) were admitted to the hospital; and although eight therapies could not be terminated within forty sessions, all but two were terminated within one hundred sessions; and, of these two, one was eventually strikingly successful. Indeed, except for Mr. Upton, no patient at follow-up showed total relapse from the position achieved at termination, and many showed

TABLE 1.   Types of Event Forecast in Rejected Patients

Event forecast	Specific danger
1. Inability to make contact.	Inability to start effective therapeutic work within a short time.
2. Necessity for prolonged work in order to generate motivation for treatment.	
3. Necessity for prolonged work in order to penetrate rigid defenses.	
4. Inevitable involvement in complex or deep-seated issues which there seems no hope of working through in a short time.	Inability to terminate.
5. Severe dependence or other forms of unfavorable intense transference.	
6. Intensification of depressive or psychotic disturbance.	Depressive or psychotic breakdown.

marked further improvement. It therefore seems reasonable to suppose that many of the specific dangers included in our implied predictions were, in fact, eliminated in our selection procedure.

Nevertheless, the differences between accepted and rejected patients were subtle and amounted to no more than a matter of degree. They are best presented as the following negative statements: No patient was accepted with whom practically *no* contact could be made; who had *hardly any* motivation for treatment; with whom the workshop could see no *conceivable* focus, however dimly; or with whom *nobody*—especially not even the therapist—believed there was the slightest chance of success.

When these statements have been made, however, there were several patients accepted who were generally believed to be unsuitable, and who were taken on to test our predictions that therapy would fail. Probably the least suitable according to our criteria was the Playwright, of whom the psychologist wrote, "This is most definitely not a focal problem but a chronic character problem." Here, nevertheless, it was felt worthwhile to use the current crisis to see if something could be achieved; but the patient was thought basically unsuitable and the statement was specifically made that the long-term aim was analysis.

A situation that sometimes developed was that the workshop member who had seen the patient thought that he could see a possible focus, against the overwhelming skepticism of the rest of the workshop; and he was then encouraged to go ahead in order to test the overall prediction of failure. This happened most clearly (1) in the Stationery Manufacturer, where the summary of the discussion states, "The general feeling was that this was outside the framework of the workshop," and where the therapist's optimism was spectacularly vindicated; and (2) in the Receptionist, where the summary states, "We all have the impression that this is not a focal therapy case," and where the improvement achieved was much more limited.

In two other severely disturbed patients who were accepted, the possibility of breakdown was clearly envisaged; but it was felt that this could be avoided either by keeping the focus superficial (Mrs. Morley) or by exploring very carefully and gradually (the Military Policeman). In both cases the implied prediction was fulfilled.

Thus, the characteristics of our sample of accepted patients can be relatively simply defined, as follows:

1. Some contact had been made and there was some response to interpretation.

2. Some conceivable focus could be seen.

3. The dangers (see Table 1) of attempting brief therapy did not seem inevitable.

Within these limits the range of patients accepted was very wide indeed. This will be confirmed in later chapters by the wide spread of scores for individual selection criteria, and also for the other important factors to be studied such as transference interpretation and focality.

Nevertheless, it is also clear that as far as *outcome* is concerned, and in marked contrast to our first sample (see chapter 7), the present sample was heavily selected in favor of *improvement*. Here, from a scientific point of view, we are fortunate in having the original sample to turn to for examples of total failure. The reason for this difference between the two samples will be discussed further in chapter 7.

5

The Clinical Material

A major disadvantage of many large-scale studies of psychotherapy is that only the minimum clinical material is published, if any, so that the reader is in no position to judge the kinds of patient selected, the techniques used, and above all, the quality of the therapeutic results. The bare statistics conceal much that is vital to judging any study as a whole. One of the strengths of *SBP* was perhaps that clinical material was given on all the patients treated, and that as much as possible was published of the evidence on which individual judgments were based.

In the present study I have also aimed to publish clinical material on all the patients followed up, but unfortunately this cannot be done in a single volume. In the clinical companion to the present book, *The Frontier of Brief Psychotherapy* (Malan, 1976), eighteen case histories were presented, to which the reader is referred. To avoid duplication, only the other twelve can be given here. They include the four "false" cases (see p. 178), four patients who went on to long therapy, one "short, favorable" and three "short, unfavorable" cases. Some details of the whole sample of thirty-nine patients in the second series (i.e., including those who failed follow-up) are shown in Table 2. The patients included here are marked with a superscript letter "a."

The following notes may be helpful:

1. The material is set out in Assessment and Therapy Forms as in *SBP*, arranged in alphabetical order of pseudonyms. Each form begins with a brief summary so that the reader can choose those of most interest.

2. In this summary I have included an indication of the contribution of each therapy, whether positive or negative, to the main significant correlations with outcome, i.e. those given by motivation, focality, and the transference/parent link.

TABLE 2. List of Patients

Patient	Sex	Age	Marital status	Complaints	Time of onset	Psychiatric diagnosis	Number of sessions	Outcome
Patients followed up								
Almoner	F	22	Single	Difficulty in deciding and remembering.	A few months	Mild depression.[b]	11	3.25
[a]Au pair girl	F	21	Married	Fatigue; irritability; headaches.	6 months	Depression.	9	2.5
Bird lady	F	35	Divorced and remarried	Phobia of birds.	Lifelong	Phobic anxiety.	9	1.375
Buyer	M	27	Single	A single blackout.	2 days	Hysteria.	18	2.75
[a]Car dealer	M	48	Married	Pains in feet and legs.	5 years	Hysteria, reactive depression.	54	2.25
Cellist	M	32	Married	Stiffness in his bowing arm.	Several years	Phobic anxiety.	9	1.875
[a]Company secretary	M	43	Married	Indigestion, impotence.	6 years	Character disorder.	12	1.0
[a]Contralto	F	34	Single	Wanted cosmetic surgery.	?	Character disorder.	>400	0.9375
Mrs. Clifford	F	23	Living with a man	Temper tantrums.	Some years	Marital problems.	90	2.75
Mrs. Craig	F	37	Married	Frigidity.	Many years	Depression, frigidity.	76	2.875
Dress designer	F	26	Married	Crippling panic attacks.	3 months	Acute anxiety state.	>200	1.25
Factory inspector	M	41	Married	Impotence.	11 months	Impotence.	19	0.83
Gibson girl	F	18	Single	Agoraphobia.	5 months	Phobic anxiety–hysteria.	28	2.875
[a]Gunner's wife	F	23	Married	Nausea and vomiting.	5 years	Hysteria, depression.	6	2.125
[a]Mrs. Hopkins	F	35	Married	Frigidity.	Many years	Anxiety–hysteria.	33	0.875
Indian scientist	M	29	Single	Premature ejaculation.	6 years	Anxiety state.	12	3.5
[a]Mrs. Lewis	F	23	Married	Nonconsummation of marriage.	5 years	Anxiety–hysteria, depression.	20	2.83
[a]Maintenance man	M	39	Married	Panic attacks.	5 weeks	Acute anxiety state.	30	3.0
Military policeman	M	38	Married	Acute anxiety attack.	Few weeks	Acute on chronic anxiety state.	5	1.375
Mrs. Morley	F	60	Widowed	Difficulties with her grown-up daughter.	Many years	Character disorder, potential severe depression.	9	2.25
Oil director	M	49	Married	Anxiety.	1 year	Anxiety state, depression.	46	2.0

Occupation/Name	Sex	Age	Status	Complaint	Duration	Diagnosis		
Personnel manager	F	40	Single	Phobia of driving her car.	Few months	Phobic anxiety.	62	3.25
[a]Playwright	M	28	Single	Severe panic attacks.	5 years	Anxiety attacks; severe character disorder.	93	2.25
Pesticide chemist	M	31	Married	Outburst of rage.	4 weeks	Obsessional personality.	14	2.5
Receptionist	F	21	Single	Depression, irritability.	1 year	Character disorder, depression.	9	1.875
[a]Representative	M	21	Single	Blushing.	2 years	Phobic anxiety.	3	2.125
Sociologist	F	25	Married	Dermatitis on neck, frigidity.	5 years	Character disorder, depression.	26	1.25
Stationery manufacturer	M	45	Married	Preoccupation with his wife's former relation to another man.	7 months	Incipient psychosis ("jealousy paranoia").	28	3.75
Mr. Upton	M	18	Single	Anxiety, depression.	1 year	Anxiety state, depression.	5	−0.625
Zoologist	M	22	Single	Conflict over his studies.	2 years	Character disorder, reactive depression.	32	2.5
Failed follow-up								
Character actor	M	34	Married	Panic about forgetting his lines.	Some years	Phobic anxiety.	15	
City solicitor[c]	M	28	Single	Headaches, hot flushes, depression.	1 year	Character disorder.	7	
Mrs. Curtis[c]	F	20	Married	Abdominal pain, depression, since miscarriage.	10 months	Hysteria.	5	
Interior decorator	M	26	Married	Inability to consummate marriage.	3 months	Impotence.	18	
Manicurist	F	26	Single	Shyness and loneliness.	Some years	Character disorder.	11	
National assistance officer	F	40	Married	Worry about hair on her face.	Some years	Character disorder.	20	
Rhodesian	M	22	Single	Fear that he was homosexual.	Few weeks	Latent homosexuality.	5	
Trawlerman	M	22	Single	Impotence.	? Some years	Character disorder.	7	
Dr. X.	M	32	Single	Loss of drive.	Few months	Character disorder, depression.	15	

[a]Patients marked thus are included in the present book. Those not marked are included in *The Frontier of Brief Psychotherapy* (1976) (excluding those not followed up).
[b]The word "depression" refers to depression at the "neurotic" end of the spectrum throughout.
[c]This patient was followed up but was clearly not telling the truth and the result was found impossible to score.

3. The case histories are, of course, disguised. The names are fictitious and are chosen from among those commonly found in England.

4. The names of therapists have been omitted in order to make patients less easy to identify.

5. The criteria, hypotheses, and assessments of outcome are those of Team 1 (DHM and EHR). They are reproduced exactly as written except for slight editing.

6. Sessions are numbered from the first interview with a workshop member, except that the projection test is not counted. The initial consultation is therefore usually the same as session 1. Unless otherwise stated, sessions were at the rate of once a week, and all patients were seen face-to-face.

7. The number of sessions is measured from session 1 to termination.

8. Length of follow-up is measured from the date of termination.

9. In order to link the clinical material more closely with the statistical evidence, I have laid emphasis on four important variables: (a) motivation, (b) focality, (c) interpretation of the transference/parent link, and (d) interpretations about termination.

10. The *projection tests* given were either the Rorschach or the Object Relations Test (ORT, Phillipson, 1955). The latter is similar to the TAT in that it consists of a series of pictures for which the patient is asked to make up stories. If differs from the TAT in that the pictures are drawn less distinctly, thus giving more scope for the patient to impose his fantasies on them; and also they are deliberately designed to bring out the kinds of feeling and anxiety commonly encountered in psychoanalytic therapy.

The Au Pair Girl

SUMMARY

Category. "False" (9 sessions, outcome 2.5).

A young woman of twenty-one complaining of depressive symptoms since her marriage six months ago. The therapist concentrated on trying to penetrate her "charming" façade and to reach the instinctual feelings underneath. This had some success, but, in retrospect, it seems that the momentum of therapy was largely supplied by the therapist. The patient found an excuse to break off after nine sessions. She then relapsed severely, and the final improvements seem to have been brought about by life experience (i.e., "spontaneous remission").

CONTRIBUTION TO THE CORRELATIONS WITH OUTCOME

Motivation: Disagreement between the two judges.
Focality: Positive (high focality, satisfactory outcome).
Transference/parent interpretations: Disagreement between the two judges.

DETAILS OF PATIENT AND THERAPIST

1. Patient

Sex	F.
Age	21.
Marital status	Married.
Occupation	Clerk in a firm of solicitors (she became an Au Pair Girl during the follow-up period).
Complaint	Fatigue, irritability, headaches, and fear of having a baby, since her marriage six months ago.
What seems to bring patient now	The patient did not seek treatment herself, but was sent by her G.P. in response to an appeal for a patient suitable as a psychoanalytic training case.

2. Therapist

Code	E.
Sex	M.

PSYCHIATRIC DIAGNOSIS

Mild depression in a hysterical personality.

DISTURBANCES

1. Symptoms. (a) Fatigue, irritability, headaches, since her marriage six months ago. (b) She overeats and has put on twenty-one pounds in weight. (c) Fear of husband's unexpected death and of her mother's new baby dying.

2. Sexual Difficulties. (a) She is afraid of having a baby. (b) She and her husband practice coitus interruptus and she never has an orgasm. She is ashamed that she feels sexually excited during her periods.

3. Gross Idealization and Denial. Her mother and husband are idealized. The sexual relation is "perfect." Her fear of having children will "sort itself out in time"; a little practice will put her sexual difficulties right. She does her best to maintain a smiling and friendly façade throughout the assessment period. She makes light of her difficulties and denies the need for help.

ADDITIONAL EVIDENCE

1. She was the eldest child. Her mother was boss in the home; and it seems that her father did not allow her close to him.

2. She was evacuated at the age of nine.

3. At fifteen she was raped by two boys. She says this is why she is afraid of motherhood.

4. Her mother had a new baby, twenty years younger than the patient, just before the patient's marriage six months ago, and was therefore not able to come to the wedding.

5. She describes her two bosses as just like babies; she has to look after them and they never think of her needs.

6. She and her husband are very busy decorating their house, which makes them very tired at night and interferes with their sexual relations.

7. In the initial interview she presented a charming and casual façade. The interviewer (later to become the therapist) told her she was a "bright liar" and interpreted her need to deny the existence of dirty, turbulent, sexual and aggressive feelings. This enabled her to become sad and serious for a short time, only to replace her façade by the end of the interview. She agreed without enthusiasm to come for treatment (poor initial motivation). In session 2 the therapist again brushed aside all denials and concentrated on aggressive feelings: jealousy of her siblings, anger with her mother for having a baby just before the patient's wedding, and anger with her husband who spent his time

painting the house instead of coming to bed with her. These interpretations brought out her fears of people dying: her mother, her husband, and her mother's new baby.

HYPOTHESIS

Gross fear of any "bad" or disturbing feelings. We think that this has to do with feelings about unsatisfactory mothering and fathering, together with jealousy of her siblings.

She defends against these feelings and the consequent depression by denial, idealization of her mother, and a false identification with motherliness.

CRITERIA

1. (a) Loss of fatigue, irritability, headaches; (b) she should stop overeating and recover her normal weight; and (c) no serious current depressive episodes.

2. Ability to drop her defenses of denial and idealization and (a) to admit her own needs, and her disappointment and unhappiness where appropriate, and to seek appropriate satisfactions for herself; (b) to enjoy sexual feelings with orgasm; (c) to lose her fear of having a baby; and, if she has one, to enjoy being a mother, while being able to admit "bad" feelings for her baby where appropriate; (d) to be able to admit anger, and to express it and assert herself in a way that improves a situation (this should apply particularly to the relationship with her mother); and (e) there should be evidence of a greater closeness and companionship between her and her husband.

REASON FOR ACCEPTANCE AND THERAPEUTIC PLAN

This patient was referred by a G.P. who showed a long-standing pattern of pressing not very willing patients into treatment. Nevertheless, the interviewer was encouraged by his ability to penetrate her defenses by forceful interpretation, and he wanted to take her on. The workshop were apprehensive both about the degree of her denial and her symptom of overeating and felt that these might hide a deeper depression than was apparent. She was thus taken on as an experiment, with the focus of exploring ambivalent feelings, particularly about her husband and her mother.

SUMMARY OF COURSE OF THERAPY

In session 3 the therapist once more interpreted denial of aggressive feelings, and succeeded in leading the patient toward anger with her husband at his lack of sexual attention. This led to her admitting that she preferred coitus interruptus to actual intercourse and that she preferred being stimulated with her husband's fingers rather than with his penis. The therapist then related her *resistance in the transference* to the *relation with her husband,* interpreting that she played around on the outside of any subject that meant anything to her, and refused to allow anyone to go deeply into her feelings, especially her aggressive ones. She made an angry response to this, saying that the therapist was experienced and she knew little. He then linked the *transference* with her attitude to *men in general,* suggesting that she was envious of a man's role. This produced a venomous outburst against all men, with the feeling that it was unfair on women to have to bear babies. The pattern in session 4 was similar: An interpretation of anger at the therapist again led to an outburst against all men. The therapist led her back to the family pattern, and got the patient's view of her father as a weak man, and her mother—though idealized—as a firm disciplinarian, especially on the subject of her going out with boys or having late nights.

In session 5 she was again trying to deny her feelings, but interpretation of this led to her telling how her twenty-first birthday party was spoiled by her mother who became ill toward the end of it. This led in turn to the story about the wedding, and how her mother—preoccupied with her own baby—didn't help her to prepare on the wedding morning. Nevertheless, her mother appeared to be wonderful. The therapist pointed out the contrast between the criticism of her mother and idealization of her. This led to the story of how her father was away during the war, and when he returned he was a disappointment to her, not making her daddy's girl. Session 6 started with her questioning whether she needed to come for therapy at all. Eventually she spoke of fears of pregnancy, childbirth, having a deformed baby, and then fears of her husband being run over. The therapist interpreted that she was not so sweet and nice but was afraid of her murderous wishes. It eventually came out that these fears began when she first learned of her mother's recent pregnancy. In the next two sessions the emphasis was on anger at the husband's sexual neglect, fears of men's violence, and sexual jealousy of men.

The climax of therapy came in session 9, with a shift in focus toward *sexuality* rather than *aggression.* During this session the *triangle of insight* was completed with respect to sexual feelings toward her father, the therapist, and her husband. She began once more by questioning whether there was any point in coming for therapy. Eventually therapist and patient got onto the subject of her *father,* with the information that after her wedding her father seemed to be upset at the thought of her sleeping with another man. This led in turn to the information that she shuddered if her father kissed her—not quite nice. The therapist linked this with the transference (*transference/parent interpretation* implied), saying that she felt *him* to be a dirty old man, and that "this was a projection of her being a dirty young woman, with promiscuous ideas." She admitted that she disgusts herself with promiscuous thoughts, which include the therapist. He then interpreted promiscuous thoughts toward her father. This led to mention of the fact that she had been raped at the age of fifteen; and then to her saying that she had taught her *husband* to be less loving and more active sexually. The therapist pointed out that she wants her husband to be a dirty old man, older, firmer, and she confirmed this rather seriously.

Therapy was then interrupted by the London bus strike. It seems typical of this patient that when the strike finished she wrote, "I believe I am expected to continue my appointments with you. I have decided I would like to discontinue unless you think it is absolutely necessary." The therapist offered her another appointment, but she phoned saying she would not come.

This therapy was important in the statistical study of transference/parent interpretations. In session 9 there were two places where the transference/parent link was clearly made and this was obviously understood by the patient; but because of the therapist's rather terse phrasing, it was a matter of opinion whether or not what he wrote actually met the criteria necessary for a transference/parent interpretation to be scored. Malan scored one such interpretation; Rayner, interpreting the criteria more strictly, scored none. The result was that, over the twenty-two therapies completed in under forty sessions, Rayner's values for the correlation between *outcome* and *transference/parent ratio* just failed to reach significance.

There were no interpretations concerned with termination.

Total number of sessions	9
Total time	3 months

FOLLOW-UP

1. 4 Months. She said that treatment had helped her considerably: Her deep depressions had disappeared, and her crippling headaches had become quite tolerable. She still had an unaccountable fear of childbirth and could not envisage having a baby. She refused to answer any questions about her sexual life, but said that her life in general was quite tolerable and she didn't think she needed further help.

2. 7 Years 11 Months. Subsequent history: The whole situation deteriorated severely during the next four years. The relation between her and her husband grew colder and colder, with him staying out increasingly late and returning to sit in silence. Her headaches and depressions returned in full force, and on one occasion—in a half-deliberate way—she had taken a small overdose of tablets. Eventually they decided to part, and she went to Rome to help look after the children of a wealthy family. Her woman employer tried to exploit her and in addition was involved in all the activities of a corrupt society, and the patient was left to cope not only with the children but with various disasters to the employer herself as well. She was thus forced to assert herself. Eventually she walked out. She kept herself going with several different jobs on the Continent for a further year. All this amounted to being thrown in at the deep end, and, she felt, forced her to grow up.

In the meantime she had kept up a quite friendly correspondence with her husband (who, she discovered later, was furthering the process of his own growing up by sowing some of the wild oats he had previously left unsown). In these letters he began to ask her to come back to him, and eventually she agreed. During the period before she left her husband, her attitude to having children had changed, and it had then transpired that it was now her husband who didn't want them. She now made it a condition of her return that they should start trying to have a child at once, to which her husband willingly agreed. She became pregnant within three months of returning, and gave birth to a little girl now aged eighteen months.

CRITERIA

1. (a) Fatigue, irritability, headaches, depressions: These symptoms have virtually disappeared. (b) She still overeats. (c) She still has irrational thoughts about her child or her husband dying. (d) Other symptoms: She always faints if blood is taken from her, and had one hysterical fainting attack recently after some people had been rude to her.

2. (a) Ability to drop her defenses of denial and idealization, etc.: As far as these manifestations were concerned, the interviewer wrote that it was hard to believe that she was the same person. She was forthright, honest, full of pungent phrases, and willing to discuss everything frankly and without embarrassment. She was able to speak of her sadness and misery when she first left her husband, though she then said she didn't like to think of these things and changed the subject. She freely admitted stresses in her relation with her husband, her child, and her mother. She was clearly able to find satisfactions for

herself within the limits of her situation. [For some contrary evidence see (f) below.]

(b) Her sexual relation with her husband is restored, and she said it meant quite a lot to her, but she still has never had orgasm. She does not mind this. She now wears a diaphragm, and they no longer practice coitus interruptus.

(c) She has completely lost any conscious fear of having children and now wants one or possibly two more; but she suffered from severe vomiting during the first three months of her pregnancy.

To the psychiatrist she spoke with genuine pleasure of her little girl, but the P.S.W. who visited her said that she showed considerable unconscious hostility toward the child, e.g., teasing her quite unnecessarily and refusing to pick her up though she hadn't been well. She was able to some extent to admit "bad" feelings toward her child and did not try to idealize her.

(d) Ability to be angry and self-assertive: This criterion seemed to be completely fulfilled (e.g., she had finally been forced to assert herself with her employer in Rome; she insisted on having a baby; she said she flared up with her husband in a way that improved the situation instead of making it worse). Her mother was no longer idealized, and she said each is able to be aggressive to the other.

(e) Relation with husband: She was honest about both the improvements and the limitations here. She said that she was still in love with him, but she didn't feel he was still in love with her. Nevertheless, he is kind and considerate, they share pleasure in the house and their daughter, and he will now talk about the future between them (which he would never do before). She gave examples of their having fun together. It is interesting that before their parting he used to suffer from quite severe attacks of what sounds like urticaria, which she said was obviously nervous in origin, but that this now hardly occurs at all.

(f) In answer to questions about her treatment, she said that all she could remember was the inconvenience of having to go there; and that she was quite sure she hadn't been helped, as she didn't need treatment, anyhow.

SUMMARY AND DISCUSSION

The main symptoms (headaches and depressions) have disappeared; less important symptoms remain.

The main defenses of denial and idealization have disappeared, and the whole "feel" of the patient is of a major character change.

The general relation with her husband is greatly improved, though the sexual relation seems little changed.

Since her symptoms returned in full force before she went to Rome, we may question whether the *tendency to react to stress with symptoms* has improved at all (see also the recent fainting attack). Yet, the situation with her husband was saved from disaster by what seems to have been highly adaptive behavior on both their parts.

We feel that the way she denied the importance of therapy was immature and unreflective. At the same time, since the improvements occurred long after termination, after a serious relapse, and in response to apparently quite independent events, we may question how much her therapy had anything to do with them.

Team 2 laid more emphasis on the indications of residual disturbance (the P.S.W's evidence about her relation with her child, the lack of orgasm, and the recent fainting attack), wondering if her story was entirely consistent.

SCORES

Team 1	3.0	3.0
Team 2	2.0	2.0
Mean	2.50	

The Car Dealer

SUMMARY

Category. Long, favorable (54 sessions, outcome 2.25).

A married man of forty-eight complaining of pains for which no physical cause could be found, caught in an unsatisfactory marriage. Relatively long therapy enabled him to deal more realistically with his marriage, which remained highly unsatisfactory, and his pains disappeared.

CONTRIBUTION TO THE CORRELATIONS WITH OUTCOME

Motivation: Strongly negative (poor motivation, relatively satisfactory outcome).
Focality: Positive (fair focality, intermediate outcome).
Transference/parent interpretations: Positive (intermediate score, intermediate outcome).

DETAILS OF PATIENT AND THERAPIST

1. Patient

Sex	M.
Age	48.
Marital status	Married.
Occupation	Dealer in secondhand cars.
Complaint	Pains in his feet (five years), spreading to his knees (two years).
What seems to bring patient now	The patient has spoken about his pains to a friend who was a doctor and had had some connection with the Tavistock Clinic. The friend suggested that he come to see us.

2. Therapist

Code	E.
Sex	M.

PSYCHIATRIC HISTORY

In addition to the above complaints, he has clearly become depressed during the last two years. This manifests itself as loss of ambition and drive, with suicidal thoughts at times. The only obvious manifestation of depression at interview was that on one occasion he broke down into prolonged weeping. He has had many investigations for his pains but no physical cause has been found.

DIAGNOSIS

Mild reactive depression with hysterical conversion symptoms.

DISTURBANCES

1. Symptoms. Pains as above. These prevent him from doing a full day's work.

2. Depression. During the last two years he has lost his ambition and drive, and is now content to watch television all evening in a state of mild depression. He has felt suicidal at times.

3. Inhibition of Instinctual Feelings and Denial of His Own Needs. He has a lifelong problem of denying his own needs and primitive feelings, and subordinating himself to others. He has an extremely moralistic attitude to his own sexual and aggressive feelings. He feels he must accept his wife's nagging, frigidity, and lack of warmth without protest. He is afraid that his sexual demands, even if he wanted intercourse once a week, would wear her out.

4. In contrast to 3, he has forced his son, who wanted to learn a skilled trade as a carpenter, to go into the family business in order to provide for his, the patient's old age.

5. He is shy and feels socially inferior.

6. His behavior with interviewers was extremely obsequious.

ADDITIONAL EVIDENCE

He was one of the younger members of a fairly large family. When he was small his father was rather indulgent toward him. His father, however, got involved with another woman; and when the patient was twelve his mother left his father, taking the younger children, including the patient, with her. He went out to work at fourteen, and from then on has always been his mother's main financial support, with very little help from his siblings. He now continues to give his mother money and visits her, in secret, because his wife strongly disapproves of the help he gives her.

His wife appears to be frail but has a powerful personality, and she nags him, never gives him a kind word, and dominates him. His attitude to this is that he must learn to put up with it, and after all, it is only his side of the story. Equally, he must put up with the fact that she is an "iceberg," and he must be careful to control his sexual feelings or it might wear her out.

The patient has built up his business to be very successful, and until his recent illness he took great pleasure in this and in the outward signs of his success, his yacht and his smart car. He has always been conscientious and honest in his business, and gentle with his employees, wanting no trouble and avoiding quarrels.

The main features of his approach to the interviews with the psychiatrist and psychologist were (1) his obsequiousness—"I'll tell you everything, Doc"; (2) his attempts to deny the emotional significance of the whole story, while steadfastly asking for help for the pains in his knees; but (3) an important breakthrough of feeling in the initial interview. This latter happened as follows: The therapist made it clear to him that he was unable to handle other people except by accepting their criticism, suppressing his own feelings—both sexual demands and anger—and remaining uncomplaining and dutiful. The therapist related this to his childhood, in which he had had to look after his mother. At this point he burst into tears and wept for a long time over his mother's miserable life after his father left her. As he went on, it seemed that at least in part he then changed over to weeping for himself, as he realized his own utter loneliness throughout his life, and his unfulfilled longing for tenderness from a woman.

In session 2 he spoke with admiration about his father's strong body, and with disapproval about his father's infidelity. He made clear that his strict business morals were derived from his mother's teaching. He admitted that he now felt burdened by his mother. With the therapist's help he was able to see how he disapproved of his father but admired and liked him, and was slavish toward his mother's teachings, which he hated. He admitted to daydreams of masculine adventurousness and even perhaps of his own infidelity. He admitted to fears of doing harm sexually to his poor little wife, and argued that the woman had to rule in the house or else there was great danger for her.

A further piece of information that emerged in session 2 was that his father's business had recently failed despite the fact that the patient had given him very considerable financial support.

HYPOTHESIS

Guilt about triumph over his father has led to the renunciation of sexual and aggressive feelings, and to the need to assuage his guilt by being a dutiful son to his mother. This has led to resentment about being burdened by her, which in turn he has had to repress, and this has led to a vicious circle of resentment and guilt. This situation is now being repeated with his wife.

CRITERIA

1. Loss of symptoms, with ability to work efficiently and enjoy it.
2. Loss of depression, with recovery of his ambition and drive.
3. Extensive reorientation of his attitude to his own needs, which should be accepted as a legitimate part of him, and should no longer be compulsively held in check by a moralistic attitude.

This should enable him at least to control his wife; and if possible to get some sexual satisfaction from her. He should feel able to assert himself constructively both with her and in other situations. At the same time this ability to fulfill his own needs should be neither compulsive nor destructive to others, e.g., he should allow his son freedom to make his own life.

4. Increase in self-confidence generally, including social situations.

REASON FOR ACCEPTANCE AND THERAPEUTIC PLAN

The therapist saw the patient privately for the initial interview and made contact with him in one dramatic moment. It was possible to see the patient's character problems, but these appeared to be rather diffuse and it was not clear exactly what focus to choose. The therapist wrote that he proposed to see the patient a few more times and then to reassess the situation, and the truth is that he drifted into therapy without ever clearly formulating a plan. The overall idea can be said to have been to try and work through the patient's feelings about his childhood and to relate them to the present situation, particularly the relation with his wife.

SUMMARY OF COURSE OF THERAPY

For the first period of therapy, which lasted for eighteen sessions, the therapist managed to put his plan into effect with some success, though the sincerity of the patient's responses, and the true basis of his improvements, always remained in question.

It will be remembered that the significant factors in the patient's childhood seem to have been that (1) he was close to his father when he was small; (2) because of his father's infidelity his mother left his father when he was twelve, taking him with her; (3) from the age of fourteen he was his mother's main financial support; (4) his strict conscience was derived from his mother, by whom he felt burdened; and (5) he appeared to be repeating a similar pattern with his wife. This situation, together with its Oedipal implications, was the main theme of the therapist's interpretations. The therapist brought in the transference wherever possible, interpreting the patient's passivity and obsequiousness as a defense against negative feelings, or a fear of being punished, or a wish to be punished. He also made a number of transference/parent interpretations, mostly of himself representing the father. It remains true, however, that at hardly any time were any clear responses recorded to transference interpretations, most of which were denied or brushed aside. On the other hand, after a very discouraging start, the patient responded with a clear dynamic sequence to the nontransference interpretations.

In session 3 the therapist interpreted that the patient had a secret liking for his father and his father's way of life, and that he wanted to be a man despite his mother's restrictive teaching. The only result of this was to intensify the patient's *defenses*: He went into a long passage of disapproval of his father, ending up by asking what all this had to do with the pain in his knees.

In session 4, however, there seemed to be a delayed confirmation of this interpretation: The patient spoke of messing about in his boat and getting his hands dirty, and how his father had always been interested in mechanical things, but his wife doesn't like this and he always feels guilty about it. His wife and mother live in a flat above his showrooms, and he feels as if he is in a cage. The therapist related this to his childhood, in which his mother was always against his having any use for his father, and the result is that he is ashamed of his father's manliness and his own. The patient agreed with this kind of interpretation in a way that gave the impression he could not make use of it: "By Jove, that's right. You must be right; after all, you're the doctor," etc.

Nevertheless, once more there seemed to be a delayed response to this interpretation, which now revealed part of the patient's *anxiety:* In session 5 he said that in business "if you expand too much you will burst," and the therapist couldn't resist suggesting that he was afraid of being a big man with a big penis in case it would be attacked. This led in turn to a highly dynamic sequence: The patient spoke first of having once hit his wife, but mostly he had concealed his anger and criticized himself. He went on to describe how she would go for him if he brought mud into the house, and as a result he always went in by the back door. The therapist suggested that he was afraid of intercourse and making a mess, and that he castrated himself at the woman's request.

The patient responded that he had always been afraid of forcing his attentions on his wife. The therapist asked him when he last had intercourse with his wife, expecting it to be months, or even years, ago. To his amazement, the patient hung his head, and then with boyish defiance lifted it and said, "This morning." In subsequent discussion it emerged that he always asked his wife's permission, and if she said no he was upset but accepted it. The therapist adopted a didactic role, telling him he was a stupid man for not understanding that a woman's no doesn't always mean what it seems, and relating this to the way in which he had been discouraged by his mother and had accepted her ban on sexuality. Later the patient spoke of having often wanted to leave his wife, but how that would only lead to ruin. The therapist pointed out that the patient felt his father's leaving his mother had led his father to bankruptcy.

This led in session 6 to what appears to be the climax of the first phase of therapy, though it is not quite certain how much it meant to the patient. In the early part of the session he managed to produce some criticism of the therapist because his pains were no better. On Sunday he had worked in the garden to overcome the stiffness in his legs, having given up a trip with his family. The therapist suddenly felt that everything dropped into place: the patient's inability to enjoy any-thing—smart clothes, his work, his success, parties, and weekends—and the probable interpretation that the pain in his legs was a mecha-nism for *avoiding pleasure*. He interpreted this vigorously and in detail. The response was equivocal. The therapist wrote optimistically that it "hit him like a hammer"; but the truth seems to be that he chewed it over at length and ended up turning it the other way round so as to neutralize its impact, by saying that it was only the pain in his legs that prevented him from having pleasure. The therapist emphasized that the main factor banning pleasure in his life was his mother. At the end of his account of the session the therapist wrote that guilt about success would explain why the patient broke down when he did, namely, when his business was really starting to do well.

The response to this session seemed once more to be an intensifica-tion of *defenses*, though this time they could be penetrated. In session 7 the patient appeared to be in a hypomanic state, and the therapist interpreted that he was trying to deny his feeling of guilt toward his parents. The patient admitted quite solemnly that this was so and that he dared not speak of these feelings to anyone else.

In session 8 the therapist interpreted further anxieties, suggesting that the patient was afraid of success for fear of arousing the envy of other men, who represented his father and his brothers. The patient accepted this, at least intellectually.

In session 9 the patient mentioned improvements and went on to say that these were helped if he didn't think of his parents, who made him feel sorry for them. The therapist interpreted first that he must have felt guilty in his childhood about taking his father's place, but this seemed to have no effect. The therapist therefore switched his interpretation, saying that he must have missed his father and still did so. At this, for the second time in therapy, the patient began to weep. He spoke about his father's kindness toward him; and then went on to give what seems to be a delayed response to the first interpretation, saying that "he had been a devil" to his father. At eleven he stole his father's motorbike, at twelve he stole his car, and earlier than this he had broken into his father's shop and deliberately done a great deal of damage. For these things his father had given him terrible beatings.

In session 12 this Oedipal theme was reached once more, via hostility toward the forbidding mother. The therapist interpreted that the patient was subservient to both his wife and his mother yet was angry with them. This led to the first occasion on which the patient had made any criticism of his mother: She offends him when she gossips about other people's faults. The therapist suggested that the patient hated his mother's criticism of his father and himself, particularly over sexuality. The patient said his mother was quite right to warn him against his father, who lost his money and ruined his life. The therapist suggested that the patient felt guilty about his own ability to make money, almost as if it was stolen, while his mother was left in poverty; and consequently he had to hide his manliness and success.

This was the main work done in the initial phase of therapy. The patient himself then suggested termination. The therapist was unhappy about this, feeling it represented a flight into health, but no interpretations were of any avail. In session 18 the patient made plain that he would like to discontinue treatment, though adding that he was not discontented with what he had got. He was due to come the next week but sent a message to say he couldn't do so and would write. This was the last that was heard for eleven months.

Improvements. He reported improvements in his pains in sessions 3 and 4, a relapse in session 6, and further improvement in sessions 7 and 8; in session 10 he reported being able to *run* for the first time for several years; and in session 12 he reported that he had been free from pain *on a Saturday* for the first time for years. In addition to these symptomatic improvements, he reported an improvement in the sexual situation with his wife (session 8); an increased ability to assert himself, particularly with employees (sessions 9 and 10); and the ability to enter places that he would not have dared to enter before, e.g., shops and a hotel (sessions 9 and 12).

Total number of sessions	18
Total time	6 months

Subsequent Events. Nothing was then heard from him for eleven months, when he asked for another appointment and was taken on for further treatment. Exactly why he sought further treatment at this point is not clear from the notes. In fact most of the gains that he had made in the first eighteen sessions seemed to have been maintained. The therapist wrote that the pains in his legs were improved (but not recovered), he was less submissive toward his wife, and more active at work. Further work concerned the same basic problems: renunciation of his manhood, and submission to women. Two months after the beginning of this second course of treatment, the therapist wrote a further report on him: He has become able to deal with customers more openly and in a less placating manner, has stopped hiding his anxiety under buffoonery, is assuming some authority with his wife, and his depressions no longer bother him much. In this report it appears that in some of his previous depressions he had felt suicidal. The therapist wrote, however, that he was not really happy about these improvements, which seemed to be based on obedience to the therapist rather than on true insight. This second course of therapy consisted of thirty-six sessions over a period of one year two months. There is no record of what happened in it.

Final total number of sessions	54
Total passage of time	2 years 6 months

FOLLOW-UP
(3 years 3 months since termination of regular therapy)

1. Symptoms. These have disappeared.

2. Depression, Recovery of Ambition and Drive. He is no longer depressed. He has been able to work well and behave in a different way from before: He can now be self-assertive and can take command. His hobbies are adventurous.

3. Acceptance of His Needs; Loss of Moralistic Attitude. (a) As far as his business life and his relations outside his marriage are concerned, this criterion is fulfilled. He can enjoy his leisure on his own. *(b) In relation to his wife,* his marriage remains quite unsatisfactory. He is freer with his wife in the sense that he can demand things of her, but she remains unresponsive. She was in fact seen in consultation at the patient's request, and was seen as a helpless, chronically self-centered woman, impoverished in her relationships, socially withdrawn, and inaccessible to insight. She refused the offer of treatment in her own right on the grounds that the journey was more than she could manage. The patient accepts this situation, feels cheated, is in despair about his wife ever changing, and does not put into practice his occasionally expressed fantasy about leaving her. He is no longer dominated by her whims, nor is he terrified of her; but insofar as he restricts his life on her account, he may still need her to form an external representative of his restricting conscience. The change seems to be that, whereas previously he accepted slavishly the burden that she placed on both their lives, now he accepts it unhappily. *(c) He is allowing his son to lead his own life,* and now no longer seems tied to him in any way.

4. Increase in self-confidence, including social situations. There has been a change in his attitude to the therapist, in that he can honestly say that he has no further need of treatment, and that he is disappointed that his wife has not been helped. He does, however, still treat the therapist with undue respect; and is self-conscious, rather like a naughty little boy, when making any aggressive remarks to him.

His former panics in social situations have disappeared, but his social life is still restricted because of his wife.

DISCUSSION

Team 1 found this difficult to score because it was impossible to tell how much of his need to restrict himself was still expressed for him by his wife.

One member of Team 2 took a much less optimistic view of him than did the other three judges. This was based on the judgment that he was still tied to an extremely unsatisfactory relation with his wife, and could neither leave her nor deal with her effectively.

SCORES

Team 1	3.0	3.0
Team 2	2.5	0.5
Mean	2.25	

Mrs. Clifford

SUMMARY

Category. Long, favorable (90 sessions, outcome 2.75).

A woman of twenty-three, complaining of temper tantrums and violent quarrels with the married man with whom she was living. One of the main foci of an extremely complex therapy was her guilt about taking this man away from his wife. The couple eventually married and the husband had treatment in a group, and the story ended with four sessions of conjoint marital therapy. The final result was a considerable improvement in the relation between the two of them.

CONTRIBUTION TO THE CORRELATIONS WITH OUTCOME

Motivation: Positive (moderate motivation, increasing; favorable outcome).
Focality: Positive (moderate focality, favorable outcome).
Transference/parent interpretations: Positive (the highest score of all therapies in the series, favorable outcome).

DETAILS OF PATIENT AND THERAPIST

1. Patient
Sex	F.
Age	23.
Marital status	Living with a married man (referred to below as her husband).
Occupation	Housewife.
What seems to bring patient now	She has been persuaded by her husband to seek help because of her temper tantrums, which are making the relation intolerable. He has himself recently benefited from psychotherapy for a psychosomatic symptom.

2. Therapist
Code	J.
Sex	M.

PSYCHIATRIC DIAGNOSIS

Character disorder leading to severe marital problems.

DISTURBANCES

1. Temper tantrums with her husband that she fears will lead to the breakup of the relationship. In one of these she smashed up the kitchen.

2. She is very jealous of her husband's real wife, and the thought of her occurs during intercourse, partly spoiling her enjoyment. She claims to enjoy intercourse despite this.

3. She tries hard to please her husband and does not seem to be aware of her own needs.

ADDITIONAL EVIDENCE

1. She was the eldest of the family. She did not get on well with either of her parents, who quarreled constantly with each other.

2. A younger brother got more attention than she did.

3. She left home at eighteen to come to London to work, where she met her husband. He told her he was single and she fell in love with him. Later he admitted he was married but promised to get a divorce, so they started to live together.

4. She clearly understood an interpretation linking her husband's real wife with the image of her mother forbidding sexual pleasure.

5. In her projection testing (ORT) the psychologist made a number of comments in the early stages designed to emphasize that *she* really needed help, which she only experienced as underlining her guilt. Later he made the simple comment that she seemed to be very lonely, after which she made it clear that she wanted help for herself.

There were three main themes: (a) seeking relief from intolerable guilt; (b) loneliness; and (c) fear of burglars and of men waiting to assault her.

HYPOTHESIS

1. She suffers from severe guilt about stealing a man from his wife, which is probably Oedipal in origin.

2. She is angry with her husband for not having told her he was already married.

3. She defends herself against both these feelings by trying to suppress her own needs and to please her husband.

4. When her husband criticizes her, this defense breaks down and she becomes overwhelmed with rage.

CRITERIA

1. **Aggression.** Replacement of the temper tantrums by the ability to assert herself effectively when appropriate.

2. Relations with Men. Ability to take active steps to solve the present problem once and for all. Evidence that she is capable of forming a satisfactory and lasting relation with a man whom she can have (which might include her present husband). Satisfactory sexual relation, not interfered with by thoughts of other women. No undue preoccupation with jealousy.

3. Guilt. She should be able to stand criticism and to find the balance between serving her own and her partner's needs.

REASON FOR ACCEPTANCE AND THERAPEUTIC PLAN

She seemed to have a fairly good basic personality and although the original pressure for treatment came from her husband, she responded to interpretation with a clear increase in motivation, asking help for herself. The current crisis seemed to be clear-cut and could be seen in terms of the past.

Having been offered treatment with the psychologist who tested her, she persisted in attempts to contact him by telephone despite difficulties.

The therapeutic plan was to link the current difficulties with Oedipal problems. We realized that it might be difficult to treat her without also treating the husband, whose contribution to the present situation was unknown.

SUMMARY OF COURSE OF THERAPY

Sessions 2–5. Here there were two main themes: (a) the relation with her husband, Ken, in which she seemed to be trying to idealize him and believe everything he said, while at the same time being maddened by the ways in which he tricked her into appearing the guilty party; and (b) her guilt at having broken up Ken's marriage. Interventions concerning (a) were met with stubborn resistance; but she was able to work with (b), and she then began to speak openly of her anger at the way in which the children of Ken's marriage had been neglected. The therapist suggested that she might herself have felt neglected as a child, which brought a flood of memories about how her sickly younger brother got more attention than she did. When her anger against her mother about this was interpreted, she seemed to respond with relief.

During this period the therapist made a number of transference interpretations, mostly of a tactical kind, e.g., about her being resentful at being transferred to him, and her feelings about his going on holiday soon after therapy began. She agreed with some of these without making any very clear response.

Sessions 6–9. The patient now began to complain of Ken's children intruding on her privacy. This led to memories of how she herself could not sleep alone as a child, so that she had to be allowed to sleep in her parents' room during much of her middle childhood and observed their sexual life.

Sessions 10–18. It began to appear that much of what she and Ken did together was an elaborate game of make-believe, in which each pretended to be a perfect wife or husband, and when the pretense broke down there were violent quarrels. This led the therapist to make a tentative link with childhood sexual fantasies, and it now emerged (a) that her mother had been an inveterate flirt, (b) was given to suicidal gestures, and (c) that the patient had quite consciously had fantasies of her mother dying, of stepping into her mother's shoes, having her father to herself, and bringing up her younger brothers better than her mother had done. Her relationship with Ken, who had boys of his own, was repeatedly interpreted as a guilt-laden reenactment of this fantasy.

Sessions 19–21. During the summer holidays the patient visited her parents' home together with Ken and his children, the first time this had ever happened. She was appalled and sad at how messy her mother had allowed her home to become. She said how sorry she felt for her, realizing how much her mother had tried to do for her while being in such a muddled state herself. She realized she (the patient) had been cruel and vindictive to her, and she felt particularly guilty because she now seemed to be so much better off in her own family life. The therapist pointed out that she was really not very sure of this, at which she spoke of her fears that Ken was not entirely honest in business. This led to her reflecting sadly that her father was an honest man despite his weaknesses; and then, for the first time, she began to admit how much her father meant to her.

Sessions 22–25. The climax of therapy came in session 22. She arrived in a very tense mood, bitterly saying that the therapist was teasing her, that she didn't know what he wanted of her, and that she would have stopped coming if she had had the guts to make the decision herself. The therapist replied with considerable heat that he was sure he was not teasing her, and then added that she seemed to be afraid that he was in a hurry and would stop treatment before she was ready. At this she broke down into tears and wept for most of the session. She said she was afraid of becoming like her mother, who had been young and pretty but after having children had become fat, old, and muddled. Her mother had married against her parents' wishes, and the farm on which they lived had belonged not to her husband but to her father, so that the patient's father was an outsider, and this grandfather had ruled the home like a tyrant.

Later sessions linked this childhood family drama to her present situation. It was pointed out how afraid she was that she was carrying on an unreal dream with Ken, just as she had carried on a dream of being with her outsider father to the exclusion of her mother and grandfather. Her feelings about the therapist's cruelly teasing her seemed to be linked with her grandfather, who had scorned her father and had no time for her. The therapist likewise seemed to her to scorn the equivalent of her father, i.e., Ken, and to have no time for her.

Sessions 26–29. After the very active session just described the patient showed a marked change. She relaxed and seemed to glow with health. She came in new clothes and enjoyed looking attractive. The tense, defensive, suspicious attitude toward the therapist melted away and never returned. Because of this change the therapist gave her a termination date three months hence. Her associations then frequently alluded to partings of one sort or another, but she tended to shrug off interpretations about termination.

Sessions 30–33. She continued to deny any anxiety about stopping. Her main preoccupation was with the intrusiveness of Ken's children, who were secretive with her and yet overfamiliar. Later knowledge of this family makes it plain that she was justifiably worried that these children were very disturbed, but the therapist missed this.

Sessions 34–37. She spoke of how sadistic children were who were neglected by their mothers. The therapist interpreted that she herself had felt neglected as a child and must have felt sadistic toward her mother, father, and brothers; and he again linked this with termination. She took this seriously and said, "I must not do what my mother and father did, as I can see what a mess it makes of life."

Sessions 38–40. She reported having the first argument ever with Ken in which she had stood her ground without losing her temper, and had proved in the end that she was right over a matter of fact. At the same time there were hints of pleasure in taking revenge on him that did not bode well for their future together. She mentioned with a faintly gloating air that Ken was so impressed with the work done on her that he had now asked for help for his own problems. Her final attitude toward stopping was that she was really rather bored with coming and would welcome a chance to try and manage on her own. There were many interpretations to do with feelings about termination but no very clear response at any time.

It is also worth noting that there was a higher proportion of transference/parent interpretations in this therapy than in any other (18 percent), though responses to them were often not clear and their therapeutic importance is uncertain.

Total number of sessions	40
Total time	1 year 1 month

SUBSEQUENT EVENTS

These were as follows (the times given are calculated from the termination of her forty sessions):

1. A few weeks: Ken was taken into outpatient group therapy, at which he was an irregular attender for about three years.

2. Six months: Ken and the patient got married.

3. Two years: The patient contacted her therapist with a new problem, that she wanted to have a baby but was uncertain about it. Ken seemed to be putting it off, and she got very angry with him. At the same time she made clear that their violent and histrionic quarrels no longer occurred, although fierce verbal battles continued.

4. The therapist took her back into treatment, giving her about fifty more sessions over about fifteen months.

5. Two years, six months: She became pregnant.

6. Therapy terminated shortly before the birth of her child, a boy.

7. During therapy a major preoccupation was with Ken's middle child, Jim, who began being very possessive of her and showing disturbed behavior.

8. Three and a half years: The patient rang up to say that she was very worried about Jim, whose behavior had become even more disturbed. She and her husband were therefore given four sessions in a foursome made up by her therapist and his group therapist. The therapists said in effect that they couldn't help with Jim, who was not asking for treatment for himself; and that the couple didn't seem able to come to a decision to be husband and wife together. It became apparent that neither could express love for fear of deliberate rejection by the other, which would lead to quarrels.

9. There was then no further contact until the final follow-up.

ASSESSMENT AT START OF SECOND COURSE OF THERAPY
(Two years after first termination)

It must be noted, of course, that Ken had been in group treatment during most of the follow-up period.

1. (a) Temper tantrums. At the first termination she had not had any tantrums for months, and these did not recur. Physical violence had disappeared on both sides, but there were still fierce verbal quarrels with mutual recrimination.

(b) Ability to assert herself. This was improved but there was considerable residual difficulty. Her act of saying she wanted a baby was self-assertion, but she had to ask for more therapy for help with this.

2. (a) Ability to take active steps to solve the problem once and for all. She was already married to Ken, so this is fulfilled.

(b) No excessive preoccupation with jealousy. She said that the guilt about stealing Ken from his first wife had been worked through, and she was no longer troubled by jealousy of other women.

On the other hand, her rivalry with other women still seemed to be present in a compulsive need to be a better mother than Ken's first wife. There was thus probably a strong neurotic element in her worry about her stepson's disturbed behavior.

3. Ability to strike a balance between her needs and those of other people. She was beginning to sort out her and Ken's distorted perceptions of each other.

SCORES

Team 1	1.5	1.5
Team 2	2.0	2.0
Mean	1.75	

FINAL FOLLOW-UP
(One year three months since the last joint session, one year ten months since termination of individual sessions, five years since first termination)

She was seen first individually and then together with her husband.

Important events not covered in the assessment below are concerned with her stepson, Jim. His behavior had been extremely disturbed and jealous, and both the patient and her husband had been worried—not without reason—that he might attack the new baby. He finally committed a crime and has had to be detained in an approved school, where he appears to be moderately happy. The therapist acknowledged that he had not taken her worries seriously enough, to which she said, "Yes, that's true, but I don't really think there was anything you could have done about it."

1. **Replacement of temper tantrums by ability to assert herself.** This was fulfilled. The physical violence has not recurred, and she can assert herself over such things as how to bring up her son. She and Ken can discuss things rationally and see each other's point of view.

2. **(a) Ability to take active steps to solve the original problem once and for all.** This is entirely fulfilled. She has not only married Ken but has had a child, and she has thereby created a new family that seems to be a settled commitment for both herself and her husband.

(b) Ability to form a satisfactory and lasting relation with a man she can have. This seems to be largely fulfilled.

(c) Satisfactory sexual relation. Their sexual relation has changed from "mad passionate ecstasy followed by recrimination and depression" to something more muted that they both enjoy. Thoughts of other women no longer interfere. This criterion seems to be entirely fulfilled.

(d) No excessive preoccupation with jealousy. She is no longer jealous of other women. On the other hand, there does still appear to be a neurotic situation going on between them: He feels he ought to give her everything she demands and then defends himself by defiantly holding onto things for himself, which makes her angry. An instance of this happened very clearly in the joint follow-up interview.

(3) **(a) She should no longer feel she has to be above reproach and (b) should be able to stand criticism.** These both appear to be fulfilled, though there is little direct evidence.

(c) Ability to strike a balance between her own needs and those of others. There is a great improvement in mutual tolerance between her and her husband, while at the same time she has been able to assert herself. She seems to be a very good mother to her own son, and at the same time she showed genuine concern for her stepson, Jim. She shows a very balanced attitude toward Jim, and also to her husband: "I'm still crazy about Ken. I don't regret having married him, though we've made an awful mess of it in many ways."

On the other hand, the interaction described in (2) (d) above shows that this problem is not entirely resolved.

SUMMARY

The final judgment depends on how much emphasis is given to the residual difficulties.

SCORES

Team 1	3.5	2.5
Team 2	2.5	2.5
Mean	2.75	

The Company Secretary

SUMMARY

Category. Short, unfavorable (12 sessions, outcome 1.0).

A married man of forty-three complaining of indigestion and partial impotence. Final follow-up suggests that he was wrongly assessed initially and many factors in the situation between him and his wife were not elicited. The initial focus seems to have been wrongly selected, and the main response to interpretation came far later on an unexpected theme.

CONTRIBUTION TO THE CORRELATIONS WITH OUTCOME

Motivation: Positive (intermediate motivation, poor outcome).
Focality: Major disagreement between the judges.
Transference/parent interpretations: Strongly positive (low score, poor outcome).

DETAILS OF PATIENT AND THERAPIST

1. Patient

Sex	M.
Age	43.
Marital status	Married.
Occupation	Company secretary in the head office of a chain of radio and electrical shops.
Complaints	(1) Indigestion, (2) partial impotence, for six years.
What seems to bring patient now	His wife is now pressing him to seek treatment for his sexual problem.

2. Therapist

Code	G.
Sex	M.

PSYCHIATRIC HISTORY

His first attack of gastric trouble occurred about six years ago and lasted for a few months. It consisted of attacks of left epigastric pain.

Apparently for the last three and a half years he has suffered from attacks of a "heavy, hard" pain, in his lower central chest, radiating to his shoulder blade, and accompanied by a distended feeling in his stomach that made him feel that he wanted to belch but couldn't. This pain tended to come on particularly on his way home from work, and was then apparently only partially relieved by alkalies. It was severe enough to make him just want to lie still, and would tend to last for an hour and a half. It also tended to come on in the middle of the night, and was then relieved within ten minutes by his taking half a pint of milk and a cracker and cheese. About eighteen months ago he had been referred for investigation and had had a barium meal. This showed hypersecretion and gastritis but no other evidence of organic disease or hiatus hernia. The physician concluded that the dyspepsia was mainly functional in origin. It improved considerably when the patient gave up smoking and stopped trying to relieve the pain by frequent attempts at regurgitation.

As far as his impotence was concerned, he told the interviewer and the therapist respectively two slightly different stories. The thing in common between these stories, however, was that the dates on which both the impotence and the gastric trouble began seemed to coincide. According to the interviewer, his impotence dated from six years ago, that is, the time of his first attack of abdominal pain. He said that he got feelings of general bodily sexual excitement, but that often he either did not get an erection or else lost it before penetrating. If he can keep out of his mind the thought that he may fail, he can have successful inter-course. To the therapist, however, he said that his sexual trouble had begun about three and a half years ago, and at the same time as the beginning of his second type of pain. He felt that over this period he had gradually lost all interest in sexual intercourse.

Another interesting fact that he told the psychologist was that there was an inverse relationship between the severity of his dyspepsia and his impotence; i.e., the worse his dyspepsia was, the more potent he was able to be.

DIAGNOSIS

Character disorder with psychogenic dyspepsia and partial impo-tence (but see follow-up for further medical details).

DISTURBANCES

1. Gastric Symptoms. See above.

2. Sexual Difficulties. These consist of loss of sexual drive and partial impotence (see above). He has become depressed by his sexual failure, and he said that he sometimes felt like crying himself to sleep. At the same time, he maintained that he was almost entirely concerned about the effect on his wife rather than on himself. His wife sometimes weeps bitterly about it.

3. Passivity. He seems to be very compliant, to deny his own needs, and to strive always to keep the peace at all costs.

ADDITIONAL EVIDENCE

1. Very little was elicited about his background.

2. The rather unexpected event that the patient associated with the onset of his symptoms was as follows: An uncle, whom he had much idealized, had been living in the patient's home for a number of years. It is clear that this uncle had been showing signs of dementia for a long time, but the patient had apparently tried to hide this fact from himself. Six years ago he had finally begun to face this, when his uncle began smearing feces, behaving in all sorts of disgusting ways, and causing the patient's wife considerable distress.

3. In connection with the above, the patient spoke of how he had also idealized his father, who had died when the patient was twenty-five; and how some years after his father's death his mother had told him to his horror that his father had had venereal disease for many years.

4. There is a current situation of very great strain at work. He has to work closely with the managing director, whom he feels to be entirely ruthless and selfish and willing to trample on anyone for his own ends. This man is reaching retiring age, but the patient feels that he will not retire; and he is thus standing in the patient's way, for the latter is the obvious choice as the next managing director. The patient has to control all his feelings about this situation, particularly because he was the managing director's protégé in the past and was very considerably helped by him. As he described this situation, there was hatred and distress in his voice.

5. This is the patient's second marriage. His previous marriage broke up because of his first wife's unfaithfulness. Despite the fact that she was the guilty partner, it ended up by her divorcing him rather than the other way round. He felt that his first wife's unfaithfulness gave him permission to be unfaithful himself, and he had had a very passionate affair (probably with his present wife, though this is not clear from the notes) before the divorce.

6. The workshop felt that the initial interview left a number of important questions unanswered: (a) Do women exist for him as real

people at all? (b) Is homosexuality important? (c) Has he any ability to recognize his own needs at all? The projection test (ORT) was undertaken with these specific questions in mind. In fact, the answers to all three questions were favorable. The psychologist was impressed by the patient's capacity to acknowledge feelings that were very disturbing for him. A clear focus for therapy seemed to emerge: that underneath his calm and pleasant exterior there lay considerable hatred for people of both sexes, the consequences of which in his fantasy were (i) retaliation from men, and (ii) destruction of women.

CRITERIA

1. Loss of symptoms.
2. Restoration of potency with enjoyment of sexuality, and a satisfactory relation with his wife in other ways.
3. Abandonment of the compulsive need to be compliant and conciliatory, with the ability to assert himself constructively.

REASON FOR ACCEPTANCE AND THERAPEUTIC PLAN

After the initial interview the patient was thought to be probably unsuitable because he appeared to be out of touch with his feelings, but the psychologist's report reversed this view. The plan was essentially as formulated by the psychologist (see Additional Evidence, 6c): to bring out the hostility lying beneath his calm and compliant exterior.

SUMMARY OF COURSE OF THERAPY

This basically unsuccessful therapy played a major part in the statistical evidence on the correlation between early focality and outcome, and needs to be discussed from this point of view.

First it must be said that the therapist, Dr. G., ranked as one of the most successful of all those in Balint's team, and there can be no question of his overall skill. Nevertheless, the impression conveyed by this particular therapy is that he had little idea where he was going, or, if he did, that his ideas were often mistaken. A major part of the responsibility for this problem can be laid at the door of the interviewing psychiatrist (who was not Dr. G.), and this therapy illustrated in a most pointed fashion the difficulty created for a therapist who has to base his work on an inadequate initial history. This applies especially to the history of the patient's relation with women, and is shown by the fact (1) that the interviewing psychiatrist made no attempt to go into the reason for the breakup of the first marriage, which was ostensibly due to the wife's infidelity, but as emerged later in therapy, appeared to be due to the patient's sexual inadequacy in that situation as well; (2) that at follow-up the patient said that his sexual drive had begun to fall off about two years after his marriage, i.e., about three years earlier than the onset of his gastric symptoms; while (3) his wife herself, in her therapy, said that something had gone wrong when her husband had returned from the war—he seemed to have become indifferent to her—which must have been even earlier and *before* they were married. Thus, although the patient dated both his gastric symptoms and his impotence from six years before and linked them with the loss of idealization of his uncle, this was in the context of a long-standing disturbance in his relation with women. And, finally, (4) there was practically no information about the relation with the patient's mother, which might well have given a clue to the nature of his disturbance with women in general.

On the basis of all this information we can see two major problems in this man's life: (1) a disturbance of unknown origin in his relation to women; and (2) a problem with men, represented by (a) the loss of idealization of both his uncle and his father, and (b) the conflict between anger and gratitude in his relation to the managing director.

These two problems were of course seen at the time, though not in such detail, and the fundamental question is whether they were separate or were linked. The therapist tried to interpret them as linked, but in discussions in the workshop this met with considerable skepticism, which I shared at the time and still share, as did Dreyfus when he came to judge focality. However, in my own judgments of focality I had a serious problem: I knew about the history that had emerged years later in the wife's therapy, and was aware of the inadequacy of the initial assessment, but of course could not be permitted to use this information. The result was that I gave the therapist the benefit of the doubt, scored focality highly against my own overwhelming skepticism, and consequently (with the small numbers involved) went some way toward spoiling the strong correlations between focality and outcome obtained by Dreyfus.

Some idea of the problems of judging focality in this therapy may be given by the following account emphasizing what seems to be the main interpretation in each session.

Session 1. In the initial interview the interviewer made the hypothesis that the link between the patient's two problems was that he was angry with his wife for causing the breakdown of idealization of his uncle, in the same way as he was angry with his mother for causing the breakdown of idealization of his father.

The projection test indicated hidden anger against both men and women, without specifying what the anger was about, though in the case of the managing director it was about standing in the way of the patient's promotion, and thus appeared to be Oedipal in origin.

Session 2. Here the therapist's main interpretation was of the patient's compliance as a *defense* against his *impulse* not to satisfy the needs of others; and that the connection between the two problems was that he was expressing the *defense* in the relation with the managing director and the *impulse* in relation with his wife. This "splitting" mechanism was also linked with the transference. Here the focus of hostility toward both men and women is adhered to, but the use of the word "needs" implies mother/child rather than Oedipal problems, so there may in fact be an implied change of focus.

Session 3. The therapist again made the link between aggressive feelings toward the managing director and the wife, suggesting that the patient was afraid of damaging and hurtful thoughts in relation to both people; but he also made the link between hidden aggressive feelings against the managing director and the patient's father; and he ended by making an interpretation suggesting the vicarious expression of aggression, that is, that he was waiting for his wife to boil over and attack him, which is what he could not do to the managing director. The patient responded more clearly to this last interpretation than to any other hitherto, saying "I can see that I am doing that. God help me if I am."

Session 4. The main interpretation was concerned with the link between the *wife* and the *mother:* that the patient resents his wife's concern about the children because this is just what he didn't get from his own mother (who, he said, was a hard woman), and he is taking his revenge on his wife by neglecting her in turn. The patient agreed with the first half of this interpretation, saying he had thought of it himself, and half-agreed with the second part. This again adheres to the focus of aggressive feelings, but now these appear to be due to mother/child problems and the link with the managing director is abandoned.

Session 5. Here the story about the breakdown of idealization of the father emerged for the first time with the therapist (the patient had originally told this to the psychologist). The patient went on to say that when his father died he had brought flowers for his father's grave but none for his mother. The therapist's essential interpretation was complex and not very convincing, again concerned with "splitting": that the patient had turned all his hatred onto his mother in order to preserve the idealization of his father, and had then transferred his hatred for his mother onto his wife. The patient denied this.

Session 6. This session was not recorded.

Session 7. The patient said that he had "backed away" both from intercourse with his wife and from trouble at work. The therapist now made an entirely new link between the wife and the managing director, namely, that the patient felt "impotent" in his relation with both, but this did not really lead anywhere.

The difficulty in judging focality in these first seven sessions comes from the fact that (1) many interpretations are on the rather wide focus of hidden aggression, but (2) the supposed link between the problems with men and with women varies from one session to another, as does (3) the cause of the aggression, and (4) the whole is very unconvincing.

There is a further mystery: Apart from the response recorded in session 3, which in any case could simply have been an example of compliance, the patient's responses to interpretations were never very clear. Nevertheless, from session 5 he began to report improvements, particularly in his confidence at work, though not as yet in the sexual situation. These may perhaps have been due to bringing out his conflicting feelings about the managing director.

Session 8. This session was the beginning of a much more convincing passage in therapy, in which real communication seemed to appear for the first time. It was typical of this therapy that the theme was an entirely new one, namely, *dirty sexuality*. The patient spoke of his father having brought him up to be very prim and correct, and was always warning him against the dangers of VD. He then began questioning why his impotence occurred when it did; and almost for the first time some real feeling about the past relation with his wife emerged, with the information that they used to be very active sexually and had had intercourse two or three times a week. The therapist then pointed out that he had not wanted to believe his wife about his uncle's dirty habits, and made the link with not wanting to believe his mother about his father's dirty self. The patient said he had never been sure about whether or not to believe his mother, for she was a hard and vindictive woman.

Session 9. This atmosphere of deeper communication was continued and increased in the next session. First, the patient came out with the information that he had disappointed his first wife sexually as well as his second wife, and that on one occasion the former had given him a hefty kick in the genitals in retaliation. He went on to say that he had been trying to talk over their earlier relation with his wife, and that one evening he had suddenly shut up like an oyster. It emerged that this was when he had mentioned an incident in which he had taken his wife out for a picnic and had discovered that they had laid the groundsheet on top of some human excreta. The therapist interpreted that he felt his sexuality to be dirty, and linked this with the patient's uncle who had started smearing the place with feces. No response to this interpretation is recorded.

Session 10. The patient now reported that he was not only feeling happier and more confident at work, but that he had had intercourse twice with his wife last week and had been surprised at his capacity to feel happy and loving to her afterward, and that he had a more open relation with her and could discuss things with her. Another entirely new theme then arose: The therapist asked if the patient's elder brother had intervened in a malign way between the patient and his parents, just as the managing director intervened between him and the chairman. This turned out to be so: The elder brother had got a lot of attention because he had fits, and there was considerable evidence that he could put himself into a fit if he wanted to.

At this point the therapist suggested terminating treatment, which the patient accepted. They met twice more.

Session 11. He reported that he felt much happier and as if a heavy weight had been lifted from his shoulders. He went on to link his pains, which he now hadn't had for months, with hidden rage against the managing director.

Session 12. In the final session there was a return to the theme of dirty sexuality. The patient said he felt he had had a "good clear-out" of things that have been troubling him for a long time. However, perhaps ominously, he said he was still not particularly keen on intercourse. The therapist interpreted that he was afraid of doing anything that might involve loss of control, using the word "clear-out" to imply loss of control of his bowels. The patient went on to say that the way his wife enjoyed sex was not refined enough for him.

It was agreed that he could get in touch with the therapist if he felt the need, which he did not do.

Looking back on this therapy as a whole, it now seems to me that early sessions were based on an essentially incorrect therapeutic plan, the only correct part of which was the connection between the patient's gastric pains and his conflict with the managing director. The significance of the "loss of idealization" of the father and the uncle seems to be concerned with the patient's fears of dirty sexuality, which only emerged late in therapy and led to the real moments of communication, and which might have been seen at the beginning if the interviewer had not had a reluctance to make interpretations in the initial interview. And, finally, the patient seems to have had a long-standing problem with women entirely independent of problems with men in general and the managing director in particular, which was not elicited at the initial interview and was therefore never a part of the therapeutic plan.

Total number of sessions	12
Total time	7 months

FOLLOW-UP
(6 years 6 months)

The position is very greatly complicated by the intervention of severe physical illness, the symptoms of which first appeared two years and seven months after termination, and from which the patient died seven years and six months after termination. This was diagnosed after biopsy of a lymph gland as an obscure lymphadenopathy, and it was treated first with radiotherapy and later with methotrexate. In fact, the diagnosis after postmortem was simply secondaries in the lymph glands resulting from bronchial carcinoma.

This condition clearly had nothing whatsoever to do with the original symptoms of dyspepsia and impotence. Six years after termination he had a second barium meal that showed no peptic ulcer or gastric abnormality. Five months after this he suffered a hematemesis, which was probably the result of treatment with methotrexate.

1. Symptoms. Evidence suggested that his gastric symptoms remained essentially unchanged throughout the whole follow-up period. He continued to suffer attacks of pain in bouts of a few months, with free periods of a few months in between.

2. Restoration of Potency, with Enjoyment. When he was seen for follow-up he had been married to his second wife for eighteen years. He said at follow-up that he thought his sexual drive had been normal for the first two years of this marriage, but had then begun to fall off. He said that, from comparing notes with other men, he was convinced that his sexual drive from then on was below normal. Before he came to us for treatment, he tended to have intercourse about once a month. In fact, his psychotherapy altered the situation in no way whatsoever, even before the symptoms of his final illness began. After they began he was often so ill and exhausted that sex was out of the question, and he and his wife gave up all attempts at it.

3. Satisfactory Relation with His Wife. All the evidence suggested that, in recent years at any rate, he and his wife have been close in all ways apart from sex.

4. Abandonment of Compliance; Ability to Assert Himself with Superiors and Subordinates. There was a marked improvement in his ability to assert himself with the managing director. He gave no impression of passive compliance at follow-up. He said that after the retirement of his managing director he did not want to be managing director in name, but wanted to be the person with the knowledge who influenced decisions behind the scenes. This is, in fact, what happened.

He said that he had never had any difficulty in asserting himself with people in an inferior position, and he gave two examples of doing so in an effective way since termination.

SCORES

Team 1	1.0	1.0
Team 2	1.5	0.5
Mean	1.0	

The Contralto

SUMMARY

Category. Long, unfavorable at the time of follow-up (> 400 sessions, outcome 0.9375). Drifted into an analysis, outcome ultimately highly favorable.

A single woman of thirty-four with whom the therapist started with a focus concerned with her relation to her father, but who eventually was seen to be suffering from a long-standing inability to form close relationships.

CONTRIBUTION TO THE CORRELATIONS WITH OUTCOME

Motivation: Strongly negative (high motivation, poor outcome).
Focality: Positive (poor focality, poor outcome).
Transference/parent interpretations: Negative, (high score, poor outcome).

DETAILS OF PATIENT AND THERAPIST

1. Patient

Sex	F.
Age	34.
Marital status	Single.
Occupation	She sings in the chorus in opera.
Complaint	She has become sensitive about her appearance and wants a plastic operation on her nose.
What seems to bring patient now	Her G.P. insisted on her seeing a psychiatrist before deciding about the plastic operation.

2. Therapist

Code	A.
Sex	F.

PSYCHIATRIC DIAGNOSIS

Character disorder.

DISTURBANCES

1. Symptoms. (a) In discussing her wish for an operation on her nose, she said her nose resembled her father's. (b) She suffers from a need to urinate at awkward moments and may have to leave a bus or the theater. This has been less troublesome recently.

2. Sexual Difficulties. She has never had a satisfactory sex life. She has had intercourse with two men, both of whom had difficulties with their erection, and at least one of whom was homosexual. She seems to prefer taking the active part in intercourse.

At one time she used to be sexually excited by the idea of being beaten, and she got men to do this. She now thinks she has lost interest in this.

3. Ability to Fulfill Her Potential. She would like to do better in her profession but has been unable to do so.

ADDITIONAL EVIDENCE

1. She did not remember her mother, who had died when the patient was eighteen months old. She had grown up very close to her father.

2. She gave the impression that she must keep a distance from women. With the interviewer (who was in fact the therapist, a woman), she appeared hostile and rather condescending.

3. When she said that her nose resembled her father's, the therapist said that it might be better to leave her father than to change her nose. Her reply was, "Oh, poor Father, I can't do that."

4. In session 2 she produced a book on psychiatry and asked the therapist to what school she belonged. The therapist interpreted this as anxiety about the therapist's competence. This completely transformed the atmosphere, and the patient then said she would reveal some things that she had never told anybody else. These were some facts in her history confirming the presence of intense Oedipal conflicts.

5. This led to two interpretations: (a) that her urinary symptoms were linked with sexual excitement; and that there was now a *fear of* getting sexually excited; (b) that she must be jealous of other women, and therefore wished to excite men but not be excited by them; and that, in contrast to her dominant father, she probably only wanted relations now with relatively impotent men. The patient confirmed this latter. She spoke sincerely about her wish to have children and to be able to accept a dominant man.

6. At the end of session 2 the patient said she had given up the idea of having an operation on her nose.

7. In her projection test (ORT), there was emphasis on the theme of keeping the parents together. The psychologist suggested that the unconscious fantasy was of separating the parents.

HYPOTHESIS

Anxiety and guilt about the closeness and intensity of her relation to her father: She has defended herself against this by (1) not committing herself to sexuality, and (2) identifying herself with her father.

CRITERIA

1. Symptoms. (a) We suspect that the wish to have an operation on her nose is neurotically based, and if this is so, then she should give this up. (b) Loss of urinary symptoms.

2. Relation with Men. (a) Ability to leave her father while still keeping a good relation with him that is not emotionally overloaded. (b) Ability to form a close, warm, not too possessive, and mutually satisfactory relation with a potent man, including the sexual relation; if possible, to get married; no undue emphasis on masochism (or sadism) in sex.

3. Ability to Fulfill Her Potential. She should be able to do so in her career, though without compulsiveness; or, to replace her career by marriage.

THERAPEUTIC PLAN

This was never clearly stated. At discussion, there was uncertainty about whether she could be helped by dealing solely with the problem concerning her father, or whether it would be necessary to deal with primitive dependent transference. It seemed possible that the patient needed an analysis, and it was suggested that the therapist should have twenty sessions in which to decide whether or not this was so.

SUMMARY OF COURSE OF THERAPY

The main theme of therapy consisted of problems in the triangular relation between the patient, her mother, and her father, with the related problems of defenses against ambivalence. Material and interpretations relevant to these themes were as follows:

1. Guilt toward her mother for not looking after her father well enough, which brought a storm of tears (session 4).

2. Her mother's intense pride in her, and the feeling that she could never allow anyone to take her mother's place, which the therapist interpreted as leading to hesitation about committing herself to therapy (also session 4).

3. Her refusal to marry a man whose wife had died, which the therapist interpreted as symbolizing her feeling that *she* (the patient) could not take her mother's place (session 5).

4. Her father appeared to have been cruel to the women around him, including the patient as a child, but the patient had also been told that she was cruel to her father, who loved her so much. All this was linked by the patient herself with her masochistic impulses. The therapist suggested that the patient was also afraid of her own sadism, and of what she might do if she were sexually aroused. Shortly after this the patient said that she *must* stay in treatment (session 10).

5. This important session was followed in session 11 by a major alteration in her feelings about her mother. She had been reading her mother's diaries, from which there had become apparent her mother's intense attachment to the patient's father. This led her to say that she could now see that her mother could not have been so tied to her as she had always imagined, and the therapist said that therefore she need not feel so tied to her mother. Until now it seemed that she had had to spend her life fulfilling what she imagined her mother wished for her.

6. The hint of possible competitive feelings with the memory of her mother emerged in session 12. The patient spoke of having once sung at a party, and because she had been very apprehensive she had found herself praying to her mother to help her, and it had been a great success. It was important, however, that after reaching the age at which her mother had died, her singing had seriously deteriorated. The therapist interpreted that until this age she had felt her mother to be a part of her, but that after this she began to have doubts about her mother's relationship to her. This was designed to shake her idealization of her mother, and it led to her expressing fears about what would happen if her mother had not been entirely loving, and to accounts of conflicting feelings about several other women in her life.

7. The culmination of the Oedipal theme occurred in session 14, when she reported a dream in which she was in a telephone booth with her father; and a friend of hers called Mary, to whom the patient said she was devoted, came along. The first association to Mary was to a friend whom the patient had idealized and then had found to be heartless and brutal. Mary's birthday was the same as the patient's mother's birthday. Moreover, the patient's father had at one time been in love with Mary but the patient had managed to maneuver him out of marrying her. Mary reminded her of the therapist. Finally, the patient said that she hated having to submit to the therapist but that she would do so completely. The therapist interpreted (a) that the patient wanted to idealize her (the therapist) in order to escape from the feeling that she was brutal and unfaithful to her; (b) that this corresponded to the patient's feeling about her mother, whom she hated because she had had a sexual relationship with her father (transference/parent interpre-

tation); and (c) that the patient wanted to offer herself to the therapist in order to get love, to keep the therapist away from men, and to save herself from hating her as a rival (like her mother). The patient responded by saying that she thought the therapist was right: She was aggressive, and she supposed that if one hated, one wanted to kill people; perhaps this was why she was so afraid of dying.

8. In the next session (no. 15) the patient said that she now realized that she had managed to feel only loving toward some people and only antagonistic toward others, and that feelings could be more mixed than this and hence more real.

9. In session 19 she spoke of having partly idealized her teachers at school and having partly laughted at them. The headmistress had had a breakdown. The therapist pointed out her difficulty in allowing people to be as she really knew they were, and linked this with the patient's mother, who was both idealized and existed in the patient's mind as someone who continually criticized her and to whom she was answerable.

Session 19 was the last before a break and the last recorded. The patient continued to be seen twice to four times a week, and at the time of follow-up was still being seen once a week.

Total number of sessions   Probably over 400
Total time   Over 5 years

FOLLOW-UP
5 years 4 months (patient still in treatment)

1. Symptoms. (a) Wish to have an operation on her nose. She gave this idea up shortly after starting treatment and it has not recurred. (b) Urinary symptoms. These have recovered with minor recurrences.

2. Relations with Men. (a) With her father. She had shown signs of being able to break away from her father, but he then died two years after she started treatment. She is now able to regard him as a real person and not as being wholly good or wholly bad. (b) With other men. She has continued to be only able to achieve relations with ineffective and not very potent men. There has been undue emphasis on being the active partner, and on sadomasochism. She has shown signs of wanting to get away from this, but has not yet found a man with whom these aspects are not important.

3. Ability to Fulfill Her Potential. She has given up her career as a singer, which apparently she never really liked.

4. General. The therapist now sees her main problem as an inability to have real relations with people, because of the dangers inherent on getting close to them. Although she has become closer to one woman friend, this difficulty seems to have largely persisted.

SUMMARY

Symptomatic recovery, with little other change except for the changed attitude to her father.

SCORES

Team 1	1.5	1.5
Team 2	0.5	0.25
Mean	0.9375	

The Factory Inspector

SUMMARY

Category. Short, unfavorable (18 sessions, outcome 0.83).

A highly dynamic though basically unsuccessful therapy with an ambivalently motivated patient, conducted largely outside the transference. The original focus was Oedipal, but a second focus appeared in the form of guilt-laden anger about premature responsibility and lack of mothering in the patient's childhood and consequent anger against women.

CONTRIBUTION TO THE CORRELATIONS WITH OUTCOME

Motivation and focality: Strongly negative (both factors high, poor outcome).
Transference/parent interpretations: Strongly positive (low score, poor outcome).

DETAILS OF PATIENT AND THERAPIST

1. Patient

Sex	M.
Age	41.
Marital status	Married.
Occupation	H.M. inspector of factories.
What seems to bring patient now	Impotence for eleven months.

2. Therapist

Code	F.
Sex	M.

PSYCHIATRIC HISTORY

He has been married for eighteen years and has apparently enjoyed a sexual relationship perfectly satisfactory to both partners until recently. About eleven months ago he began to have sporadic difficulty in getting an erection. Eight months ago his impotence became complete. (For details of external events associated with these symptoms, see below under Disturbances.) He was referred by his G.P. to a consultant physician who in turn referred him to the Tavistock Clinic, writing that he was physically exceptionally fit.

DIAGNOSIS

Impotence.

DISTURBANCES

1. Problems over Potency. There had been no difficulty in his sexual relation with his wife until recently. In his own words, "I only remember half a dozen occasions on which I failed to satisfy her."

Eleven months ago, because of administrative problems at work, he was assigned to help a colleague of equal rank but some years older than he was. It was about this time that he began to experience sporadic difficulty with his erection. Then, eight months ago, his wife had to go into the hospital for dilatation and curettage for a vaginal discharge. When she came out of the hospital, he became completely impotent.

2. Problems over Jealousy. (a) The ORT showed complete inability to tell stories about three-person situations. (b) He does not like to take his wife out socially, and he agreed with the interpretation that this was because he wanted to keep her to himself (it is worth noting that they have no children). (c) Another disturbing factor in the work situation is that for many years he has enjoyed an exclusive relation with a superior whom he much admires, and now he has to share him with this colleague.

3. Obsessional Phenomena. He has always had a perfectionist and self-driving nature. He can only relax at home after doing several hours work in the house, though he can relax on holiday because he feels he deserves it. One of the disturbing factors in the work situation seems to have been that working with this colleague has prevented him from doing the job in the way he wants. This has resulted in a number of petty irritations that he has been unable to voice; and it has given him a tight feeling in the head. He has also begun to be preoccupied with small things that people say to him that might be taken as criticism.

ADDITIONAL EVIDENCE

1. The patient is the eldest of five children.
2. His father was a traveling salesman and was therefore away from home a great deal. When he was at home he never showed his feelings. He is a very calm person and can sit in a chair and do nothing, which the patient could never do.

3. His mother was described as rather highly strung, like the patient.

4. The patient only had an elementary education, but he went to night school and worked himself up into his present highly responsible job.

5. He seems to have coped well with problems of competition in the past. He was not anxious before exams and usually passed them, though he failed the last one and decided not to try again.

6. There has been no trouble with superiors at work; he has either felt great respect for them and gladly worked for them, or else he has felt they didn't know their job and he has gone his own way regardless of them.

7. In both the initial interview (session 1) and session 2 the patient showed a clear pattern: Starting defensive, he suddenly opened up when the end of the interview came near, and then began to communicate about what seemed to be the heart of his difficulties.

In session 1 he said he was quite sure that his trouble had been started by the situation at work mentioned under Disturbances, and he felt that his wife's operation was irrelevant. As a way of leading toward Oedipal problems, the interviewer (who was also the therapist) suggested that he needed to "prove himself," which had been shown throughout his life by his need to work hard and do jobs well. The patient agreed, and the therapist went on to say that, with the new arrangement at work in which he was no longer his own boss, he was now unable to go on proving himself; and that something had then gone wrong in another sphere of activity in which a man needed to prove himself, namely, sexuality. The patient did not agree with this. What seemed to make more sense was his inability to express anger with his colleague, and he seemed to feel that his wife received the anger rather than the man. The therapist then discussed possibilities of treatment and prepared to bring the interview to a close. The patient, however, then asked if he could smoke, and began to say that he did not like going out anywhere with his wife, but just wanted to stay at home with her. He agreed with the interpretation that he liked to keep his wife to himself and didn't want a third person present.

8. He was then seen for a projection test (ORT). The most unusual feature was that all his stories concerned two-person situations regardless of the number of the figures on the card. He thus seemed to express his need for exclusive possessiveness of the other person. For instance, he began with a story of being on a desert island with a woman— "something I have always dreamed about." Despite this, the sequence from card to card showed a very clear Oedipal pattern. He dealt with the

man or the woman but never with both together. The psychologist felt that his tolerance of anxiety was weak, and that in face of difficulty he could only fall back on mechanisms of denial and avoidance.

9. Session 2 started with an attempt at a "flight into health," and ended with the patient plunging into deep communication. He said that he now realized that a number of the things that he had felt were "silly," that he had had one partially successful intercourse with his wife, and that he didn't want to waste the therapist's time. He seemed very doubtful about accepting treatment, and eventually the therapist suggested that they should meet once or twice more and see what happened. The therapist then invited him to talk about anything that he liked. This caused a considerable disturbance in him, he obviously became nervous, and spent a long time trying to get a lead from the therapist. Then, suddenly he plunged in. He started by saying once more how he liked to keep his wife to himself; and then spoke first about the relation with men under him, which gave him little trouble; and went on to say that relations with equals were not so good. The therapist eventually interpreted that the patient must feel that his colleague was in some way interfering between him and the superior for whom he had always worked. The patient spontaneously said, "Could I be jealous?" He went on to say that when he worked for a superior he liked to feel that he was the best inspector that superior had working under him. The therapist first pointed out how the theme of competitiveness and triangular situations ran through almost all the patient had said, and when the patient agreed with this, made a tentative link to the past by saying that the situation of working well for a superior resembled the relation of a son to a father. From this it emerged that his father did not take very much notice of the children, and certainly wouldn't have appreciated anything that his children did. The patient was, however, not conscious of any resentment about this. What he did feel resentful about was that his father had not treated his mother properly and had left her to bear the whole burden of looking after the children. At the end of the session he said he would like to come for treatment, but he was certainly not wholehearted about it.

HYPOTHESIS

We think that this man cannot tolerate anxiety and guilt associated with competition. He defends against this by careful avoidance of close competitive situations, both those involving his wife and those at work.

His *anxiety* was aroused by the competition at work; and possibly his *guilt* (about having prevented his wife from having children) by his wife's dilatation and curettage.

CRITERIA

1. Recovery of potency and full enjoyment of the sexual relation for both partners. Evidence that the relation with his wife is warm and close in other ways as well.

2. Evidence that he can tolerate and participate directly in three-person situations without signs of excessive anxiety or hostility. No need to keep his wife exclusively to himself.

3. Relaxation of the compulsive element in his perfectionist and self-driving nature, without a serious falling-off in the quality of the things he does. He should be able to relax in appropriate circumstances, without necessarily feeling he has to earn this. He should be able to take criticism. There should be no other evidence of irrational guilt.

REASON FOR ACCEPTANCE AND THERAPEUTIC PLAN

After the initial interview and projection test the therapist wrote out detailed predictions, on which the following account is based. He thought the patient was highly suitable on the grounds that (1) the problem was acute and recent, (2) a clear focus could be seen in terms of conflicts about competition, (3) the patient was psychologically unsophisticated, but had shown an ability to think quite deeply about his problems and seemed to be asking for insight, and (4) he seemed to have basically a very good personality. (Here it is worthwhile noting the psychologist's reservations about his ability to tolerate anxiety.)

"The evidence suggests that he feels guilty about anger or rivalry with his father, but has hitherto successfully defended himself against this, (1) by avoiding three-person situations, and (2) by placating his conscience with hard and perfectionist work. The problem has been reactivated by (1) a disturbed relation with a man (the colleague at work), and (2) an inability to be perfectionist, since he is now working under this colleague." The psychologist felt that the wife's operation was also relevant: In the patient's fantasy she had been "interfered with" by a man, but since the gynecologist turned out in fact to be a woman, this interpretation was hardly correct!

"During the course of therapy I shall aim to interpret the whole of the above pathology, working from the present back into the past. I shall try to link this with his father and mother, but I do not expect any conscious response to this. Therapy will be almost entirely outside the transference. He will treat me as someone to whom he is coming for help, whom he trusts, and under whom he will work. Negative transference will be almost entirely absent but will be interpreted wherever found, probably without conscious response. Termination will present no difficulty. He will accept what I lay down and in any case will be anxious to get treatment over."

SUMMARY OF COURSE OF THERAPY

Therapy went almost exactly according to prediction in sessions 3, 4, and 5, in the sense that the theme was *competition*, and it was possible to relate this increasingly clearly to the patient's childhood, the transference also playing little part.

He opened session 3 by saying that he had been doing a lot of thinking since last time, and his main conclusion had been that he had always wanted to be "top of the pack." If he did any job, even including decorating his own house, he wanted it done better than anyone else could do it. The therapist here tried to lead toward Oedipal problems by suggesting guilt about competitive feelings toward his superiors. The patient said he only had such feelings toward superiors whom he did not respect. The therapist suggested that this originated in the patient's relation to his father, whom he could not respect. The patient seemed both distressed and surprised, said that he was quite sure this was the central point of the whole thing, and then immediately changed the subject back to competition in the present. He said that his wife was a very attractive woman, and at times he had cause to be jealous. In fact, he had always dealt with this in such a way as either to cut the competition short or to avoid it altogether. The therapist again directed the patient's attention toward the past by emphasizing that this probably originated in the patient's relation with his father.

This apparently had its effect, because the patient started session 4 by speaking of an incident that he had felt to be extremely humiliating, namely, that when his father had been short of money he (the patient) had once had to buy him a new suit. It emerged that his father had never been strict with him and that the patient wished he had. The therapist interpreted that as a result the patient had had to be strict with himself. This then led to a second main theme that played an extremely important part later: that since the patient was the eldest child he had to be a great help to his mother in the house, and look after the other children. His mother was not a disciplinarian but rather appealed to his conscience, and it seemed that this might be one of the origins of his compulsiveness.

The sessions so far had been essentially exploratory and as yet nothing definite had been arranged about whether the patient was going to come for regular treatment. The therapist therefore opened session 5 with this question. The patient then showed the most extraordinary example of his ambivalent motivation. He started by proposing a flight into health, saying that he wasn't sure he was getting anywhere and since he now realized his problem was "petty jealousy" he wondered if he might manage by himself. The therapist said that surely the test of that was whether he had recovered from his impotence. Much to the therapist's astonishment the patient's answer was, "Oh yes, I have." It turned out that his potency had gradually increased during the time he had been coming for treatment, and that he had now had intercourse three or four times without any setback but he hadn't thought to mention the fact! The therapist, mindful of the psychologist's opinion about the patient's poor tolerance for anxiety, decided that the best thing to do was to let the patient make his flight into health, and arranged to see him again in three weeks time. At this point, once again the patient suddenly entered into deep communication. The themes that emerged were, first, difficulty in expressing anger toward another man, and then competitiveness once more. He said that all this must have been there a long time; how would it ever be possible to understand why? By this time the session had already gone nearly an hour, but the therapist nevertheless felt it right to give a major interpretation, first of all, about the *past:* that a boy and his father could be rivals for the mother, and how every boy wanted to push his father out and have his mother to himself. If his father was too weak, he might feel that he had succeeded only too easily in pushing his father out, and would forever feel guilty about it. Perhaps this was what had happened. The patient said, "You amaze me." He then said that he had never had any real contact with his father and felt a certain contempt for the way he behaved. Later he spoke of liking to take responsibility, to which the therapist said, "Yes, but I think you are always afraid that some man will come—" and the patient completed the sentence by saying, "and knock me off my pedestal." He then himself made the *link with the present*, saying that this was exactly what had happened recently, namely, that the man in charge of him had taken him off the responsible job that he was doing before. The therapist then made a further possible link between the past and the present, saying first that in these uneasy relationships with men, there was also—at least in fantasy—a woman present. In his childhood the situation had concerned himself, his father, and his mother; in the present situation it was himself, the man at work, and his wife; one must remember that the disturbed relation with this man had disturbed his relation with his wife. The explanation of this must be that for him to win and marry a very attractive woman was really proving that he was a man, but he was always afraid that another man would come and knock him off his pedestal. This was what had happened recently. The therapist then *completed the triangle of insight,* pointing out that he, the therapist, was a man in a superior position, and that the patient probably felt that the therapist would criticize him for not wanting to be in an inferior position. The patient admitted that when he had first come he had wondered what the therapist thought of him. At the end of the session the patient said he felt they had got further than ever before.

It has been necessary to give the foregoing sessions in some detail in order to illustrate both the patient's mixed feelings and the steady progress in the depth of interpretations. Further sessions will be given in overview only.

During these sessions it had never been clear whether or not the patient wanted to undertake regular therapy, and it was only in session 6 that he finally decided to do so. The therapist set a time limit of a total of eighteen sessions.

It seemed that once the basic Oedipal interpretation had been given, and although this theme was reiterated on a number of occasions, the patient now felt free to work on his second main theme, namely, as mentioned above, the fact that during his childhood he had had to look after the other children and had seldom been able to go out and play. He had thus missed much of his own share of mothering and had never been able to be carefree and irresponsible. He spoke of all this with more open emotion than at any other time during therapy, and it seemed clear that he could not make demands for himself because his mother was so busy, and that he had transferred a similar pattern to his wife. His defense against his angry feelings about what he had missed was another important source—besides competitiveness—of his compulsive need to do jobs as well as they could possibly be done. This defense began to disappear, and in session 6 one of the themes was "laziness," and he told how recently he had found himself, instead of working as hard at home as he did at work, simply sitting around and reading.

Side by side with this there also emerged, first, anger with his wife; and then the realization that there were at least two factors leading to his complaint of impotence other than those elicited in his initial history, one of which predated the change of jobs with which his original attack of impotence had been associated.

The first appeared in session 11, as follows: About two months after he had been put on the new job and had begun to experience intermittent sexual failure, his wife had mentioned the possibility of going to work in the United States for a period. At this he had got unaccountably angry, and he now realized that he must have felt she wanted to get away from him. This was made worse when she said jokingly that she might settle down there and not come back. His answer, half-jokingly, had been, "Yes, that's why I haven't any more interest" (by which he meant sexually).

The second precipitating factor emerged in the final session. This was that sexually his wife had always been slow to arouse, and that during foreplay he tended to suffer from "leakage of sperm." On one occasion, before his transfer to the new job, his wife had felt his penis and had said "Oh, you're wet," which he took to mean that he was weak. He felt this had set up a vicious circle in him of sexual failure and fear of failure.

During this later part of therapy his potency fluctuated, but the basic situation was one of relapse and reluctance to put himself further to the test. His wife began to suffer from intermenstrual bleeding and was due to be admitted for another D and C, and he was afraid that intercourse might do damage.

At a time when his potency had returned (session 14) he reported a number of other improvements: that he was feeling more confident, could speak to people more freely, felt less critical of other people and therefore did not need to be always above reproach himself, and—surprisingly—that his writing had improved. It was never quite clear how much these improvements depended on continuing sexual success. On the other hand, a stable change seemed to be that he felt much less compulsively driven to work in the house.

The therapist made some attempt to get at feelings about termination, with little conscious response. The most important work was in session 13, where the therapist said that the patient might well go away disappointed in the end. To this the patient said he didn't think he would be disappointed as he knew that everything had to come from himself. "I don't want you to open the door and say, 'There's the birthday table for you.'" The therapist pointed out how "reasonable" the patient was being, and linked this with his childhood and his relation with his wife, where he couldn't allow his own demands to find expression. This was a further occasion on which the triangle of insight was completed.

As far as the predictions were concerned, the first main theme of competitiveness was correctly foreseen, and also the relative absence of transference interpretations and work on termination, but the second main theme of being forced in his childhood to take responsibility too soon, his consequent inability to make demands, and his anger with his wife were unforeseen.

Total number of sessions	18
Total time	7 months

FOLLOW-UP

Independent Assessment (6 weeks)

He was seen by therapist A, a woman. Practically the whole interview was taken up with the subject of intercourse. He now felt that his trouble had nothing to do with being transferred to the new job, nor with his wife's operation. He said it had started with the incident in which his wife had remarked on his penis becoming wet. He later said how careful he always had to be not to hurt her, and that unless he took great care in getting her ready for intercourse he hurt her badly. The independent assessor felt that the patient had a tremendous preoccupation with keeping other people's good opinion, that treatment had helped him overcome this in relation to men, but not in his relation with women. She felt that the patient's very great ambivalence toward women had been left largely untouched.

Retest (7 Weeks)

The psychologist could find little evidence of positive change. Three-person situations were avoided as before. The main change seemed to be that the patient no longer denied his difficulties over potency, but the only result of this was a loss of his illusions and the feeling of being left empty and hopeless. There also seemed no evidence of any improvement in his relation with men. An important piece of reality was that he was now back in his original job with the superior he liked.

2 Months

He reported that his wife had not been fit and that he had not attempted intercourse. He added that it had now become clear to him that much of the time his wife did not really want intercourse, and therefore the tension between the two of them had decreased. He went over the history of his need to prove himself. He said that before all the trouble started, he had felt confident in himself and had had no need to prove himself. When he began to have sexual difficulty, this need to prove himself had first appeared. At home he would keep wondering what his wife was thinking of him, and then would feel compelled to go and prove himself by some work in the house. Now this feeling has disappeared, and he is back to where he started. Things are also back to normal at work, and he takes great pleasure in once more putting "fourteen hours into a twelve-hour day."

In this interview the therapist made a determined attempt to get at disappointment and anger about the comparative failure of treatment, but the patient remained "reasonable" about this throughout.

1 Year 8 Months

For ten months after his last contact with the clinic, he had made no attempt at intercourse because he was afraid of failing. He had, of course, been very worried about this, and had felt that his wife must be getting very frustrated. Then, one night when she was due to go to a party the next day, he had suddenly felt that if he didn't do it now somebody else would after the party. So he did, it was very successful, and his wife was very happy about it. They then had intercourse for the next four nights, waited about a week, tried again and this time it was unsuccessful. He was now so afraid of failing that he didn't try again for several weeks. However, since then they have had intercourse irregularly, and he said that most of the time it is fairly satisfactory and his wife achieves "complete satisfaction." If, on the other hand, he has to take a long time preparing his wife, he tends to lose his erection. This is much better than when he was at his worst before treatment, but slightly worse than when he was at his best.

As far as the rest of his relation with his wife is concerned, he has now cleverly succeeded in maneuvering her to sharing an important common interest with him, and enjoying it. The result of this is that the atmosphere is much warmer between them than it used to be. Moreover, since they are no longer afraid that intercourse will be a failure, they can touch each other during the normal course of their relation without the fear that they will start something that they cannot complete.

The common interest mentioned above means that he is able to relax at home much more than he used to be. He still does a good deal of decorating, but he said this was necessary.

As far as work is concerned, he is back to how he was before the trouble started. The constant feeling that other men were criticizing him and that he was criticizing them has gone. He is expecting promotion.

6 Years 9 Months

Letter from patient:

"Please accept my apologies for not answering your first letter. I realize that it was rude of me, but since I felt that this was an intrusion on my privacy, I felt that by ignoring it I would hear no more. When I moved away four years ago, I purposely gave you no forwarding address to avoid just this. While I understand your desire for research into results of past treatment, and would not wish to obstruct this research, I feel that since no apparent change has taken place since our last interview, my comments at that interview could be used in this research. With the foregoing observations in mind, I see no further gain in correspondence or interviews and request that the matter be closed. May I take this opportunity of thanking you for your efforts on my behalf. Although I may appear ungrateful I can assure you that this is not so."

DISCUSSION

The judges agreed that they must take the one year and eight months follow-up as the point to assess.

1. Potency and Relation with His Wife

It seems clear that his actual potency has partly been restored, but not to the level that existed before his trouble started. There is strong evidence that his attitude toward his potency has always been of a compulsive kind, and there is little evidence that this has changed. On the other hand, the tensions between him and his wife have been reduced because he is no longer so anxious about failing sexually; and they have found a common interest which gives them greater companionship.

2. Tolerance of Three-Person Situations

The circumstances in which he resumed the sexual relation imply a possible new ability to compete actively. The constant need to criticize men at work, together with the feeling that they were criticizing him, has disappeared.

3. Relaxation of Compulsiveness

There seems little doubt that he is now able to relax more at home, and this seems to be a genuine gain. How deep this goes is not certain.

Both judges agreed that the final refusal of follow-up must indicate considerable residual anxiety.

Team 2 thought that the information was inadequate for a proper assessment.

SCORES

Team 1	1.0	1.0
Team 2	No score	0.5
Mean		0.833

The Gunner's Wife

SUMMARY

Category. "False" (6 sessions, outcome 2.125).

A young married woman suffering from guilt about hostility toward her mother, who responded initially, then immediately went into resistance, and then forced the therapist into premature termination. She eventually improved, many years after termination, apparently in response to life events.

CONTRIBUTION TO THE CORRELATIONS WITH OUTCOME

Motivation and focality: Variable.

Transference/parent interpretations: Strongly positive but rather fortuitously—two such interpretations recorded in a short therapy give a high *proportion,* with high intermediate outcome.

DETAILS OF PATIENT AND THERAPIST

1. Patient

Sex	F.
Age	23.
Marital status	Married.
Occupation	Shorthand-typist.
Complaint	Nausea and vomiting for five years.
What seems to bring patient now	Recurrence of her symptoms about five months ago despite an operation (see below).

2. Therapist

Code	B.
Sex	M.

PSYCHIATRIC HISTORY

Her symptoms started with feelings of nausea about five years ago when she was eighteen. The G.P. wrote that subsequently, in addition to the nausea, her symptoms consisted of "typical ulcer pain." The patient's account to the psychiatrist was different: She said that the main symptom was a "bubbling feeling" in her abdomen, followed by an increasing feeling of gastric tension that could not really be described as a pain. This might end in vomiting, which gave her relief. When her symptoms were at their worst she was vomiting about once a week. Barium meal finally revealed a duodenal ulcer, and she had a vagotomy and pyloroplasty eleven months ago. She was then symptom-free for about six months, but the symptoms returned. She has in fact vomited twice since the operation.

DIAGNOSIS

The original diagnosis was hysteria and mild depression. The final follow-up revealed that her gastric symptoms were clearly phobic in origin.

DISTURBANCES

1. Symptoms. (a) Gastric symptoms as above; (b) mild obsessional tidiness; and (c) she is easily upset and cries easily. The tears were running down her face throughout most of the psychiatric interview.

2. Problems over Aggression. She has difficulty in expressing anger, particularly with her mother.

ADDITIONAL EVIDENCE

1. She described her father as someone who stayed in the background and was not master of the house as he should be. She could not feel close to him.

2. She was married nine months ago, about two months after her operation. When asked why she chose to marry this particular man, she answered, "Because I loved him. He was the man I wanted to share my life with." When asked what sort of a person her husband was, she said, "Not like my father, he is master in the home." She said that their sexual life was very satisfactory.

3. The most important source of trouble in her life seemed to be her mother. The evidence for this stemmed from the initial interview:

Early in the interview the patient described herself as easily upset by arguments and accidents. When asked whom the arguments might be with, she said, "My mother." When asked for an example, she spoke of conflict between her mother and her over whether she should spend the money to have a white wedding. Her mother had felt that she ought to put the money down for a house. It was while the patient was talking about this that the tears started.

The next theme was how her mother had been extremely over-worked all her life. An attempt to point out the mixture of anger and guilt in this met with little response at this stage.

When she was asked about her childhood she said it was "very happy"; but when she was asked for memories, she could only say,

"Well, I enjoyed school," and "I remember the war, and running to the shelter."

An attempt to find out any factors in her life that might have led to the original onset of her symptoms, or their recurrence more recently, met with no success. Finally she said "Perhaps it's just everything—all the things that worry me." At this point the interviewer suggested that the thing that gave her most trouble was being angry. She agreed with this and said she wasn't the sort of person who could "just storm out of the house." The interviewer asked her what house, from whom? Again it was her mother. She spoke of having begun to get into conflict with her mother at about sixteen and a half, when she started feeling that she wanted to do things her own way. Quickly she veered away to how overworked her mother was. The interviewer said that she must be angry with her mother but couldn't really be angry because she was so sorry for her. This time the patient seemed completely convinced that this must be so.

4. She was given a projection test (ORT), and the psychologist wrote that her mother is seen as a possessive person who has to be got rid of if the patient is to find happiness. Although in some of the stories the patient gets rid of the woman and goes off with the man, she cannot maintain this and inevitably has to renounce her heterosexual wishes. There were two stories of the dangers resulting from a gas leak, which the psychologist interpreted as her explosive feelings of resentment that she had to keep inside herself. Many of her themes were rather like fairy stories, where some fairy godmother turns up to put everything right. Behind the themes of Oedipal guilt, there were hints of problems connected with greed, possessiveness, and rejection by a frustrating mother. On the other hand, the psychologist wrote that the patient seemed to have a foundation of secure good experience, and he did not see her as very ill.

HYPOTHESIS

There is evidence for resentment against her mother because of a feeling of deprivation, which she cannot express freely because she feels too guilty and sorry for her mother. We suspect that this deprivation applies especially to primitive love and understanding.

With this as background there may also be guilt about having a man.

CRITERIA

1. **Symptoms.** Loss of (a) gastric and (b) obsessional symptoms without development of substitutes. (c) She should not be so easily upset.

2. Aggression. She should lose the need to idealize and to present herself as "nice." With her mother she should be able to express her anger but to appreciate her where appropriate. This ability to be angry and to assert herself constructively should apply to her whole life.

3. Relation with Husband. Since we suspect that her statements about the relation with her husband are idealized, she should be able to admit strains in their relationship, and at the same time there should be evidence of a freeing of "positive" feelings toward him.

REASON FOR ACCEPTANCE AND THERAPEUTIC PLAN

Both the initial interview and the projection test centered around a conflict between anger and guilt in the relation to her mother, which seemed a clear-cut focus. The psychologist felt he had made contact with her and was willing to take her on. As his therapeutic plan he wrote: "To help her to acknowledge (1) her guilt at being greedy and leaving her mother in the lurch; and (2) her resentful feelings about the possessive, frustrating mother."

SUMMARY OF COURSE OF THERAPY

In session 2 the patient had difficulty in starting, saying that she didn't know what was wanted. The therapist made several interpretations of her fear of showing him anything beneath the "nice" exterior. This eventually brought out a good deal of detail about how her father and mother had failed her when she needed support and understanding with difficulties she was having at school with schoolwork. This was in contrast to her remarks about school in session 1.

Session 3 started ten minutes late because she did not report to the reception desk when she arrived; the receptionist had looked so busy that she hadn't wanted to bother her. The therapist suggested that she was afraid of asking anything for herself, and she said that she would like to have fun like other people. Even when she was a child she had had to study hard while her brothers had all the fun. She went on to speak about how her mother is now a household drudge, and how much more satisfying her own life is than her mother's. The therapist suggested she felt guilty at getting so much more than her mother. This brought out clear evidence that the patient's abdominal symptoms were most severe when her life was most satisfying. She described a sudden attack of nausea that had forced her to run out of a cinema—"Perhaps it was because I was so excited and happy."

In Session 4 she reported that she was now a lot better. She has not had a recurrence of nausea since beginning treatment. She has learned that her trouble is that she worries too much about other people, and she is determined to stop doing this. Her mother has been very worried over the patient's grandmother's serious illness, and the patient is very sorry about the situation but it hasn't worried her nearly as much as it would have done previously. After she had said all this she dried up and had nothing else to say. Eventually the therapist interpreted that he had become the mother who did so little to meet her demands, yet with whom it would be quite unreasonable to be angry because of her need to be grateful and to keep a good relationship with him (transference/parent interpretation). Her response to this was to talk some more about her mother's failures to provide what was needed.

In session 5 she said that although she had always told the therapist she didn't get angry, her husband had been pointing out the opposite to her. An example had been that when they were engaged she had insisted that her husband should stop unnecessarily supporting his own mother if they were to get married. The therapist spoke about her guilt at getting what she wanted in a triangular situation, and linked this to a situation involving the boss and another girl at work, when she had triumphed over the other girl and got her promotion but also got her symptoms. He also linked it with the home situation where she had wanted to demand her rights from her mother and displace her grandmother. The patient replied that she would make up her mind not to be guilty in the future at getting something that she wanted. She went on to say that she felt this was the answer to her problems, and as she is so much better perhaps she should stop coming for treatment. She deflected all attempts at interpreting her withdrawal as a defense against facing angry and jealous feelings that she did not want to know about. Patient and therapist eventually agreed to make a further appointment in a month's time.

In this final session she reported that on the whole she was still very much better, although her abdominal pain had recurred on two occasions. She has now been married nearly a year and her feeling of security increases all the time. Everything is going nicely at work. As soon as she started to look beneath the surface, however, a picture of innumerable worries emerged. These concerned particularly her anxiety about becoming pregnant, which would shatter all the financial security she and her husband had built up. She vacillated in her feeling about whether or not to continue treatment. She felt she had said everything she could, yet she did not want to cut off the possibility of more help. When the therapist suggested that they would no longer meet regularly, but that she could call upon him whenever she felt the need, she felt this was the ideal solution.

SUMMARY

The focus as initially laid down was used and was clearly entirely appropriate. Some important insights seemed to be achieved, but the moment this occurred the patient withdrew, i.e., the true underlying motivation was relatively poor. There were two transference/parent interpretations recorded out of a total of twenty. This gives the high transference/parent ratio of 10 percent, although the actual amount of working through of the transference/parent link was of course relatively small.

| Total number of sessions | 6 |
| Total time | 4 months |

FOLLOW-UP

6 Years 8 Months

The patient was located abroad, where her husband had been posted. She returned a questionnaire, from which it appeared that she was *essentially unchanged.*

8 Years 9 Months

The interviewer wrote: "She was very different from the rather frightened and distressed girl that I remember seeing nine years ago. She struck me as being much more poised, very much more self-confident, and although still with a number of neurotic difficulties, she seems basically happy."

When seen, she and her husband had recently returned from a two-year spell of duty abroad. They now have two children.

1. Symptoms

(a) Gastric symptoms. Though better, these have not completely cleared up. It is now clear that a large part of these symptoms is phobic in origin. She gets a knotted-up feeling in her abdomen, accompanied by nausea and a feeling of emotional tension, in the following situations: (i) When she is going to meet people that she does not know very well, and especially if she gets behind time preparing for such an occasion; and (ii) in cars, buses, and coaches, if she isn't driving (trains and the subway are all right, cars if she is driving). She associates the symptoms that she gets on social occasions with a lack of self-confidence, and the fear that she will do something foolish.

At the same time she made clear that her lack of confidence in social situations is considerably better than it used to be. Situations that would have been very frightening can now be tolerated after initial anxiety, and others are no longer frightening at all. Moreover, whereas she used to vomit fairly frequently in such situations, she now has not done so for at least a year.

She suffered from very severe vomiting during both her pregnancies and vomited blood on one occasion during her second pregnancy. She had to be admitted to the hospital early in both pregnancies. She had great difficulty over her first labor and had to have a Caesarean section. She finally had to be sterilized owing to her anxiety about possible further pregnancies.

(b) Obsessional tidiness and control. The tidiness seems unchanged. She told of an incident in which, because of her anxiety about her children doing damage, she had unnecessarily controlled their natural boisterousness.

(c) Easily upset, cries easily. This is still present, though it is better. There was a background of possible tears running through the whole interview, particularly at mention of the word "security." This strongly suggested that she has never really got over the impression left on her by her childhood.

2. Aggression

(a) Loss of need to idealize. She was much more forthright than in the first interview, and there seemed much less evidence of a need to idealize.

(b) Ability to express anger with her mother but to appreciate her where appropriate. She gets on better with her mother but since they now live far apart it is difficult to judge how far this represents a real improvement.

(c) Ability to assert herself. She is now much more able to assert herself.

3. Relation with Her Husband

When asked about her husband, the first thing she said was, "Oh, he is my *rock*, he is the person who means security to me." She spoke of him with real love and told how badly she misses him when he is away. At the same time she was able to admit strains in their relationship, and how they flared up at each other over small things. It was difficult to judge how much idealization there was in this. Their sexual life seems entirely satisfactory.

4. Relation to the Children

It is possible that the severe symptoms during pregnancy indicate much underlying difficulty in relation to being a mother. The evidence from the interview suggested that although she was able to be a *conscientious* mother, it was by no means certain how much she *enjoyed* being a mother; and it was clear that at times she allowed her anxious preoccupation with control and with saving money to over-ride allowing her children freedom or saving them from distress.

DISCUSSION

EHR made the following point: If she had not been sterilized after her second pregnancy, her sexual life would have been severely disrupted and this quite likely would have set up a serious vicious circle in her whole life. If we had seen her in that state, we could not possibly have regarded this as a good result of psychotherapy. Against this it must be said that no one can tell the extent to which her symptoms during pregnancy were psychogenic.

There is no doubt that her present adjustment to life is an extremely good one, though we may question her ability to stand up to any loss of the security that means so much to her. Although she has considerably matured, she seems to remain basically the same insecure, anxious, mildly depressed, and mildly obsessional person.

SCORES

Team 1	1.5	2.0
Team 2	2.5	2.5
Mean	2.125	

Mrs. Hopkins

SUMMARY

Category. Short, unfavorable (33 sessions, outcome 0.875).

A married woman of thirty-six with two complaints: (1) disturbed behavior in her daughters, and (2) frigidity. A basically nontransference therapy resulted in considerable improvements in both problems, but at follow-up the original patterns seemed to have been largely reestablished.

CONTRIBUTION TO THE CORRELATIONS WITH OUTCOME

Motivation: Fluctuating.
Focality: Neutral (moderate focality, poor outcome).
Transference/parent interpretations: Strongly positive (score zero, poor outcome).

DETAILS OF PATIENT AND THERAPIST

1. Patient

Sex	F.
Age	36.
Marital status	Married.
Occupation	Housewife.
What seems to bring patient now	Twenty months ago she consulted a child psychiatrist because her elder daughter, then one and a half, could not sleep and both parents were almost exhausted. One week ago she consulted the same psychiatrist about her frigidity.

2. Therapist

Code	H.
Sex	M.

PSYCHIATRIC DIAGNOSIS

Anxiety–hysteria.

DISTURBANCES

1. Sexual Difficulties. She has never got any satisfaction from sexual intercourse, and recently intercourse has become increasingly distasteful to her. In the past few months she and her husband have not had intercourse at all.

2. Disturbances in Elder Daughter. One and a half years ago she consulted another psychiatrist because her daughter, Katherine, could not sleep and both parents were exhausted. Now Katherine has to have her and her parents' doors open at night so that she can see her parents' bed. The patient cannot change this arrangement because she is afraid it might create anxiety in Katherine. Katherine has to get up three to four times a night to pass water, always calls out to her parents, and expects an answer. The patient usually sleeps through this and her husband answers.

3. Anxiety. The above disturbance in Katherine has almost certainly been fostered by the patient's excessive anxiety about her children. This is part of a general anxiety: She is afraid all the time that something terrible may happen, especially to her children. She takes exaggerated precautions against any harm coming to them. If she remains alone in the house, she is constantly afraid that a burglar may come in.

ADDITIONAL EVIDENCE

1. Something has gone wrong between her parents, who are now distant from each other.

2. A younger brother was born when the patient was fifteen. During the pregnancy the patient was continually asking whether her mother would still love her after the baby was born.

3. In the initial interview she started by talking about her sexual problem, but quickly went on to the problems of Katherine and sleeping arrangements. The therapist tried hard to show her that there was something highly neurotic in this, but the patient remained cheerful throughout and it seemed little impression was made.

4. However, in session 2 (the patient was not given psychological tests), the therapist was first able to point out the patient's inconsistent behavior with her children; and she then gave clear indication of her ambivalence about overcoming her frigidity. With the help of some interpretation she eventually came out with the exaggerated precautions she had to take in the home lest harm should come to the children, and then her fear of burglars. The therapist tentatively linked her fear of burglars with her fear of intercourse (in which something intrudes into her). This was a much deeper session and it seemed that progress was being made.

HYPOTHESIS

Her present disturbances seem to express a conflict between wanting a private relation with her husband on the one hand, and her anxiety and guilt about this on the other:

1. She is allowing her daughter to interfere in her sexual relation with her husband. This both expresses her guilt, and via identification with the daughter, may well express her own childhood wish to interfere in her parents' relation.

2. She is angry with her children (perhaps because they have come between her and her husband), but she defends herself against this by overanxiousness and an obsessional fear that harm will come to them.

CRITERIA

1. Mutually satisfactory sexual and emotional relation with her husband.

2. Loss of excessive anxiety in general, and particularly over the children, accompanied by: (a) ability to enjoy being a mother, and (b) ability to be firm with the children when necessary, especially in preventing them from coming between her and her husband.

3. Ideally, there should be some evidence for an increase in her ability to express deep feelings both about herself and the people close to her.

REASON FOR ACCEPTANCE AND THERAPEUTIC PLAN

Though the therapist was discouraged by what he called her "impenetrable friendliness" in the initial interview, he felt able to make a therapeutic plan. This was to use the relationship with her children as an entry into her "complicated fixation to her mother." He wrote that this might possibly lead to some relief of her frigidity, but "if this should prove too difficult I intend to stop there." He was encouraged by the much deeper second session.

SUMMARY OF COURSE OF THERAPY

If the therapeutic plan were rephrased as "to use the patient's relation with her children to lead into Oedipal and sexual problems," then it would have been remarkably accurate. The result was a complex therapy in which these three themes tended to run in parallel, and they are best considered separately.

1. Interpretations About the Patient's Relation to Her Children

It soon came out that there was trouble not only in Katherine, but in her younger sister Jane, the chief manifestations of which were that she spent a lot of time rocking before going to sleep, and also that she wetted the bed.

The main interpretations given to the patient about her relation with the children were as follows:

(a) That her attitude was a mixture of overindulgence and interference (session 3).

(b) That Katherine and the patient were in competition for the husband's attention, and that the patient—because of her own Oedipal problems—was behaving in such a way as to express her guilt about not handing over her husband to her daughter (session 3).

(c) That she was very afraid of being an inadequate mother (session 4).

(d) That Katherine was expressing the patient's own feelings, e.g., Katherine was due to go away with her father for a weekend and was apprehensive about sleeping in a strange house. It was easy to show the patient that it was she who didn't like the idea of her husband and Katherine being away together (session 6).

(e) In response to (d) the patient mentioned that when Katherine was born she had the feeling of wanting to do something against her. It was therefore possible to interpret that the overindulgence was a defense against aggressive feelings.

(f) The therapist suggested that Jane's rocking was a result of being overstimulated (session 9). This was abundantly confirmed; Jane was a very attractive child and it was difficult for her parents to keep their hands off her. On one occasion when she was put to bed by her grandmother she didn't rock at all.

2. New Ways of Handling the Children

Work of the kind listed under 1. above seems to have resulted in a number of elementary discoveries on the part of the patient and her husband about how to handle the children:

(a) On one occasion, when Jane was got up at night as a precaution against her wetting the bed, she had screamed, and her father had come in and told her to shut up (session 7). To everyone's amazement this worked like a charm! The therapist pointed out how the patient was unable to be gentle and firm at the same time.

(b) In session 23 the patient reported that Katherine had been very aggressive when Jane had been ill, because of all the attention the latter had got, and that she had said she wanted different parents and a different house in which to live. To this the patient had said that she didn't want to have a different girl from Katherine, she wanted her Katherine. This had completely resolved the situation.

(c) Jane had asked her mother whether it mattered if she rocked, and much to her surprise her mother had answered that it didn't matter at all, Jane could do what she liked (session 25).

(d) While they were on holiday, Jane had been very aggressive toward everybody. One night her father had sat down on her bed and asked what was wrong; was she unhappy because she had been trying to give up rocking and had succeeded? He suggested she should have a good rock, which she did, and she hasn't rocked since (session 28).

3. The Patient's Feelings About Sexuality, and the Link with the Past

(a) In connection with Katherine's Oedipal feelings, the therapist suggested that the patient also must have been in love with her father (session 3).

(b) It emerged that after marriage the patient somehow lost her freedom over sex: The situation is now that she can't bear to undress in front of her husband or to have him touch her unless she is fully dressed. The therapist interpreted that she finds her body unattractive (session 7).

(c) Session 8 started with feelings of being useless, which the therapist suggested expressed her feeling about her own body. It then emerged that her father was very fond of her and the therapist suggested that she felt despair about being stimulated by him but never satisfied. Session 9 included the interpretation mentioned under 1(f) above about *Jane* being overstimulated. In session 10 the therapist interpreted that both the patient and *Katherine* had been stimulated sexually but not satisfied. This brought out some of the patient's earlier sexual history: She had started smoking and masturbating, with mild fantasies about men, in her adolescence, but she had known nothing of actual intercourse until marriage, and this had been a shock to her.

(d) It emerged in session 15 that her father had been a philanderer and that she once saw him in town with another woman. The therapist interpreted that she wanted to take revenge on men by frustrating them.

(e) A very important session was no. 18. Katherine had wanted to know what happens to the clothes of people who have died. The therapist interpreted that Katherine wanted to inherit everything from her mother, and that mother and daughter may be rivals for the father. Haltingly, the patient brought out evidence for how much her two daughters were in love with their father. She said that her relation with her own father was quite different: She couldn't stand being near him. It eventually came out that her father used to like Katherine but has now transferred all his affection to Jane because he likes cuddly babies but can't stand cheeky little girls. The therapist suggested that she once had a good relation with her father but later lost it.

(f) It gradually became clear that she had a severe distaste for her own body and also was largely ignorant of her own genital anatomy. In session 26 the therapist gave her an anatomy lesson, with diagrams. In session 27 she reported that she had used a mirror to explore her own genital anatomy, and had found it revolting.

(g) When, in session 29, she said that she could have orgasm when her husband masturbated her, but found intercourse itself distasteful, the therapist interpreted that since her clitoris was a kind of penis she could enjoy it being stimulated, whereas the rest of her body was feminine and that was disgusting. This led to her saying that women's bodies smelled even if they took regular baths, whereas men's didn't smell even if they didn't take baths.

4. Changes in the Patient's Sexual Relation with Her Husband During Therapy

(a) After session 10, in which there emerged the history of her loss of sexual freedom after marriage, she reported (sessions 11–13) a slight increase in sexual feeling; but it also became clear that she could tolerate a sexual approach only if she didn't get excited herself.

(b) In session 15 the patient, without warning, brought her husband with her, and both were seen together. In this session it came out that her husband suffered from premature ejaculation; and the therapist also remarked that he was apparently incapable of "manhandling" her.

(c) In sessions 17 and 18 she reported that she had encouraged her husband not to be so considerate with her sexually. As a result his premature ejaculation improved and so did her sexual interest, but she did not have orgasm.

(d) She then reported that her distaste for intercourse had disappeared, and that she had got very near to orgasm, but her husband finished too soon (sessions 19 and 21).

(e) There was then a progressive increase in her sexual involvement, from (i) getting to orgasm fairly easily through masturbation by her husband, though she doesn't like this (session 28); through (ii) the most successful intercourse of her whole life though she did not quite reach orgasm, which followed session 29, in which her distaste for women's bodies was brought out; to (iii) regular intercourse with orgasm, though she said she didn't really enjoy it.

5. Ending of Therapy

In session 27 the patient herself suggested stopping for the time being to see if she could make use of what she had learned, and the therapist agreed, though privately believing that she needed further help, and would ask for it.

There was then a four-month break. The therapist wrote to her and she came for session 28. Here she brought out that although she had been the instigator of the break she had been very upset by the fact that the therapist had agreed, feeling that he had lost interest in her and she was a hopeless case. The therapist made no interpretation but assured her that this was a misunderstanding, and that the aim had ben for her to experiment with the knowledge that she had gained.

Therapy was again left for four months, after which the patient asked for another appointment (session 29). During the next few sessions it became clear that there were considerable improvements in her relation with her children; but although there were clear improvements in her sexual feelings, she seemed unable to enjoy actual intercourse. She finally admitted that she was only seeking help over her sexual problem because she was afraid her husband might leave her. She then proposed that treatment should stop on condition that she could come back if she needed further help, to which the therapist agreed.

6. Comments

The reader may have noticed that the above account contains hardly any reference to the transference. This was, in fact, true of the therapy as a whole. The therapist often felt that the patient was inviting him to be forceful with her, but he deliberately refrained from this because he did not want to get into competition with her husband, nor did he interpret it. There were *no* transference/parent interpretations recorded. Since, despite the remarkable initial improvements, this was judged to be a basically unsuccessful therapy, it made a strong positive contribution toward the correlation between T/P interpretations and outcome.

Total number of sessions	33
Total time	1 year 8 months

FOLLOW-UP

9 Months

There seemed to have been a considerable degree of relapse. Although she and her husband have intercourse two or three times a week, and although she has no revulsion, she has little interest. She would like it less often. She does not like being touched and considers her body uninteresting. Things are better if she is slightly drunk.

Katherine's behavior has been sensible, but Jane's much less so. She has been making trouble over going to school, and recently has started having restless nights and coming into her parents' bedroom. Katherine insists on wearing bathing trunks when having her bath. An improvement that has been maintained was that the patient seemed much less anxious about all this.

5 Years 1 Month

1. Mutually Satisfactory Sexual and Emotional Relation with Her Husband

She is now able to allow her husband intercourse without the help of whisky, but she remains completely frigid and her aversion to physical contact remains extremely strong. She would be happier if nobody, neither her husband nor her children, wanted to touch her.

There was little evidence in the follow-up report about the relation with her husband apart from sex.

2. Loss of Anxiety in General, Particularly with the Children, Etc.

(a) A number of the manifestations of anxiety are very much improved. She can now let the children come home alone from school by public transport, and she can stay alone at home quite unperturbed. Instead of listening intently for the burglars who are bound to come, she can sit comfortably watching television.

(b) On the other hand, although Katherine ceased to interfere with her parents' sleep for a period after termination, she then started to wake up in the night and come into her parents' bedroom. She was eventually sent for treatment in her own right, after which this behavior ceased. Moreover, it seems that some problem in the parents is still being acted out in the family. Thus, Jane, now aged eight, cannot sleep alone and insists that she must sleep with Katherine. Katherine hates this but the parents have given in to Jane's wishes. This, together with certain other evidence, suggested to us that the parents cannot tolerate the idea of their children having to face and overcome anxiety about separation. Moreover, when Jane was ill, her mother slept with her and allowed Katherine to sleep in the double bed with her father. This was despite the fact that there was a spare room available for Katherine. This suggests that the patient is still colluding with her daughter's wish to interfere in her parents' relation. The parents' behavior over their daughters' sexual education also suggests that they were trying to do the enlightened thing against powerful underlying anxiety.

Jane gave up her rocking spontaneously, but still bites her nails.

3. Increase in Ability to Express Deep Feelings, Etc.

Here there was little evidence; but the parents' behavior over problems of separation in their children suggested little change.

SUMMARY

1. She has lost many of the *symptoms* of her anxiety.

2. She is trying to do the right thing both in her daughters' upbringing and in the sexual relation.

3. However, the anxieties in both of these areas seem basically unchanged.

SCORES

Team 1	1.0	1.0
Team 2	1.0	0.5
Mean	0.875	

Mrs. Lewis

SUMMARY

Category. "False" (20 sessions, outcome 2.83).

A young married woman apparently suffering from "Oedipal" anxieties, with very doubtful motivation, with whom the therapist seems to have had little idea where he was going. She improved dramatically many years after termination in response to leaving her husband for another man.

CONTRIBUTION TO THE CORRELATIONS WITH OUTCOME

Motivation and focality: Negative (both factors low, favorable outcome). *Transference/parent interpretations:* Negative (low score, favorable outcome). The dynamic factors were thus far lower than would be expected from the favorable outcome.

DETAILS OF PATIENT AND THERAPIST

1. Patient

Sex	F.
Age	23.
Marital status	Married.
Occupation	Telephonist.
What seems to bring patient now	A few weeks ago she went to her G.P. (who was Tavistock-trained) complaining of chilblains, and in passing asked if there were any reason why she might not conceive. The G.P. noticed an extreme inhibition in talking about sexual matters, and referred her to the clinic.

2. Therapist

Code	K.
Sex	M.

PSYCHIATRIC HISTORY

She was married five years ago, at the age of eighteen. She only learned about the "facts of life" from a woman friend immediately before her marriage. Her husband thought that she should not have children as she was too young, but later they decided to start trying. Two years ago she started to have irregular periods, and she went to an antenatal clinic. The consultant there wrote, "Vaginal examination was quite inadequate as she seemed extremely tender with possibly an intact hymen. I should think she is undoubtedly pregnant and I have booked her for confinement here." She attended the antenatal clinic for about five months and then was told she was not pregnant. The G.P. wrote, "I am sure this was a proper pseudopregnancy." Since then she and her husband have continued to try to have children, but she does not conceive. At initial interview, she said that she had never been able to relax enough to let her husband in, as far as she knew there had never been any blood on the sheet, and she thought her hymen was probably still intact. She and her husband continue to have intercourse two or three times a week, on the basis that her husband gets part of the way in and has an orgasm, and she is relieved when it is all over.

Ever since she was married, she has suffered from vomiting in the mornings in spells of a week or two with intervals of a week or two. The vomiting does not occur when she is menstruating.

She described herself as the sort of person who flares up and then it is all over quickly. Recently this has been worse, and she also cries for no apparent reason. She was tearful throughout much of the initial interview.

She has never liked being left at home alone, and her husband always makes sure that there is someone in the house if he isn't going to be there.

DIAGNOSIS

Anxiety-hysteria with mild depression.

DISTURBANCES

1. Sexual Difficulties. It seems most likely that her complaint of inability to conceive is in fact because she has not allowed consummation of the marriage. She allows her husband to get only part of the way in, and is relieved when intercourse is over. She says she is afraid of the pain; but she also sometimes tells her husband that it is hurting before it is in fact.

2. Symptoms. (a) False pregnancy (see above); (b) "morning sickness" (see above); (c) phobic anxiety, fear of being left alone (see above); and (d) recent attacks of crying for no apparent reason.

3. Difficulties over Aggression. (a) Recently she has been irritable and has tended to flare up. But she is also very afraid of rows and of her own temper. (b) After session 1 the therapist wrote that she had to fit in with other people's needs and "had no life of her own."

ADDITIONAL EVIDENCE

1. She is an only child.

2. With her father she experienced a great deal of companionship when she was a child—in her own words, "I am afraid I idolize him."

3. Her husband is eight years older than she. She said of him that he was happy-go-lucky like her father; and that, like her father, one could not be angry with him for long but found oneself laughing.

4. There is severe tension between the patient and her mother. They quarrel frequently, and when this happens her mother first flares up and then won't speak to her for a week or more at a time. Her mother does things for other people before she will do them for the patient. Soon after the patient got engaged, her mother told her that she didn't want her to have children. In the initial interview, when the patient spoke of her mother, her face twisted and almost twitched. In contrast, it was particularly when speaking of her father that she became tearful.

5. The psychologist wrote of her *projection test (ORT)*, "A hysterical frigidity based on Oedipal conflicts, focusing on her guilt and the internalization of a forbidding mother, who thus acts as a control over her guilt-ridden sexual wishes. The key to her problem is probably her fear of her mother's envy and retaliation."

6. A theme in session 2 was her fear of her own temper. The therapist pointed out that she expressed no annoyance despite the fact that it had taken her two hours to get to him. When he later asked what she felt should be done about her, she replied that it was up to him. He then suggested to her that she had no life of her own, and for the first time she seemed to appreciate that this was unsatisfactory, and the therapist felt she came to life.

HYPOTHESIS

There is evidence of deprivation of love and understanding from her mother and bitter resentment about this. She has turned for love to her father, whom she has idealized, and has married a man very like her father. Her mother has openly expressed disapproval of the patient's having children.

We cannot be sure why she is unable to enjoy sex and have children, but we think that one of the factors is fear of her mother's retaliation.

CRITERIA

1. Ability to allow full sexual intercourse with full enjoyment and orgasm.

2. Loss of symptoms: vomiting, fear of being alone, crying.

3. Ability (a) to experience anger with both women and men in a way that improves the situation and (b) at the same time to appreciate their good qualities.

4. Ability to feel she can live her own life and acknowledge and satisfy her own needs.

REASON FOR ACCEPTANCE AND THERAPEUTIC PLAN

At initial interview the signs were ambiguous: The pathology seemed fairly clear and it was not difficult to formulate a focus in terms of guilt about Oedipal hostility toward her mother; but on the other hand, there was little response to interpretation, and when she was asked what she wanted help for she said she did not know, thus showing limited motivation. The projection test confirmed the psychiatric opinion of the pathology, and suggested a sound ego, but the psychologist was more impressed than the psychiatrist with the patient's motivation. Therapist K offered to see her.

After session 2 the therapist formulated a rather different focus, writing: "It seems to me that she is terrified of her primitive aggressive drives. My immediate aim would be to link the fact of her not having a life of her own with her conflicts over her temper, and to help her claim and possess these feelings. I would try to do this in the transference, e.g., her denial that she is annoyed at having to come so far to see me, etc."

SUMMARY OF COURSE OF THERAPY

This was a very unsatisfactory therapy in which there was limited contact and limited progress throughout, much of the work being done unsuccessfully on the patient's resistances.

From the beginning she was unspontaneous and had little to say. The therapist first tried to link this with her feeling that she had her mother inside her, criticizing her (session 3). It emerged that her mother expressed her own anger by silence, and the therapist suggested that the patient's "dumbness" expressed an attack on him (session 4). She agreed that she had thought of this herself in relation to her husband, but she couldn't really believe it.

An early theme was the patient's *vomiting*, which tended to occur on the way to the sessions. It seemed that this symptom had first occurred when she had moved to secondary school at the age of eleven (session 3). In session 5 she made clear that she could not allow herself to experience anything exciting between herself and another person, but had to store it up and examine it on her own. The therapist interpreted her vomiting as expressing anxiety about something too intense happening between her and him, and she agreed. It then emerged that last week she and her husband had had intercourse, and not only had he got right in but it was her fertile period. She said that if she became pregnant she would conceal it from her mother, as otherwise she would feel it would be taken away from her.

In session 6 it emerged that the onset of her vomiting had also coincided with her father's return from the war. This led to her speaking loudly and volubly about jealousy of her mother, but in such a way as to imply that she herself was blameless. Thus, even here her resistances were much in evidence, and the therapist used the word "slippery" in referring to her way of avoiding responsibility for her own feelings. She agreed with this and said that her husband had used the same word.

In session 7 there was again much material about jealousy in which she was never involved. The therapist pointed this out and she admitted that she took pleasure in slipping out of everything. It later emerged that her vomiting had improved, though she put this as her husband's statement and not her own.

In session 9 the therapist made what ought to have been a major interpretation, suggesting that her refusal of responsibility for her own feelings was her attempt to deny that she wanted to excite her father and steal him from her mother. He then had to point out that she did not apparently react to his more or less accusing her of being a thief. She admitted that in such situations she always controlled herself and only later might explode. She spoke of an intense row between two of her relatives, in which she had to control herself for fear of getting involved. Toward the end of this session her stolid passivity had changed to a certain degree of animation.

In session 10 she seemed as resistant as ever. In session 11 she then spoke of having discussed her sexual ignorance with an elderly woman friend; and she went on to speak with intensity of never having learned about sex nor of having become aware of sexual feelings as a girl. The therapist tried to link her need to have such feelings forced out of her with the situation in therapy, in which she seemed to be largely drifting; yet, he said, if he set her a time limit she would just remain obstinate. She agreed but remained helpless.

The nearest that the therapy came to real progress seemed to be in sessions 13–15. The therapist suggested that in her attitude of "not caring" she was pushing away painful, resentful thoughts, and that this included him. She said that if she became angry she could never apologize, and if she became angry with him she could never come back. He suggested that the anger was about not being cared for, and when he related this to himself her eyes filled with tears. She admitted that she was near to breaking down but in fact did not do so.

There was by now a definite change from the atmosphere of previous sessions, and in session 14 she was somewhat depressed and often on the brink of tears. Since the last session she had had attacks of trembling and of her legs feeling useless. The therapist suggested that she had been angry with him, and though she agreed she said she could never express it to him. She went on to speak of much resentment against her mother, the theme being of trying to get some love from her mother but always failing.

There was then a two-week break, and in session 15 she spoke of having to leave her dog by itself and how it might howl. The therapist related this to her feelings about being left alone last week, but though she agreed she indicated that she would always suppress her feelings. He then said that the whole problem of her facing her real feelings might become more real if he set her a time limit, and they agreed on a further five sessions. Later in the session he made a major interpretation making the therapist/parent link, saying that she had kept both the therapist and her husband from "getting into" her, and that this was in order to deny her wish to have her father because of her guilt toward her mother. She seemed to consider this more seriously than before.

However, this was then followed by three sessions of resistance. Finally, in session 19, she reported a terrific row with her husband over her mother. She said she realized that she was displacing her conflict with her mother onto her husband and that she really must have it out with her mother. She said she was terrified of doing so, but was afraid that unless she did her marriage might break up. She felt she might possibly be able to write to her mother rather than speak to her, and the therapist suggested that she might write to him about her feelings.

Of course, she didn't write. Session 20 was the last. She insisted that she could never be any different, and the therapist insisted that it wasn't that she couldn't but that she wouldn't. They eventually agreed that she would write for an appointment in three months (of course, she didn't do so).

In this session the therapist noted that she had lost 35 pounds during therapy and seemed more alive, energetic, and exciting.

Total number of sessions   20
Total time   7 months

FOLLOW UP

10 Months

Three weeks after termination the patient went to her G.P. and told
him that she was unchanged. He suggested that she go to a psychiatrist
nearer home, which she did, but she disliked him and left after the
second session. When seen again by the therapist, she had then maintained her loss of weight. The important thing that had happened was
that she had started an affair, short of intercourse, with another man.
Her husband had found out about it and had told her that either she
stopped the affair or else they separated. She had stopped the affair,
was continuing with her husband, and their relation seemed much the
same as when she first came.

6 Years 4 Months

General. She was seen for follow-up by therapist F., who had
originally seen her for consultation. He wrote that apart from her build
she seemed to be an entirely different person. In place of the quiet,
passive woman who cried throughout much of the interview, she was
straightforward, forceful, earthy, at times even brassy, and had a certain hardness. The events of her story, as seen by her now, took on an
entirely different aspect:

She felt now that when she and her husband got married, he was
almost as ignorant about sex as she was. She said she had been "shaken
rigid" by the examination at the hospital in which she had been told
she was still a virgin. From then on, she felt, there had been open
tension between her and her husband, flaring up regularly into open
rows. This situation got steadily worse for about four years. Roughly
three years ago she became pregnant for the first time, and she now has
a daughter aged two and a half. The patient realized that, as soon as her
daughter became old enough to notice, she was badly affected by her
parents' rows. The patient therefore bottled up her feelings from then
on, agreeing with anything her husband might say in order to get the
row over as soon as possible and keep the peace. Two years ago, her
husband bought a tobacconist's shop, she helped serve in the shop, and
they moved into the house above. Domestic circumstances were such
that they had very little privacy, and she began to feel that she was in
danger of a breakdown; she was getting shaking attacks and acciden-
tally breaking things.

One of the regular customers in the shop was a man called Philip.
She and Philip fell in love, and they began to go out together. Finally,
five months ago, she left her husband and went to live with Philip. He
is a fitter in the R.A.F., and has now been sent abroad. She and her

husband are getting a divorce, and she is going out to join Philip and marry him as soon as the divorce is made absolute.

She said that the only thing that she regretted was the fact that this meant leaving her daughter behind. They have decided that life in the Forces is unsettled and would be likely to disturb her, and that the best thing to do is to leave her to be looked after by the patient's husband and her parents. Moreover, there would be legal difficulties over custody, since her husband is divorcing her for adultery and she is leaving the suit undefended. The interviewer felt her regret about her daughter was genuine, but did not go very deep.

Since leaving her husband, she said, she has found a strength that she never knew she had. She has been able to face everybody despite what they think of her, and she has even succeeded in winning her parents round to accepting Philip.

As far as the direct relation with Philip was concerned, a graphic picture emerged of two people with a lot in common and passionately in love with each other. Her description left no doubt whatsoever that this included the sexual relation. The only reservation here was that when the interviewer asked her whether she had orgasm, a queer expression passed over her face and she said "Yes" in a way that left him unsure whether to believe her or not.

As far as the relation with her mother was concerned, it seemed that her mother's attitude to her had entirely changed from the point at which she first became pregnant. From then on they seemed to get on well together. In view of her mother's previous statement that she did not want the patient to have children, this was a complete mystery.

As far as symptoms were concerned, the patient said that she had vomited every morning of her life from six months after she was married until she went to live with Philip; since then she has not vomited once. Moreover, during her pregnancy with her daughter, she had suffered from vomiting quite severely. Since going to live with Philip she had in fact become pregnant, but had had a miscarriage at twelve weeks. During this pregnancy she had not vomited at all. The other two symptoms, being afraid to be alone, and depression, had also continued up to the time she started living with Philip and then had disappeared.

She emphasized with obvious feeling and almost with astonishment the enormous personality change that had taken place in her since she left to live with Philip. Above all, she emphasized how she could now go out and face difficulties and overcome obstacles, whereas before she had tended to be much more passive and frightened—"I am not that girl who used just to sit in a chair and cry any more, am I?" She said spontaneously that she felt her symptom of vomiting had been basically due to sexual frustration, since it started soon after she was married, continued uninterrupted, and then disappeared completely once her sexual relation with Philip started.

In answer to the question of what she had felt about treatment, she said that she had liked her therapist very much, and although it had not been noticeable at the time that he had helped her, she had later realized that some of the things he had said were true. Asked for an example, she could only recall that he had said she had married her father in her husband.

DISCUSSION

Before she left her husband and went to live with Philip, the only changes were (1) the apparent ability to allow full intercourse, and the fact that she became pregnant; and (2) the change in the relation with her mother, which seems to have been caused by a change in her mother rather than in her. Apart from this she seems to have been entirely unchanged.

Since her cohabitation with Philip, all the original criteria appear, on the face of it, to be completely met. EHR, however, put forward the following important reservation: We know that before therapy the patient's main background problem was a sense of deprivation in relation to her mother. Now she does not feel deprived by her mother or anyone, but she is depriving her two-and-a-half-year old daughter by the act of going away with Philip. It is not unreasonable to suggest that the accusations that she has made against her mother will be repeated against herself in the years to come by her own daughter. Thus, it could be argued that she has done no more than transfer the problem of deprivation from herself to her daughter. Not only this, but she does not show very much concern about what she may be doing. It was also true that she showed no recognition of any contribution she may have made toward the situation between herself and her husband. In view of all this, EHR felt the result was impossible to score.

Team 2 also had reservations. They emphasized that the improvement was very recent; that the future of her child was in jeopardy; and that a possible dynamic interpretation of the present situation might be that the relation with Philip was idealized while all the bad feelings about men were left behind in her husband.

SCORES

Team 1	3.0	No score
Team 2	3.0	2.5
Mean		2.833

The Maintenance Man

SUMMARY

Category. Short, favorable (30 sessions, outcome 3.0).

A working-class man of thirty-nine caught in a marriage with a dominating wife, suffering from an acute attack of anxiety in relation to a symbolic act of emasculation by her. Therapy was directed toward bringing out this situation and linking it with his childhood. Late in therapy there was a dramatic moment of self-assertion with his wife, followed by one with his therapist. At follow-up there were remarkable improvements in the situation.

CONTRIBUTION TO THE CORRELATIONS WITH OUTCOME

Motivation: Strongly positive (high motivation, favorable outcome).
Focality: Positive (fairly high focality, favorable outcome).
Transference/parent interpretations: Positive (high score, favorable outcome).

DETAILS OF PATIENT AND THERAPIST

1. Patient

Sex	M.
Age	39.
Marital status	Married.
Occupation	Maintenance man in industry.
Complaint	Panic attacks for five weeks.
What seems to bring patient now	One week ago he had a severe panic attack at work and had to be taken home by ambulance. He is still not working.

2. Therapist

Code	G.
Sex	M.

PSYCHIATRIC HISTORY

No previous abnormality was elicited except that he had some *déjà vu* feelings at the age of eighteen.

DIAGNOSIS

Acute anxiety state.

DISTURBANCES

1. Symptoms. (a) Panic attacks; (b) fear of dying, having TB or cancer, going mad, going in a bus or public transport (but he can use his motorbike; (c) disturbed sleep, frightening dreams, e.g., of his daugher dying; (d) headaches, difficulty in swallowing, frequency and difficulty of micturition; and (e) present inability to work.

2. Problems of Masculinity and Aggression. Relation to Wife. (a) He is dominated and sexually frustrated by his wife but is unable to be angry about this. (b) He feels he is a coward, not ambitious enough, and not a real man.

ADDITIONAL EVIDENCE

1. Background. His mother was described as unforgiving and disgusted by sex. His father was promiscuous. When he was thirteen, his father left his mother. His mother said that if his father returned she would leave. The father did return and his mother left, taking the patient with her and leaving his father to look after the other siblings. The father married again later and the patient described the second wife as insane.

2. Wife's History. She had polio as a child. She divorced a previous husband on the grounds of sexual cruelty. There was a son by this first marriage, now aged sixteen, whom the patient has adopted. She married the patient eleven years ago, and they have a daughter aged nine of whom the patient is very fond.

The patient sees his wife as getting even with the world. She is always quarreling with neighbors, and she and the patient have had to move many times because of this.

3. Relation with Wife. His wife made him promise before they were married that he wouldn't make many sexual demands on her, and she allows him intercourse once a month or less. She seems to gauge when he is at the end of his rope and allows him intercourse then.

He said that if he tried to hit her she would throw something at him, and that he was a coward, anyway; he would stand up to anybody in an argument but he didn't like to have to use his fists.

He said that his wife always made the decisions and always turned out to be right. He had had a motorbike and sidecar for eighteen months, but she had eventually persuaded him to give it up because she was frightened of traveling in it. He finally sold it six weeks ago, and this seems to have been the precipitating cause of his present illness.

4. Initial Interview. The therapist made a number of interpretations about the current situation: e.g., that some of his physical symptoms were due to keeping his rage against his wife inside him; that he took his revenge on her through being ill; that he was afraid of showing his anger because he was afraid of being abandoned; and that his illness had been precipitated by the feeling that he had been castrated by her when she made him give up his motorbike. There was no dramatic response to any of these interpretations, but he considered them all thoughtfully and seriously.

5. Session 2. He said that he was feeling better and was going to start work again tomorrow. He added that the therapist's words last week had made a big impression on him, and they have been going round and round inside him ever since. The therapist had conveyed to him that he had got into this state because of his own fault, that he had let his wife sit on him, and that he really had to stand up for himself more. An interpretation about the way his violent feelings had disappeared but had come back in fantasy led to his saying that after his father had left his mother, he had been the go-between between them. There had been a court order against his father and he, the patient, had had to go and get the money from his father for his mother. He had been torn between them but had adhered to his mother. The thought then suddenly occurred to him that he was afraid that like his father he would go for other women. He went on to say that he had had the thought that perhaps his own marriage was going to break up now; about the same period had elapsed as when his parents' marriage began to break up.

HYPOTHESIS

The evidence suggests that for a long time he had been afraid of, and guilty about, his sexuality and aggression. He married a woman who he knew disliked aggression and would ration his sexuality. The result has been accumulating resentment and fear of loss of control, which has led to his breakdown. A number of his symptoms can be interpreted in terms of death wishes.

CRITERIA

1. Loss of all symptoms.
2. (a) He should be able to prevent his wife from dominating him, should be able to assert himself with her, and should be able to enjoy it. It is difficult to say how much this should include the sexual relation, as this will also depend on his wife. (b) He should be more able to assert himself with men and to enjoy it. (c) This self-assertion should not lead to anxiety or other symptoms. (d) He should feel more of a man.

REASON FOR ACCEPTANCE AND THERAPEUTIC PLAN

The therapist was impressed by the way in which this unsophisticated man could use interpretations, and by the clear progress between sessions 1 and 2. However, his plan was modest: "To concentrate on the present situation and the way he is dealing with it, and to try and avoid too much going into the personality background."

SUMMARY OF COURSE OF THERAPY

This long and complex therapy is best presented as a number of interrelated themes.

Urinary Symptoms. In session 3 there emerged a new aspect of the onset of his symptoms. His wife meets a lot of wealthy people, with cars, at work. The patient has always had an ambition to have a car but feels he cannot afford one. Two days before the onset of his symptoms his wife brought two of these men home, apparently in order to show him he need not be jealous.

In this session the therapist made the transference/parent interpretation that coming to treatment and then going back to his wife aroused feelings in him like being the go-between between his mother and his father in his childhood: First he could ally the therapist against his wife, but then he had to go back and face his wife by himself.

The patient made no clear responses in this session but in session 4 he reported that he had been very bad during the past week and had had a panic attack. He had been in a pub with his wife and brother-in-law, had become afraid that he would not be able to control himself, and had had to rush home to his mother. The essential interpretation given here was that he had to suppress his rage against his mother for not allowing him to be a sexual man like his father. There was also a parallel situation between him and his wife, and the therapist again interpreted the motorbike that his wife had made him give up as standing for his penis. This led him to reveal that ever since he was a child he had suffered from difficulty in traveling because of the fear that he would have to urinate. The therapist interpreted this as an expression of sexual excitement and the fear of losing control.

During the rest of therapy a good deal of work was done on this urinary symptom. In session 5 he spoke of being ill in terms of keeping things in or letting them out, and the therapist linked this with fear of urination. In session 11 the patient remarked that he was feeling more independent of his wife and was doing things in his own time instead of immediately when she told him to. The therapist linked this first with the wife's control of the sexual situation, and then with the patient's impulse to urinate when he wasn't supposed to, suggesting this was a sort of defiance. The patient said immediately that it had struck him that it is mostly when he is with his wife that he gets this symptom. In session 12 it emerged that three times recently he had had nocturnal emissions when there were clean sheets on the bed. The therapist interpreted that if she wouldn't allow him to use his penis as a man he would regress to being a child and make her clean up after him.

In session 13 he reported being as bad as he had ever been, which he attributed to mentioning homosexual feelings in a previous session (see below). In this session, however, he also reported that whereas he used to have a recurring dream of panic at being unable to urinate, after session 12 he had had a dream in which he was urinating to his heart's content, so much that he couldn't stop, and had woken up afraid that he was wetting the bed. He said he thought this was some sort of breakthrough.

In session 16 he said that he never knew what he was going to say before he came, but it just "poured out of him." The therapist related this to urination, and said that the patient needed to reassure himself that he was potent by being able to urinate effectively, symbolically speaking, in the sessions. There was then a link between this symptom and *homosexuality*, in that the patient said that his difficulty in urinating in public lavatories might be because he had been seduced in public lavatories as a boy.

In session 23 he reported that twice recently he has woken up to find himself on top of his wife and ejaculating, and has apologized in the morning. When the therapist asked him why he had to apologize, he said that he felt he was messing her up; and he went on to say that deep down he felt she wanted sex as much as he did, and he was depriving her by not giving it to her. This made a link with his *fears of inadequacy*, because he then admitted that he was afraid of not being able to satisfy her, and that he had at times failed in the past and this was one of the reasons why she did not want sex with him now.

Compliance and Rebellion. In the above work on urination the therapist frequently made or clearly implied the link between the patient's *wife* and his *mother*. This was even more clearly made over the related problem of *rebellion* and his *defense* of *compliance*.

In session 6 he reported that his wife had refused him intercourse and that he had been silent and hurt afterward but unable to do anything about it. The therapist suggested that he had to be a good boy for his wife as for his mother, and that he was afraid of losing control of his rage if he let himself go.

In session 7 the patient brought out for the first time impulses to defy authority, e.g., how during the war he went with girls in brothels and never told his wife, and then a long-standing fantasy of having intercourse with a colored woman. The therapist suggested that he wanted to do all sorts of exciting and dirty things, like his father.

This theme of identification with the "bad" side of his father was continued in session 14, in which he said that his father had been sent to prison for encouraging him to steal a bicycle, and that he himself had been sent to a detention home for encouraging another boy to steal some money. The therapist pointed out the identification, and the patient said he had thought of this himself, and was afraid it would mean that he would have to leave his wife just as his father had left his mother. The therapist suggested that it was exciting to be like his father, and that his mother was the restrictive one who wouldn't allow him his own sexual feelings, and that he felt the same about his wife.

Oedipal Problems and Homosexuality. In session 8 he spontaneously mentioned the question of *outdoing his father* in the way he brought up his own children; and he went on to tell of feeling in competition with his brother-in-law, whom he felt to be a fake and a boaster. The therapist linked rivalry with the brother-in-law with rivalry with the father, suggesting that out of guilt he needed to defeat himself.

In session 9 he said that he often had sexual dreams about men as well as women. The therapist interpreted that the patient's wife confirmed that his penis was no good, and that he was always comparing his potency with that of other men and feeling inferior. The therapist went on to suggest that the patient was afraid his homosexual feelings for the therapist might become too strong, and that he felt envy at the feeling that the therapist had a better penis than he had and would not share it with him.

In session 13 the patient spoke of a number of homosexual episodes, in most of which he had been the passive partner to an older man. Later he mentioned the time when his parents had separated, and he spoke with real feeling of the anguish that he had gone through, going from one parent to the other, loving both, wanting them to be together; but later saying that really his love had been for his father and he had stayed with his mother more out of a sense of duty. The therapist interpreted that the homosexual episodes were an expression of still seeking his father.

In session 15 there was a very important passage concerned with Oedipal anxieties. This started with the patient's reporting jealous fantasies about his wife's relations with men at work, after which he had woken up in the night to find himself "all over" his wife, very sexually excited. The therapist interpreted that he was very excited by his wife's ability to have contact with the big penises that he himself much admires and longs for. The patient responded by telling of a childhood memory of injuring his scrotum on a nail, and how some men who were in the house had told him that he should look after this organ and make sure he didn't lose it. It then turned out that he had never thought of his penis as being small, but he had always thought what a "beaut" it is. Then he himself said that perhaps he had always needed to think this, and that any woman would be horrified at the size of it, and that this was really a "delusion." Later he said with considerable anger that he wondered why he wasn't able to be really angry with his wife and tell her that she mustn't go out with other men, or even to beat her up. The therapist asked him who he would be like if he did this, to which he said that it could only be his father. The therapist interpreted that the patient's fantasy of playing the role of father was a defense against his fear of his father's attacking him for his misdeeds. He responded with a memory of his father catching him and his sister at sexual games, and he went on to say that he saw a pattern in all this: that he has to be the one who obeys everybody, whom nobody will tell off, always punctual and efficient.

In session 19 the therapist interpreted homosexual feelings toward himself: that the patient came hoping that the therapist would be like a good father who would fondle him and plant things in him that would work in him later (*transference/parent interpretation*). The patient responded by speaking of his tender side, which he expressed particularly with his daughter, and added that he was very sentimental about such things as books and films.

In session 24 he said that he wondered if his fear of sexual inadequacy had anything to do with his mother. He then mentioned, first, that when he was sixteen he had found his best friend, a boy of eighteen, having intercourse with his mother; and then that when he was small he had slept in his parents' bedroom and had often heard them having intercourse, and that his fantasy had been that his father was attacking his mother.

Climax of Therapy. This came in sessions 25–27 with the theme of self-assertion and domination. In session 25 the patient reported with considerable anger that his wife would start lovemaking with such remarks as "Come on, get it over with, I suppose you want to perform now," and the therapist pointed out to him the hidden invitation to him to dominate her. In session 26 he said that although he could not dominate his wife he could assert himself with other men at work.

In session 27 he reported with an air of satisfaction that to his own great surprise he had really blown his top with his wife last night. She had told him off for taking some money from the housekeeping that he was going to return, anyway, and he had shouted at her to stop treating him as a child and had banged the table. During the course of this he emphasized how the thought had crossed his mind that he could come along and discuss it with the therapist the next day. The therapist therefore—perhaps insensitively, but fortunately, as it turned out—suggested that he had this row in order to do what was expected of him. At this the patient picked up his paper and shook it at the therapist, banged his chair with the point of his finger, and said that the therapist was trying to take *this* away from him now; he hadn't done it for the therapist but had really got wild with his wife and had done it for himself.

Termination. Session 10 was the last before a fortnight's break, and the therapist made interpretations about jealousy of his other patients. There then emerged for the first time some negative feelings about the therapist: the patient was sometimes dissatisfied and felt there was no point in coming. The therapist eventually suggested that the patient felt frustrated because he could not have the therapist to himself as he wanted his mother to himself (*transference/parent interpretation*).

In session 20 the patient reported that his phobic symptoms had disappeared and the therapist suggested tapering off treatment. From then on sessions were spaced irregularly, at one- to four-week intervals. In session 21 the patient was worse again, and he himself related this to the idea of stopping.

In session 24 he reported a dream in which he had burst into tears and a woman had taken him by the hand and asked him what was wrong, and he had said that it was because he had got to leave the Army and his mates. The therapist related this to giving up treatment.

After the climactic session 27, little further important work was done and termination came uneventfully.

Total number of sessions	30
Total time	1 year 1 month

FOLLOW-UP

5½ Months

He reported that he had been symptom-free except for one short episode of anxiety. He is able to go to pubs and travel on public transport. A remarkable change has occurred in his relation with his wife. Their sexual relationship has become exciting, vigorous, and frequent. This apparently began as a result of the change in *her*, in that she began to want it in a way that she hadn't before. He had become anxious because he had thought she might be trying to make up to him for being unfaithful to him. He therefore taxed her with it, but she denied this and said that she had had a frightening dream in which he had died, which made her feel guilty toward him. She admitted that her behavior had contributed to his illness. However, a few days before the interview he had attempted intercourse and had had premature ejaculation. He had become very upset at this but he thinks that he can manage the situation.

4 Years, 9 Months

1. Symptoms

(a) He has had only a single anxiety attack since termination. This occurred while he was driving his car, and he is fairly sure that it followed a disagreement with his wife.

(b) He has had a period of suffering from hesitancy of micturition, sometimes taking as long as a minute before he could start, and then suffering from weak flow. He had a cystoscopy, was told there was nothing organically wrong, and since then the above symptoms have been replaced by a tendency to precipitancy.

Apart from the above he has been entirely symptom-free.

2. Relation with His Wife

In many ways he seems to have reached a compromise in his relation with his difficult and dominating wife. Where what happens is under *his* control, he is able to take decisions against her wishes—e.g., buying a car, doing the job he wants (see below). Where it is under *her* control, he states his position firmly and is satisfied with this even if he doesn't get his own way. There are rows between them, but they don't linger on, and he doesn't take it out on other people. In the area of spare-time activities he seems to have reached a very reasonable compromise between seeking his own enjoyment (e.g., football matches or attending to the car) and activities in which his wife can share. He has determined not to get hurt by being rejected sexually, but senses when she is willing for intercourse and then it is enjoyable. Sometimes they may go for months without intercourse, at other times it is frequent. He says his wife would allow him intercourse much more frequently if he did more things for her, like taking her out to a show, etc. He says he is determined not to buy love in this way.

The only reservation is that he still gives the impression of being a "small man daring" in his relation with her, but what else can one expect, given their two personalities?

3. Self-Assertion with Men. Feeling of Being a Man

His work history has been somewhat complicated. Whereas when he first came, he was just a maintenance man working under supervision, for the past three years he has been working in a different factory in a supervisory capacity. This has meant more regular hours, but also less chance of overtime work. This job is recognized as difficult, and he chose to do it because he wanted to show people that he could. He says there is a way of managing people, which is that instead of *telling* them to do things you *ask* them, and he has had no trouble and has thoroughly enjoyed it. He has been told that he can continue, but he has preferred to go back to his old factory and his old job. The greater chance of overtime means that he can earn more money that way. Two years ago he had been offered promotion to an even higher rank, but he refused this because the conditions of work were not so satisfactory and he could earn as much money by putting in overtime. His wife criticized him for this at the time but he did not let her influence this decision.

During the interview he said that he was very disappointed that the therapist had not sent for him two years ago, because he wanted to tell him that he now had a car. This was said with some triumph, and it was clear how much the car meant to him. With a great deal of determination in his voice he told how much he had wanted it, and how he had been determined to master it. He had had one serious accident—apparently not his fault—but as soon as the car was repaired again he got into it and drove off. It was against his wife's protest that he bought it, but she now enjoys going out in it and he drives her all over the place.

SUMMARY

Most of the criteria seem largely fulfilled, but there are reservations in his relation with his wife, and it is difficult to sort out reality from neurotic decision-making in his refusal of promotion. The differences between the judges follow from different emphasis on the reservations.

SCORES

Team 1	4.0	3.0
Team 2	2.5	2.5
Mean	3.0	

The Playwright

SUMMARY

Category. Long, favorable (93 sessions, outcome 2.25).

A highly gifted but disturbed man of twenty-eight who was taken on in the full knowledge that he appeared to be highly unsuitable for brief psychotherapy. Relatively long-term therapy of a somewhat informal kind seems to have produced considerable favorable changes.

CONTRIBUTION TO THE CORRELATIONS WITH OUTCOME

Motivation: Positive (intermediate motivation, intermediate outcome).
Focality: Strongly negative (very low score, intermediate outcome).
Transference/parent interpretations: Positive (intermediate score, intermediate outcome).

DETAILS OF PATIENT AND THERAPIST

1. Patient

Sex	M.
Age	28.
Marital status	Single.
Occupation	Playwright.
Complaint	Severe panic attacks (five years).
What seems to bring patient now	His panics are getting worse and have recently been crippling. He is also about to face what was construed as a severe test in his life (the nature of which is not given for reasons of discretion).

2. Therapist

Code	K.
Sex	M.

PSYCHIATRIC HISTORY

Home Atmosphere. This was very unhappy.

Previous Symptoms. At the age of ten, probably in connection with being given talks about internal anatomy, he fainted twice. Ever since then he has had the panic-stricken feeling that he would faint whenever he was in social situations or other situations from which he couldn't escape. He has always hated the sight of blood.

Present Illness. Five years ago, at the time of an unhappy and guilt-laden relation with a girl, he began to experience panic attacks of a different kind. These were of the utmost severity and essentially without content, though they gave him the feeling that "everything was going to stop," that he would commit suicide or go mad. These had now become so bad that he felt he was fighting for his life; hence the urgency of his demand for help.

DIAGNOSIS

Very severe anxiety, some of it phobic, in a man with a severe character disorder.

DISTURBANCES

1. Symptoms. As above.

2. Difficulties with Women. He has never been able to form a close relation with a woman, though he has led an active sexual life. The report on the projective test mentioned a feeling of contempt for women that bothers him.

3. Sense of Aimlessness. He has made an elaborate plan for his life, but it no longer makes sense and he doesn't know what he wants.

4. Aggressiveness and Intellectual Defense. The interviewing psychiatrist described him as "fearful, puzzled, ready to be antagonistic, all covered by excellent verbalization." The therapist in the first therapeutic session felt an "extreme competitiveness." All his feelings were covered over by intellectual arguments.

ADDITIONAL EVIDENCE

1. All details except those under 2. below are omitted for reasons of discretion.

2. In his projection test (ORT), he was unable to tell real stories to the cards, but just said what he saw in them with many alternatives at once. The only exception was that he told the story of a wizard in a fairy tale, who had given up love for success and power. When it was pointed out that this must be what the patient felt about himself, he did not argue, though he made many scientific and philosphical qualifications to most of the other things the psychologist said. Many of the cards evoked an intense sense of mood such as ennui, real fear, or sinisterness. An example of the latter was "hooded mourners in grief," who were spoiling the relations between young lovers by laughing at them. This particular percept combines in a most succinct way depres-

sive, paranoid, and Oedipal fantasies. In his material he seemed to have created an extreme split between father-figures, who were portrayed as ideal, and mother-figures, who were totally bad and sinister. The psychologist wrote that there was very strong evidence of his fear of complete disintegration. "This is most definitely not a focal problem, but a severe character problem."

3. When in the first therapeutic session the patient described his fear of fainting, the therapist asked if it wasn't rather that he was afraid of something *coming out of him*. He literally gasped at this reversal of his usual way of looking at things, and for a moment it seemed that real contact had been made.

4. Throughout the assessment period the patient showed, side by side with his intellectual defenses, a desperate demand that something should be done about his panics at once.

HYPOTHESIS

All the evidence suggests that this is a very disturbed man, troubled by primitive anxieties in relation to people, which we believe are ultimately derived from his relation with his mother. These anxieties are probably both depressive (guilt and concern about his own primitive destructive urges), and paranoid (fear of sinister forces in the world directed against him). As defenses against his anxieties he has adopted (1) extreme intellectualization, and (2) the replacement of any close involvement with people by a need to dominate and feel superior to them. The panics must represent some kind of breakdown in his defenses and the threatened breakthrough of primitive feelings.

CRITERIA

1. Loss of symptoms.
2. Marked reduction in (a) his need to intellectualize, (b) his paranoid attitude, and (c) his extreme competitiveness, accompanied by:
3. An ability to admit his feelings and to allow himself to become close to people, especially women, and to feel love for them, while being able to tolerate ambivalence.
4. At the same time he should retain his ability to do well, and should show an increase in his ability to be creative.

THERAPEUTIC PLAN

This is a case in which the workshop's motives for taking the patient on seem to have been largely irrational. The patient had been referred by a Tavistock G.P. specifically for brief therapy, clearly because of the severity of the current crisis. He was seen privately by therapist E. All the evidence in the initial interview and projection test, however, suggested that this patient was not suitable for brief psychotherapy. Our motives probably consisted of an interest in this exceptionally intelligent and gifted man, and a response both to the challenge that he presented and to his extreme pressure for help. At the end of the report on the first therapeutic session, the therapist wrote that his immediate aim was to try and help the patient meet the approaching test in his life, but the patient denied, almost certainly correctly, that this was of any significance. Very soon after this, the theme in the workshop discussions was that the aim should be an attempt to prepare the patient for a full-scale analysis, although this was not really rational either, as he could not afford it.

SUMMARY OF COURSE OF THERAPY

Much of this complex therapy consisted of interpreting the patient's defenses against emotional involvement. These were never at any time more than partially penetrated, but when they were it became clear that the underlying feelings and anxieties were of a very primitive kind.

In session 5 the therapist pointed out his need to keep his feelings to himself, and this led him to describe how as a child he used to have attacks of weeping in his sleep that led his father to come in to him, and how he felt all right if he could wake up with his father at his side. The therapist said that there must be something "inconsolable" in him, with which he agreed. At the end of this session the therapist wrote that the patient formed a very complex relation with him, containing (1) a "bewitching, appealing charm" expressing his need for help, (2) a defensive intellectual attack, and (3) a refusal to become deeply involved. The therapist proposed to make (3) his main focus, with the aim of getting the patient to accept a full-scale analysis.

In accordance with this focus, in session 8 the therapist made use of the above-mentioned crying attacks to suggest that if the patient really asked for help he would become involved in fears of dependence. The patient made a clear response, speaking of fears of losing control, going mad, or jumping out of a window.

In session 10 there was for the first time a major breakthrough of anxiety. With much tension he spoke of having attacks of *jamais vu*, feeling about a familiar object that he had never seen it before. Usually these attacks were horrifying to him. As he was telling this he became more and more anxious and finally had to leave the room. When he came back the therapist tried to link this anxiety with the transference, to which the patient said that he did not agree: His feelings about the therapist consisted of indifference. The therapist then made a transference/parent interpretation, saying that this was the same as the patient felt about his mother. The patient then said that it was true that his mother was indifferent to him, indeed hostile; and the therapist pointed out that hostility was more than indifference.

The next few sessions were concerned with further defenses and the primitive feelings lying behind them. This included: (session 13) the need to be constantly on the move to avoid being tied down; (session 14) his inability to stop himself from intellectually demolishing everything the therapist said; (also session 14) his inability to tolerate any demands, especially for love, and the feeling that unless he could give only when *he* wanted he had to run away; (session 16) the feeling that it was essential that the therapist's only purposes were those that fitted in with his own, probably for fear of being let down, betrayed, and disappointed, as by his mother (transference/parent interpretation); (session 17) his need to be interesting all the time in order to feel he could be accepted at all; (session 18) several external events that had made him feel extremely insecure, with the result that there had been another breakthrough of anxiety with the fear of involuntarily committing suicide.

At the end of session 20 the therapist wrote that he could perhaps work with the patient's overwhelming demands, and that the patient might use the experience of termination to work through disappointment and resentment that his demands could not be met.

During the next few sessions some historical facts emerged that made some sense of his difficulties. These were that before the onset of his anxiety attacks he had been able to deny his feelings completely, and in particular his feeling that his mother did not love him, to which he now attributed his difficulties. The therapist suggested (session 25) that therefore he could never commit himself in case he was rebuffed, which seemed to mean something to him.

In session 30 there was an important change. The patient returned to a feeling, mentioned previously, that he had to be intellectually interesting all the time because really he was empty and there was nothing lovable in him. He spoke of his fear of people making any demands on him in case they discovered that he had nothing but his brain with which to respond. The therapist wrote that for the first time the patient had given up his intellectual poise and had allowed himself to be seen as pathetic.

In session 31 it emerged that he was feeling much better and had not had any anxiety attacks for weeks. He was still taking tranquilizers but only as a precaution. The therapist pointed out the obvious analogy between this and his therapy.

In session 33 there was a partial breakthrough of feeling. The patient said that he had begun to experience again something that had happened at about the age of eleven, namely, that his mind would become filled with horrible images, such as an eye being cut into slices by a plate of glass. The therapist made an attempt to interpret this in terms of the "eye" being really the patient himself—"I"—which the latter quickly demolished by intellectual argument.

However, in session 34 the patient again appeared to be in touch with much distressing feeling. He started by announcing that he would have to go abroad twice in the next few months, and although this was in fact a piece of reality that had been arranged long before, the therapist felt that the patient had forestalled the question of termination. After a short silence the patient described an incident in childhood in which he had lashed out at someone because of frustration at his own failure to achieve something he was trying to do. The therapist suggested that when he was silent in treatment he was really wanting to scream. The patient agreed with this and told of an incident at school in which he had suddenly heard screaming and had come to realize it was himself. Another boy had played a practical joke on him without realizing the extreme pain and even danger that it would lead to. The patient had felt ashamed at his screaming, and no anger against the boy, because it was the school tradition to keep a stiff upper lip in all circumstances. He linked this with his feeling unable to complain to his parents when he was evacuated during the war. The therapist linked this in turn with his inability to express his dissatisfaction about treatment. The patient denied this, saying that the therapist had never rebuffed him. The therapist then suggested that they might consider doing something that he would really feel as a rebuff, namely give him a termination date. The patient said that he couldn't really believe that the therapist would ever do what he, the patient, did not want. In fact no actual termination date was mentioned.

Session 39 was the last before a six-week break due to one of the patient's absences abroad. Suddenly there was an atmosphere of intense communication. Here it must be said that at the time the patient was involved with an extremely "fraught" relation with a girl that was in fact almost certainly the immediate precipitating factor for the recent severe exacerbation of his symptoms and hence for his seeking treatment. The significance of this only emerged at follow-up and—inexplicably—seems to have been entirely missed during therapy. The patient excitedly read out a letter from this girl, saying that he needed to dominate his partner in any relationship and use her entirely for his own ends. He was amazed at her insight and had to confess it was true. The therapist said that he wanted to be cared for in therapy entirely on his own terms, and the patient said he felt a guilty triumph at always succeeding. He realized that he must keep everything under his own control, which the therapist linked (probably unjustifiably) with the patient's absences.

There was then a six-week break, two sessions, and then another six-week break. In the next session, no. 41, in connection with this current love affair, which was now breaking up, he began to realize his feeling that two people in love must possess each other entirely, and his terror at feelings of jealousy if anyone came between him and someone he loved. The therapist tried without success to relate this to termination.

Not long after this the patient was involved in a number of activities away from London, and it was left that he would get in touch with the therapist when he was in a position to resume treatment, but in fact he did not do so.

Total number of sessions	43
Total time	1 year 2 months

FOLLOW-UP

3 Years 7 Months

(At this point the patient consulted a nonworkshop psychiatrist who took him on for further psychotherapy. Our assessment is based on this psychiatrist's report at the beginning of his treatment.)

1. Symptoms

(a) Panic attacks. Although the severe panic attacks seem to have stopped by the time he terminated with therapist K, it seems that they had by now started again, since "very severe anxiety attacks" were among his complaints. At the final follow-up, however, the patient said that at this time his anxiety attacks were less frequent and less severe. He still suffered from claustrophobia as before.

(b) Fear of blood and other symptoms. The fear of blood was unchanged. In addition, he now complained of insomnia and headaches.

Overall severity of symptoms. Probably essentially unchanged.

2. Intellectual Defense and Aggressiveness

(a) Need to intellectualize. This seemed to be "somewhat improved." He was now aware of his isolation, and he sought further psychotherapy in order to get closer to people.

(b) Paranoid attitude. This was very difficult to assess.

(c) Extreme competitiveness. He gave up some of his activities that meant for him the gaining of power, and it is therefore clear that there was some improvement here.

3. Ability to Admit His Feelings, to Allow Himself to Become Close to People, and to Tolerate Ambivalence

There is evidence of greater ability to admit his feelings in the fact of his more genuine motivation for help. On the other hand, his main complaint was of isolation; and he still had not been able to relate deeply to a woman. We do not know about ambivalence.

4. Ability to Do Well, and Increase in His Ability to Be Creative

Both parts of this criterion were fulfilled.

SUMMARY

Some reduction in defenses, symptomatically probably unchanged, marked improvement in creativity with possible reduction in competitiveness; basic isolation and inability to get close to people, especially women, unchanged.

SCORES

Team 1	1.0	0.5
Team 2	1.0	0.5
Mean	0.75	

5 Years 6 Months

The patient was interviewed by the workshop psychologist who had originally tested him. He had had a total of fifty sessions with the nonworkshop psychiatrist whom he had consulted, over a period of one year four months (total number of sessions in his two courses of therapy, ninety-three). He was now seen six months after the termination of this second period of therapy. The second psychiatrist handled him by making contact with his extremely intelligent ideas, responding warmly to him as a real person, and not trying to analyze him in any great detail. There seems little doubt that this was the right approach.

1. Symptoms

(a) Anxiety attacks. The very severe anxiety attacks have ceased but he still suffers from claustrophobia. This anxiety is more controllable than it used to be.

(b) Fear of blood and other symptoms. The fear of blood seems

probably unchanged. Insomnia has disappeared. We do not know about headaches.

Summary: Symptomatically "much improved."

2. Intellectual Defense and Aggressiveness

(a) *Need to intellectualize.* There is a marked reduction in this. He now seems very much in touch with some of his inner feelings; and he clearly realizes his difficulties with people, though he has not been able to resolve them.

(b) *Paranoid attitude.* Comparing the atmosphere of the follow-up interview with that of the original projection test, the psychologist said that there was a very marked change. There was now an atmosphere of "easy happiness" as opposed to the previous feeling of underlying extreme aggressiveness. On the other hand certain paranoid attitudes are still present, e.g., when seeing a play he has the feeling of being attacked by the dramatist.

(c) *Extreme competitiveness.* The improvement noted at the previous follow-up has been maintained.

3. Ability to Admit Feelings, Etc.

There is considerable improvement in his ability to admit feelings. The easy atmosphere at the interview must indicate an improvement in his ability to get close to people. On the other hand, he has never managed to get really close to a woman.

4. Ability to Do Well, Creativeness

This criterion is completely fulfilled.

SUMMARY

Considerable symptomatic improvement; marked reduction in the tenseness of his relation with people; reduction in competitiveness with increase in creativeness; but he is still unable to get really close to a woman.

SCORES

Team 1	2.0	1.5
Team 2	2.0	3.5
Mean	2.250	

The Representative

SUMMARY

Category. "False."

A very brief therapy with a young man of twenty-one, during which the patient reached insight about the meaning of his symptom, made a flight into health, and broke off treatment. At follow-up he was found to have been able to build upon this in a quite impressive way, though there were some reservations about the depth of the changes that he showed. This was thus one of the "false" cases in which the improvements found at follow-up appeared out of proportion to the dynamic quality of the therapy.

CONTRIBUTION TO THE CORRELATIONS WITH OUTCOME

Motivation and focality: Strongly negative (ranked exceedingly low on these factors, high intermediate outcome).
Transference/parent interpretations: Strongly negative (score zero, high intermediate outcome).

DETAILS OF PATIENT AND THERAPIST

1. Patient

Sex   M.
Age   21.
Marital status   Single.
Occupation   Representative for a plastics firm.
What seems to bring   Blushing and social embarrassment, two years.
    patient now

2. Therapist

Code   E.
Sex   M.

PSYCHIATRIC DIAGNOSIS

Phobic anxiety.

DISTURBANCES

1. Blushing and Social Embarrassment. The first attack that he could remember occurred about two years ago when he was sitting in a café with a number of his male friends. A very attractive girl of fifteen came and sat down at their table and he became embarrassed and confused. A more recent incident occurred when a girl teased him in the office, and his boss joined in. He wrote in his application form that women only have to be mentioned in a conversation for him to blush. He may also blush in the middle of a conversation for no apparent reason at all. He cannot join freely in a conversation without the fear of blushing. It is worse when anyone of the opposite sex is present, even relatives. The result is that he now no longer wants to make friends or to have anything to do with the staff at work. Until the onset of these symptoms he had always been sociable and enjoyed life.

2. Attitude to Sex. He appears to have a very anxious and censorious attitude toward his own sexual feelings. Interpretations about them either made him anxious (in the projection test), or else were taken as severe moral criticism.

3. He has felt inferior all his life.

4. He gave the impression of a considerable degree of passivity.

ADDITIONAL EVIDENCE

1. He felt his father had been hard and stern and had never given him the approval and affection he wanted. He had always tried hard at manly things, but his father would always tell him where he went wrong. His mother and siblings were hardly mentioned.

2. He was brought up very religiously by both his parents to lead a clean life. Until his present illness he had always regarded himself as a confident, successful, clean, open-air, healthy type.

3. He had enjoyed the rough and tumble of life in the Navy, where he did his National Service. He was proud of his courage in various dangerous situations that had arisen during this period.

4. A factor possibly contributing to his present illness was that during his period in the Navy, he had written home regularly to a girl friend; but that soon after his discharge this girl got involved with another man and he gave her up.

5. He and his girlfriend had occasionally got sexually excited together, but for him the idea of sexual intercourse before marriage was wrong. He said that he was ashamed of sexual thoughts and tried to fight them off. He told the psychiatrist who saw him first that he felt very guilty about masturbation and felt that it was harmful and showed in his face as a haggard look. In the initial interview with the therapist, however, he said—without apparent guilt or embarrassment—that he masturbated "the same as everybody."

6. He had originally been seen by a nonworkshop psychiatrist. His next contact with the clinic was his projection test (Rorschach). His

detachment from feelings was so marked at the beginning of the test that the psychologist quickly interpreted to him that there were two aspects of him: (1) the healthy, efficient bit of himself; and (2) another part that was shameful, perhaps connected with sex, and that showed in his blushes. The patient's reaction to this was mixed: He both seemed to become warmer and closer, and at the same time seemed disturbed and the Rorschach seemed entirely concerned with his anxieties. He seemed to be anxious both about sexual feelings and primitive aggressive feelings.

When he was then seen for the first interview with the therapist, his reaction to the projection test seemed to be that he had been strongly criticized for his sexual feelings. When the therapist did not take up this attitude, the patient read him a little sermon about the inappropriateness of sexual thoughts before marriage.

HYPOTHESIS

He is very ashamed of all his instinctual needs. This has been derived from a very strict and religious upbringing. He has used an identification with this strict system of values as a defense against his instincts. In face of authority figures he identifies them with the strict morality and passively submits to them; if they act permissively he has to express the moral values himself.

There is plenty of evidence that sexual feelings figure largely in the instincts against which he is defending himself; but we think that rivalry and all kinds of aggressive feelings, including primitive ones, are very important as well.

CRITERIA

He should abandon his defenses and feel free to accept and use (without compulsiveness) both his sexual and aggressive feelings in all appropriate situations. This should lead to the following:

1. He should lose his symptoms and become able to enjoy social life again.

2. There should be no further need to denigrate sexual or aggressive feelings either in himself or other people.

3. He should be able to become active and to assert himself constructively with both men and women, especially authority figures, while remaining on good terms with them. He should be able to face rivalry without anxiety.

4. He should develop a mutually satisfactory sexual and emotional relation with a woman.

5. He should have an inner feeling of self-confidence as a man.

REASON FOR ACCEPTANCE AND THERAPEUTIC PLAN

This patient was referred to the workshop after being seen by a nonworkshop psychiatrist, the simplicity of his complaints making him a candidate for a focal approach. He was therefore next seen by a workshop psychiatrist. In response to an interpretation concerned with sexual feelings, he then produced a series of responses that seemed to be largely expressing pregenital anxieties. Therapist E volunteered to explore this further. No therapeutic plan was made.

SUMMARY OF COURSE OF THERAPY

This was the least dynamic of all our therapies, the patient consistently denying all interpretations. Since the final result scored relatively highly, the contribution to all the important correlations was negative.

As already reported, the patient took the psychologist's interpretations about sexuality as moral criticism. In session 1 he tried to extract the same meaning from the therapist's remarks, and when he could not do so he provided the moral criticism himself.

In session 2 the therapist made a determined attempt to continue on the subject of the patient's anxieties. He made interpretations about the patient's fear of sexual thoughts, fear of women, and longing for a father's forceful approval and love. Whatever the therapist said the patient took calmly, first denied its truth, and then partially agreed in such a way as to be unhelpful. The therapist felt that the patient was being steadily obstructive and that no progress was being made. Comments about this obstructiveness were discussed with irritating reasonableness.

Session 3 was even more difficult. The patient said, "Ask me anything you like and I will tell you," but in fact gave no fresh information. The therapist tried to interpret (1) the patient's need to retreat from women whenever there is a danger of his going too far, and his relative ease with men; (2) the loss of confidence as a self-castration with fear of his father as its basis; (3) his fear of the therapist and need to render him harmless. The response to all these interpretations was to contradict them.

The patient canceled the next session at short notice, and then wrote the therapist a letter from which the following is an extract:

> The object of this letter is to ask that we postpone our talks for a while. So far we don't seem to have obtained anything informative and I confess that sometimes I am a little bored. That's why I think a rest would be useful. Please don't think I am not grateful, because in some ways you have opened my eyes; for that I thank you. I would however be very much obliged if you would allow me to contact you some time in the future. You see, I have a strong feeling that I can overcome my difficulty.

Total no. of sessions   3
Total time   5 weeks

FOLLOW-UP
(7 years 9 months)

He did not in fact contact the therapist, but returned for a follow-up interview with another member of the team very willingly. It was interesting that, in marked contrast to his hostile attitude toward therapy, he now said that he had come to us when he was in trouble and if there was anything he could do for us in return it was a debt that he was glad to repay. He said that he was now an entirely different person: He was "cocky" again, and now felt free and able to enjoy life. He was extremely honest about the connection between his symptom and sexual guilt, though this was not easy for him to speak of. His immediate answer to the question how the rest of his life had gone was, "Like a bomb." He added that he was very happy in his job, there were prospects, he was married ("the best thing that has ever happened to me"), and he had three smashing children. But when he was pressed for details it became clear that he was not entirely satisfied with his position at work.

1. Symptoms
(a) *Blushing.* He said that when he had first come to us he was very immature and very shy. It had quite suddenly come to him during the treatment period, but not in an actual session, that the reason for his blushing was guilt about masturbation. He had not been able to speak of this to his therapist, and instead had rung up and said he knew what the trouble was and that he didn't want to come any more. (This does not entirely agree with our information, see above). He had then decided that he must conquer this habit. A few days later he had gone to a party at which a number of his female relatives were present and had suddenly discovered that he felt entirely different, quite free, and did not blush. During the next two years, there had been some "slip-backs" in which he had masturbated and found himself blushing afterward, but after this time the problem had been entirely conquered. When asked what he had done about sex during this period, he said that he had played a lot of sport, mainly cross-country running. He added that it was an old joke among athletes that if a man was off form one day, then he had "been with his wife" the night before.

It thus seems clear that although he overcame his symptom, the basic problem of sexual guilt remained unchanged.

(b) *Solitariness.* He now enjoys social life and this problem seems to have entirely disappeared.

2. Denigration of (a) Sexual and (b) Aggressive Feelings

(a) Sexual. The above remark about sexual intercourse weakening a man's athletic performance was repeated later when he told the interviewer that he never had intercourse if he was going to run the next day. He said that one could overcome it for a time, as one could if one ran while one had flu, but it usually affected one in the end. This suggests that the guilt about masturbation is carried over in his attitude toward sexual intercourse even in marriage (see 4. below).

(b) Aggressive. This seems entirely fulfilled.

3. Ability (a) to Become Active and Assert Himself, (b) to Face Rivalry

(a) Self-assertion. This seems to be largely fulfilled at work. He was apparently able to get on with a difficult boss without submissiveness, and to deal with a difficult colleague while remaining on good terms with him. In addition to this, he said that his relation with his father had changed: Previously they had been uneasy with each other but now they are much closer.

(b) Facing rivalry. He was able to win his wife in face of competition from another man, apparently without undue anxiety.

4. Satisfactory Sexual and Emotional Relation with a Woman

He has now been married for five years, and to all outward appearances this criterion is entirely fulfilled. It was also true, however, that all the women in his life were idealized; e.g., he said, "Of course, everyone's mother is wonderful." It was difficult for the interviewer to get a picture of what his wife was really like. EHR emphasized that he did not feel that the patient was able to regard his wife as a separate person apart from his own fantasies. In contrast to this, his attitude toward his three children, who seemed to be doing very well, appeared to be much more genuine and spontaneous.

5. Feeling of Self-Confidence as a Man

He tried to exaggerate his success at work, and blushed when the fact was brought out that he felt he was not earning as much as he should. He tried to make out that the prospects in his job were better than they really were. These facts suggest that at least some underlying uneasiness remains.

SUMMARY

The two judges of Team 1 agreed that to all outward appearances he was "cured." There were also some more reliable indicators that at least some of this improvement was genuine: (a) his ability to face rivalry, and (b) his ability to be assertive with men.

On the other hand, both judges—EHR especially—found much to

criticize in the overall picture: (a) The problem of guilt about masturbation was apparently never overcome; (b) there was still a denigration of sexuality; (c) he idealizes women; and (d) he still uncritically identifies with his parents' strict moral values.

EHR felt that this was essentially a false solution, though a very valuable one. DHM wrote that he would like to score less than 3.0, but on the formal evidence didn't see how he could. Both judges were contaminated by the knowledge that therapy had been very short.

Team 2, who were not contaminated by any knowledge of the length of therapy, also had considerable doubts about how deep the changes went.

SCORES

Team 1	3.0	1.5
Team 2	2.0	2.0
Mean	2.125	

6

The Observed Improvements, Clinical Considerations

It is often very difficult to obtain evidence from purely clinical consider-ations about the factors responsible for observed improvements. With statistical treatment it is a different matter, and this will be presented in the next few chapters. However, clinical scrutiny of these patients does provide some important observations, and these will be considered now.

THE INFLUENCE OF EXTERNAL EVENTS AND CHANGES OF ENVIRONMENT—"SPONTANEOUS REMISSION" AFTER PSYCHOTHERAPY

A major problem arises when the patient appears to have improved, often long after termination, through the influence of either (1) external events not under his own control, or (2) a change to a more favorable environment, which usually is under his control. This leads to a preliminary consideration of an important issue, namely, the evi-dence in the present series for factors resembling spontaneous remis-sion. The relevant details in six patients are shown in Table 3.

To these six there should be added a further patient, the Represent-ative. Here the improvements that occurred seem out of proportion to what happened in his three-session therapy. His complaint was blush-ing, and during therapy he apparently acquired just one piece of insight, namely, that his symptom was due to guilt about masturba-tion. At this point he broke off treatment, determined to overcome his

TABLE 3. Improvements in Response to External Events

Patient	Disturbances remaining at termination	Event associated with improvement	Length of time since termination	Nature of improvement	Final score for outcome
Indian scientist	Still stuck in job far below his potential.	1. Had leadership thrust upon him. 2. Emigrated to a country where color bar was no problem.	Several years	Effective and satisfied in responsible job.	3.5
Personnel manager	1. Afraid to drive at night. 2. Adventurousness leads to anxiety. 3. No relation with a man.	Death of her mother.	4 years	1. Able to drive at night. 2. Adventurousness without anxiety. 3. Relation with a man.	3.25

Buyer	Tension at work; difficult relations with male colleagues. Felt he would "go under."	Forced by the political situation at work to set up his own business.	5 years	Effective and satisfied at work. Able to deal with men.	2.75
Mrs. Lewis	Extremely unsatisfactory relation with husband. Frigid.	Left her husband for another man.	6 years	Satisfactory relationship; passionate sexuality.	2.833
Au pair girl	Progressively deteriorating relation with husband; headaches and depression.	Parted from her husband; enforced maturation while working as au pair girl in foreign country.	3–4 years	Return to her husband, much improved relation.	2.5
Gunner's wife	Gastric symptoms, especially in social situations.	A period as the wife of an officer abroad.	7 years	Improved self-confidence; improved symptoms.	2.125

problems by stopping masturbation. Symptomatically speaking, this worked, but it has all the credentials of a flight into health. Nevertheless at follow-up (nearly eight years), though the original sexual anxiety could certainly still be detected, his improvements involved the ability to face various specific stresses in the form of challenges to his manhood, which included self-assertion with bosses and the achievement of a satisfactory marriage in the face of competition from a rival. He was certainly no longer the kind of person whom one would consider as needing treatment.

On the basis of events in therapy these seven patients can be divided fairly sharply into two groups. There were (1) three "satisfactory" therapies (Indian Scientist, Personnel Manager, and Buyer) in all of which the patient showed high motivation, and therapy resulted in intense interaction on a clear-cut focus; and (2) four "unsatisfactory" therapies. Of the latter, Mrs. Lewis showed poor motivation throughout, and the therapist seems to have had little idea where he was going; the Au Pair Girl, despite some apparently intense work (which was probably imposed on her by the therapist), made an excuse to break off therapy after nine sessions; the Gunner's Wife, after responding to interpretation in sessions 3 and 4, went into impenetrable resistance and pushed the therapist into premature termination in session 6; while the Representative showed the lowest motivation for insight of all our patients and broke off treatment after session 3.

Thus, the main candidates, on clinical grounds, for the argument that improvements were due to factors other than therapy are these four latter patients. Clinical arguments, however, have a tendency to become circular—no one knows that "unsatisfactory" therapies may not contain powerful therapeutic factors—and the only way of escaping from this is by use of statistical methods on the whole sample. In fact, the statistical evidence that these four patients are in some way anomalous is considerable, and these patients will be put in a special category referred to as "false." The evidence will be presented in later chapters.

If for the time being we accept this tentative conclusion, then we can now add to the list of mechanisms of spontaneous remission given in our paper on untreated patients (Malan *et al.*, 1975) as follows:

1. Finding a more satisfactory partner (Mrs. Lewis);

2. Being forced to meet a challenge requiring self-reliance (the Au Pair Girl and the Gunner's Wife—possibly, with more help from therapy, also the Indian Scientist and the Buyer); and

3. Breaking the vicious circle between a crippling symptom and its social effects (the Representative). This mechanism bears a strong

resemblance to one of those postulated for the Research Chemist reported in our above-mentioned paper, and as discussed there, it also supports the claims of behavior therapists for permanent benefit from a type of therapy directed exclusively at a patient's symptoms.

EVIDENCE ON THE VALIDITY OF PSYCHOTHERAPY FROM TIME FACTORS

There is a very important type of clinical evidence about the validity of psychotherapy, which was used in *SBP* (see p. 169), and which needs to be examined in the present series. This comes from the coincidence in time between improvements in disturbances of *long duration* on the one hand and therapy of *brief duration* on the other. We may call the ratio of the first duration to the second the "duration ratio." The greater the value of this ratio, and the greater the proportion of patients showing a high value for it, the more does it seem likely that *some* factor in therapy was responsible for the improvements, since the argument that spontaneous remission "just happened to occur at this point" begins to look more and more implausible.

This kind of evidence needs both to be taken seriously and to be used with caution, since no one can say what changes might be shown by a sample of truly untreated patients over a period of time such as a year. Yet, major and lasting improvements in what appear to be character problems of long duration, which occur within a few months or even weeks of starting therapy, cannot be dismissed lightly. Examples of improvements in such problems are shown by the Indian Scientist (inability to get on with other men), Almoner (need to keep everything "nice"), Maintenance Man (inability to stand up to his wife), Pesticide Chemist (inability to stand up for his rights at work), Mrs. Morley (possessive relation with her daughter), Cellist (inability to assert himself with his mother). In all these cases the disturbance is presumed to have lasted more than ten times as long as the time taken to relieve it. The evidence in the whole sample is shown in Table 4. Only those changes are included that were at least partially maintained throughout the whole of the subsequent period.

An interesting observation here is the high proportion of problems of self-assertion in the list, suggesting the important and clinically valuable conclusion that problems of this kind are among the most amenable to therapeutic intervention.

TABLE 4. Temporal Relations of Therapeutic Effects During Therapy

	Age	Therapeutic effects during therapy	Score for outcome	Approximate duration of disturbance at consultation	Duration: consultation to improvement	Approximate duration ratio
Stationery manufacturer	45	Several times during therapy he spoke of having a better relation with his wife than *ever before in his life*, but this had been only partly maintained at the time of termination.	3.75	6 years	Duration of therapy 1 yr. 10 mos.	3
Indian scientist	29	After confessing in session 4 that he had read his father's love letters to his mother, he experienced an extraordinary sense of relief, and later reported (1) disappearance of anxiety attacks, and (2) great relief of tension between himself and other men. Both these improvements were apparently permanent.	3.5	(2) ? 12 years	2.6 months	55
Personnel manager	40		3.25			
Almoner	22	In session 9 she reported a major quarrel with her parents, after which she walked out on them. She had previously never been able to criticize them. The long-term result was a major, permanent improvement in her relations with them.	3.25	? Many years	5 months	10+
Maintenance man	39	In session 11 (3 months) he reported more independent behavior with his wife; in session 20 he reported disappearance of his phobias; in session 27 (1 yr.) he reported a major row with his wife. He had previously been entirely dominated by his wife, apparently as long as they had been married (11 years).	3.0	11 years	1 year	11

	Age		Score			Follow-up
Mrs. Craig	37	Wish for and enjoyment of sexual intercourse. Previously no sexual contact for 3 years.	2.875	3 years	4 months	9
Gibson girl	18	Major improvements in agoraphobia—able to attend wedding (session 14); able to get a job (session 24).	2.875	5 months	4.3 months	1
Mrs. Lewis	23	Claimed that she allowed consummation of marriage (session 5).	2.833	5 years	2.6 months	23
Mrs. Clifford	23	Undoubted improvements in relation to her husband but too gradual to be dated.	2.75	?	?	
Buyer	27	Anger against a woman for the first time in his life (sessions 17 and 18).	2.75	Many years	6.5 months	10+
Pesticide chemist	31	Ability to assert himself at work (session 6).	2.5	Many years	4.3 months	10+
Au pair girl	21		2.5			
Zoologist	22	He made active efforts at resuming his studies and making contact with girls soon after the first termination (about 8 months). Formerly girls had existed almost entirely in his fantasy.	2.5			
Mrs. Morley	60	Major improvement in her relation with her daughter (session 5). The former problem was an inability to allow her children to live their own lives.	2.25	Many years	7 weeks	20+
Playwright	28		2.25			
Car dealer	48	Asserted himself by firing an employee for the first time in many years (session 10). Also symptomatic improvement.	2.25	Many years	3 months	10+
Gunner's wife	23		2.125			
Representative	21	Made a clear flight into health, having reached the insight that his blushing was due to guilt about masturbation. Nevertheless, this was the turning point in his overall improvement.	2.125	2 years	5 weeks	20

Continued

TABLE 4. (Continued)

	Age	Therapeutic effects during therapy	Score for outcome	Approximate duration of disturbance at consultation	Duration: consultation to improvement	Approximate duration ratio
Oil director	49	There was considerable fluctuation in his overall anxiety but an overall trend toward relief, starting most dramatically in session 21 when he said he felt "calmer than *ever before*."	2.0	11 months	3.5 months	3
Cellist	32	Sudden realization of the absolute necessity of asking his mother to leave his house, apparently soon after the end of therapy. Time relations not clear, but it is probable he had never been able to assert himself in such a way with her before in his life.	1.875	?	?	?
Receptionist	21		1.875			
Bird lady	35		1.375			
Military policeman	38	Considerable remission of symptoms (session 4).	1.375	14 years	3 months	56
Dress designer	26		1.25			
Sociologist	25	Dermatitis recovered (session 13)—though this also seems to coincide with her pregnancy.	1.25	5 years	4 months	15
Company secretary	43		1.0			
Contralto	34		0.9375			
Mrs. Hopkins	36		0.875			
Factory inspector	41		0.833			
Mr. Upton	18		-0.625			

It is important to point out that all this evidence does not necessarily suggest either what the factors in therapy were that led to improvement, or that they were specific to therapy of a psychoanalytic kind. Insofar as problems of self-assertion in particular are concerned, it is as well to remember the evident effectiveness in certain cases of assertive training as practiced by the behavior therapists, or of such mixed approaches as that of Browne (1964), which included not only interpretation (mainly of current rather than past conflicts) but also hypnosis and a good deal of exhortation. Where, in our own patients, the technique included interpretation of the transference and the link with childhood, there is no evidence from the purely clinical data that these specifically psychoanalytic elements are *necessary;* perhaps merely bringing out the lack of self-assertion, with the implied permission or even implied exhortation to be assertive, might be all that is needed. Incidentally, it is interesting to note that Browne uses exactly the same argument to support the value of his therapy as was used above, quoting as evidence a 76 percent improvement rate with very brief therapy in a sample of patients who had been treated medically for the same symptoms for an average of nearly ten years.

There are only two patients in whom the evidence for specific psychoanalytic factors is clear: (1) the Indian Scientist, whose improvements followed a dramatic moment (session 4) in which he experienced great relief after a marked response to an Oedipal interpretation; and (2) the Gibson Girl, who showed two such moments: first, when she found herself able to attend a wedding without anxiety following interpretation of her envy of the bride (session 13); and second, when she got a job immediately after she finally admitted (session 23) that her symptoms had started when her boyfriend began pestering her for intercourse, and then openly admitted her sexual ignorance.

Nevertheless, it must also be pointed out that the improvements observed were in almost all cases preceded by *relevant* therapeutic work. Thus, the Almoner's highly therapeutic row with her parents followed a series of sessions in which she had been able to admit hostility toward them for the first time; the Pesticide Chemist's new ability to demand his rights followed repeated interpretation of his mechanism of leaning over backward to meet everyone else's demands as a cover for his own resentment, and so on. Moreover, even those improvements that followed a flight into health did so after clearly relevant events brought about by therapy: Thus, the Representative began to overcome his problem of blushing after reaching the *insight* that it was due to guilt about masturbation; and the Military Policeman's symptomatic improvement seems to have begun during therapy when he had the courage to speak of his "weakness" to a fellow officer, whom he discovered to have had a breakdown similar to his own.

Such moments in therapy have always been included in the Assessment and Therapy Forms, so that the reader can judge the clinical evidence for himself.

7

Further Follow-up on the First Series

Before any statistical work on the second series can be discussed, it is necessary to ask the crucial question of whether the original hypotheses stood the test of further follow-up on the first series. If they did not, there is nothing to cross-validate.

Of the eighteen patients used in the original correlation studies further follow-up has been obtained on all but one, and it has been necessary to change the score for outcome in nine. Since these later scores have been judged by myself single-handed, I have in most cases preferred to give an upper and a lower limit rather than an exact score. The information, together with that on the three patients not included in the correlation studies, is given in the following pages and is summarized in Table 5.

ARTICLED ACCOUNTANT
(Male, 22, single. 27 sessions. Original score for outcome: 0.)

Initial Disturbances. (1) He was referred for treatment because of the acute appearance of uncontrollable homosexual feelings, which had led to his being arrested for homosexual behavior in public. (2) He was largely unaware of heterosexual feelings. (3) This incident had caused him to become depressed and to plan suicide, though he did not actually attempt it. (4) He had an uneasy relation with older men at work, being unable to stand up to them, and being constantly afraid of making small mistakes. (5) He showed a pattern of denying his feelings and not really knowing where he was going.

TABLE 5. Further Follow-up on SBP Cases

	Information given in *SBP*				Last follow-up in *SBP* (since first termin- ation)	Original score for outcome of brief psycho- therapy.
	Number of sessions brief therapy	Time of start of further treatment (since termination)	Nature of further treatment	Number of sessions, further treatment		
Biologist	10	—	—	—	4 yrs 11/12	3
Lighterman	17	—	—	—	4 yrs 1/12	3
Neurasthenic's husband	14	—	—	—	3 yrs 3/12	3
Falling social worker	40	—	—	—	3 yrs 0/12	3
Railway solicitor	30	—	—	—	3 yrs 8/12	3
Girl with dreams	18	7/12	Brief therapy, same therapist.	10	7/12	2
Civil servant	12	—	—	—	2 yrs 11/12	1
Surgeon's daughter	18	—	—	—	2 yrs 0/12	1
Unsuccessful accountant	7	—	—	—	2 yrs 0/12	1
Draper's assistant	11	1 yr 11/12	Brief therapy, same therapist.	14	1 yr 11/12	0
Storm lady	19	3/12	Individual, same therapist.	34	3/12	0
Tom	4	3/12	O.P. at mental hospital, then admission.		3 yrs 3/12	0
Pilot's wife	19	—	—	—	1 yr 0/12	0
Student thief	11	—	—	—	—	0
Paranoid engineer	13	Immediate	Individual, same therapist.	45	—	0
Violet's mother	15	1/12	Group treatment.	Continuing	3/12	0
Articled accountant	27	—	—	—	2 yrs 7/12	0
Student's wife	9	c. 1 yr	Individual, with 2 therapists in hospital.	25+	3 yrs 1/12	0
Hypertensive housewife	20	2/52	Individual, same therapist, then 2 admissions.	20	1 yr 0/12	0
Clown	5	2 yrs 10/12	Psychiatric O.P. treatment.	?	9/12	No score
Dog lady	10	1/12	Group treatment.	?	4 yrs 3/12	No score

Latest Follow-up in SBP (2 Yrs. 7 Mos.). (1) His homosexual feelings had considerably receded, but it was clear that they were still there beneath the surface. (2) An attempt to form a relation with a girl during therapy was revealed as an attempt to please the therapist, and came to nothing. He remains largely unaware of heterosexual feelings. (3) His depression has disappeared. (4) In his relations with older men at work, there has been a considerable improvement in his confidence,

Time of start of further treatment	Nature of further treatment	Number of sessions or duration of further treatment	Final follow-up (since first termination)	Final follow-up (since later termination)	Final score for outcome	Direction of change from original score
6 yrs 5/12	Individual, with original therapist.	21	6 yrs 5/12	—	1–2	Minus
—	—	—	13 yrs 9/12		1–2	Minus
—	—	—	4 yrs 5/12 | 11 yrs 8/12 |		3–4	
—	—	—	10 yrs 8/12		3–4	
—	—	—	5 yrs 2/12		4	Plus
3 yrs 10/12 (since 2nd termination)	Individual, with another workshop therapist.	3	6 yrs 0/12	4 yrs since 2nd termination	0	Minus
—	—	—	10 yrs 4/12		0	Minus
6 yrs 2/12	Individual, with nonworkshop therapist, then joint family therapy.	36 (individual) 5 joint family.	12 yrs 8/12 12 yrs 8/12		0	Minus
—	—	—	4 yrs 9/12		0–1	
—	—	—	6 yrs 8/12	4 yrs 4/12	0	
—	—	—	7 yrs 5/12	6 yrs 4/12	1–2	Plus
—	—	—	3 yrs 9/12		0	
—	—	—	7 yrs 1/12		0	
	No further information.		—		No score	—
—	—	—	—	None	1–2	Plus
—	—	—	4 yrs 7/12	2 yrs 4/12 since leaving group	No score	?
—		—	3 yrs 9/12		0	
?	O.P. drug treatment continuing.		4 yrs 5/12	c. 1 yr 6/12 since end of psychotherapy	0	
	1. O.P. treatment at neurosis unit. 2. Individual psychotherapy with G.P.	c. 2 yrs		3 yrs 5/12 since 2nd termination	No score	—
	No further information.				No score	
	No further information.				No score	

and he went through a period when he was no longer worried about small mistakes. Nevertheless, his relation with his boss ended in a serious row. He eventually got a new job in which he gets on well with his new boss, but his worry about mistakes seems to have returned. He has given up all idea of taking his final exams and becoming a chartered accountant. (5) As for denial of experience, he seemed little in touch with his feelings and had considerably withdrawn from social life.

Further Follow-up (3 Yrs. 9 Mos.). The position was essentially unchanged. He still gives the impression of having little idea where he is going, and he has a fantasy of taking up an entirely different kind of work. There was a suspicion, which the patient did not deny, that he felt this might make homosexual contacts easier.

Latest Assessment. No further change.

Score. 0.

BIOLOGIST

(Male, 27, married. 10 sessions. Original score for outcome: 3.)

Initial Disturbances. (1) Eating phobia; (2) sexual difficulties: (a) partial impotence, (b) compulsive fantasies with a homosexual flavor, seriously interfering with his life; (3) difficulties with older men; and (4) difficulties over achievement.

Latest Follow-up in SBP (4 Yrs. 11 Mos.). (1) Eating phobia disappeared; (2) (a) marked improvement in potency and relation with wife, (b) fantasies much less frequent but still occur; (3) and (4) happy in new job, in which he receives a good deal of support from his boss.

Further Follow-up (7 Yrs.). (1) Eating phobia: no recurrence; (2) (a) heterosexual problem: complete relapse; (b) fantasies: has "grown out" of them and they no longer occur; (3) and (4) no further trouble.
Patient refused private treatment with colleague of original therapist and referred himself to an eclectic psychotherapist.

Latest Assessment. Apparently there has been no true resolution of his sexual problem; and, in view of the supportive nature of his job, it is not certain that his problems concerned with men and achievement have really been solved. Nevertheless, two serious symptoms have disappeared.

Score. 1–2.

CIVIL SERVANT

(Male, 22, single. 12 sessions. Original score for outcome: 1.)

Initial Disturbances. (1) Nausea and anxiety in claustrophobic situations, particularly eating in public; (2) extreme shyness with girls;

(3) difficulty with male authority in that he is constantly worried about making small mistakes, and gets irrationally angry if told off for making a mistake; and (4) problems over achievement: failing his final exams twice.

Latest Follow-up in SBP (2 Yrs. 11 Mos.). The essential change was that his fairly severe anxiety symptoms had disappeared, though he still suffered from the feeling of a lump in his throat most of the time. In other areas the changes were minimal.

Further Follow-up (10 Yrs. 4 Mos.). He asked for a further interview because over the past three years he has had four apparently unconnected and relatively trivial physical symptoms, each of which has lasted for some months and has then disappeared. He was worried that this might add up to a major physical illness. The essential impression that he conveyed was that things were very little altered for him since the previous follow-up. He still has some difficulty eating in public, and he still has to see to it that he is not in a situation where there is no exit. He is, however, now able to complain to the boss when he feels there has been an injustice. The therapist felt that he was keeping things back from her, and wrote, "This makes me feel that he may be containing very severe paranoid anxieties." He was referred for private treatment. The therapist's fears seemed amply justified when, after being seen for a consultation in private, he wrote an extremely paranoid letter to the psychiatrist who saw him.

Latest Assessment. On the above evidence, the score of 0 is indicated unequivocally.

Score. 0.

DOG LADY
(33, married. 10 sessions. Original outcome: no score.)

Initial Disturbances. (1) Intense fear of dogs since the age of six; and (2) she arranges things so that everybody is nice and kind to her, and she cannot tolerate it if people do not fit in with this.

Latest Follow-up in SBP (4 Yrs. 3 Mos.). This patient was regarded as unsuitable for brief psychotherapy, and was taken on with the sole aim of enabling her to accept group treatment. This was successful, but was not regarded as a legitimate aim for our kind of brief psychotherapy. She attended group treatment for three and a half years, and finally left the group in a state of great anxiety, after speaking for the first time of fantasies about the therapist's sexual relations with another woman. Finally, four years and three months after the termination of the individual therapy, she asked for individual therapy in private, but when there was some delay over offering her an appointment she refused to come.

Further Follow-up. There is in fact no further follow-up, but some details not given in *SBP* are worth including. Her group therapist wrote: "Her problem is part of a very extensive paranoid personality . . . at the same time it seems that her family life is a little freer." She also said that her fear of dogs was now not quite so paralyzing as it used to be.

Latest Assessment. This patient was really rejected for brief psychotherapy. The opinion that she was unsuitable was amply confirmed by subsequent events.

No score.

DRAPER'S ASSISTANT
(Female, 21, married. 11 sessions. Original score for outcome: 0.)

Initial Disturbances. (1) Inability to allow her husband to penetrate in intercourse; and (2) mild phobias, e.g., of being alone in the house or in the street, which in fact have never prevented her from doing anything she wanted to do.

Latest Follow-up in SBP (1 Yr. 11 Mos.). Although at two-and-a-half month follow-up she had claimed that she had had intercourse, she now admitted under pressure that in fact she never had. She was taken on immediately for further treatment by the same therapist and given a further twelve sessions, making twenty-five, including the first two follow-ups. In addition, her husband was seen for three sessions by Therapist E, and then broke off treatment.

Further Follow-up (6 Yrs. 8 Mos. Since Original Termination, 4 Yrs. 4 Mos. Since Second Termination). (1) Her husband has now left her and is petitioning for annulment of their marriage on the grounds of nonconsummation. He has been associating with other women and apparently has no sexual difficulty with them. The patient herself has another boyfriend, and she is quite sure that everything will be all right this time. (2) From the way she spoke at interview, it appeared that her mild phobias had really persisted up to the time her husband left her. She now again claimed that they had disappeared.

Latest Assessment. The evidence is unequivocal that she has never allowed intercourse. Even if her phobias have in fact disappeared, they were never of much importance in her life.

Score. 0.

FALLING SOCIAL WORKER
(Female, 27, single. 40 sessions. Original score for outcome: 3.)

Initial Disturbances. (1) Phobia of falling and fainting; (2) severe "split" in her relations with men: specifically, sexual relations short of intercourse with disreputable men and inability to have sexual relations with "decent" men; (3) emotionally tied to her possessive father; and (4) compulsive overwork.

Latest Follow-up in SBP, Letter from Patient, (3 Yrs.). (1) The phobic symptoms persist with less intensity, but do not worry her any more. (2) She had apparently given up the relations with disreputable men and was now able to have sexual relations short of intercourse with marriageable men. Nevertheless, she still refused intercourse itself, and this resulted in the breakup of her relation with one of her boyfriends. (3) She now seems to have broken free completely and is able to lead her own life. (4) Compulsive overwork has disappeared.

Further Follow-up (1), Letter from Patient (4 Yrs. 3 Mos.) At three years and seven months she suffered a temporary but severe relapse of her symptoms. This occurred during a flu epidemic when many of her colleagues were ill and she was greatly overworked. She all but collapsed and had to be taken home. When she returned to work she was still severely phobic, but she then got real flu herself and her symptoms disappeared and have not recurred.

She is still in the position of not being able to make up her mind which of two men to marry.

Further Follow-up (2), Letter from Patient (10 Yrs. 8 Mos.). She is now married and has two children. She painted an idyllic picture of her marriage. She said that there were still occasions when she became agitated because of having to do too much, but that now she just cried about it on her husband's shoulder and immediately felt better.

Latest Assessment. We were a little unhappy about the amount of idealization in her letter, and this and the lack of a follow-up interview precluded a score of 4. Otherwise the result seems very good.

Score. 3–4.

GIRL WITH THE DREAMS
(24, single. 18 sessions. Original score for outcome: 2.)

Initial Disturbances. (1) Symptoms of general anxiety, nightmares, panic attacks, one of which was epileptiform; (2) difficulty in asserting herself, particularly with women; and (3) sexual problems, specifically she feels safer with less masculine men, and is always left with a strong feeling of dissatisfaction after intercourse.

Latest Follow-up in SBP (7 Mos.) (1) Anxiety improved. No panic attacks. (2) The relation with her mother seems much improved. No information about her ability to assert herself. (3) During therapy she became pregnant, and she married the father of her child. She feels her husband is weak, her physical response to him is limited, and she is still left with a sense of dissatisfaction after intercourse.

She was then taken on for a further ten sessions with the same therapist. During this period her husband was also taken on for brief psychotherapy with another workshop therapist.

Overall total of sessions: twenty-eight + husband's treatment of eleven sessions.

Position at Second Termination (Session 28). The important gain seemed to be that she was now getting on very well with her mother. Her sexual relation with her husband was sometimes very good, but at other times it disgusted her and she pushed him away. She had recently, out of the blue, had another panic attack while her husband was actually making love to her. There was no evidence about her ability to assert herself.

Further Follow-up (3 Yrs. 10 Mos. Since Second Termination). Six months ago she had a major symptomatic relapse. She had another panic attack accompanied by shaking in her arms. Since then she has been fairly severely claustrophobic, has had a number of panic attacks when feeling restricted, and cannot travel by train when alone. It was clear that there was a good deal of strain between her and her husband, and the situation seemed to be that she dominated him but resented the fact that he allowed her to do so. There was a good deal of trouble between them sexually. She described hysterical symptoms that seemed to be a consequence of an inability to express anger against a doctor who had examined her. There was no further information about the relation with her mother.

She was seen for three sessions in all, the last one being four years since the second termination. She was symptomatically slightly better and could now drive her car into her local town, but could not contemplate driving it to London.

Latest Assessment. At this point the only gain seems to be the improvement in her relation with her mother. However, the major symptomatic relapse must indicate that her problems are essentially unresolved. There seems little justification for a score greater than 0.

Score. 0.

HYPERTENSIVE HOUSEWIFE
(34, married. 20 sessions. Original score for outcome: 0.)

Initial Disturbances. (1) Headaches; (2) tendency to form relationships with disturbed men (for details, please see *SBP*): left her husband for a lover nine years ago who died four years ago and two months ago she returned to her husband; (3) severe depression, with hand-wringing and retardation, since the death of her lover four years ago, and two years ago a suicidal attempt with tablets; and (4) uncontrollable outbursts of temper.

Latest Follow-up in SBP. After her twenty sessions there was a marked improvement in headaches and depressive symptoms. She was seen for an independent assessment, and this was very quickly followed by a relapse. She was taken on again by the original therapist one month after the first termination and given a further twenty sessions (forty sessions in all), but she became so depressed that she had to be admitted to a neurosis unit. When the time came for her to be discharged she took a small overdose and was transferred to a mental hospital. When last heard of she was soon to be discharged.

Further Follow-up (3 Yrs. 5 Mos. Since Second Termination). Shortly after her discharge from her second admission (see above) she again took an overdose and was admitted a third time, to yet another hospital. She discharged herself against medical advice the next day (this was one year and eight months since the second termination) and then continued to be seen as an outpatient at the original neurosis unit.

She had the good fortune to be under an extremely insightful G.P. who was Tavistock-trained. He eventually took her over and continued to see her once a week for two or three years. He writes: "While still idealizing her dead lover, she became able to face some realities (that he was a thief, sometimes knocked her about, etc.), and she became able to be aggressive to me without being overcome by excessive guilt." She was helped in addition by a woman health visitor, one of the few good relationships with a woman that she has ever made, and as an aid to her need to make reparation her G.P. got her a job as helper in an old people's home. Her psychotherapy was supplemented by a long course of phenelzine, and up to the present she continues to take four hundred mg of barbiturate nightly.

Her G.P. eventually retired and moved away, but he gave her good warning, and this did not result in any further acting out. She is still living with her husband. She has become able to do her own shopping and housekeeping and is doing a part-time job. She tolerates, and sometimes hungrily enjoys, sexual relations. The main deficiencies are that she is still very guilty and afraid of the violence of her own impulses, and the overall relation with her husband is not a good one.

Latest Assessment. In view of the extensive and varied subsequent treatment that she has had, it does not seem relevant to score this result. No score.

LIGHTERMAN
(30, married. 17 sessions. Original score for outcome: 3.)

Initial Disturbances. (1) Background problems: (a) severely compulsive character; and (b) relation with his mother severely affected by compulsiveness. (2) Following recent mild head injury: (c) and (d) severe and short-lasting, and less severe and longer-lasting, anxiety attacks accompanied by confusion; (e) attacks of rage against his children; (f) agoraphobia, claustrophobia, fear of going out on the open river; and (g) depressive attacks.

Latest Follow-up in SBP (1 Yr. 7 Mos.). (a) Compulsive phenomena much improved and replaced by reparative acts, especially acting as foster-father. (b) Relation with his mother much improved and no longer affected by compulsiveness. (c) and (d) No severe anxiety attacks, though he still gets short-lasting attacks of tension. (e) He can now cope with his children's demands and deal with them firmly when necessary. (f) Phobias remain largely unchanged. (g) He has apparently recovered from depressive phenomena.

As reported in *SBP*, this patient was written to four years and one month after termination, but wrote that as he was so much better he felt he did not want to visit the clinic again.

Further Follow-up (1) (5 Yrs. 7 Mos.). This patient still refused to be seen by any member of the clinic, and could only be followed up by his G.P., who was careful not to probe too deeply. The patient seems to have been stabilized in a chronic somewhat hypochrondriacal and anxious state. He visits his G.P. fairly often, usually anxious about some minor physical symptom, and receives meprobamate regularly.

Further Follow-up (2) (13 Yrs. 9 Mos.). The above situation seems to have been entirely maintained. The patient still comes regularly for prescriptions for meprobamate, having become anxious and tense over some minor matter. Apart from this, the G.P. described him as being "well-adjusted." He and his wife have continued to act regularly as foster-parents. There have been no complaints from the wife about their relation, nor any disturbance in any of the children.

Latest Assessment. Assessment is very difficult without further information, but it seems there has been some symptomatic improvement, together with an improvement in the patient's personal relations. However, the chronic anxiety implies a good deal of unresolved problems, and it looks as if the original score of 3 was optimistic.

Provisional Score. 1–2.

NEURASTHENIC'S HUSBAND
(54, married. 14 sessions. Original score for outcome: 3.)

Initial Disturbances. These consisted essentially of a life-long inability to assert himself or value himself at his true worth.

Latest Follow-up in SBP (3 Yrs. 3 Mos.). There was a remarkable improvement in his basic problem. He has (a) been able to assert himself at work; (b) been able to assert himself with his wife in those areas where it is possible, and to accept philosophically those areas where it is not; and (c) has earned the respect of his children.

Further Follow-up (1) (4 Yrs. 5 Mos.). There was no essential change in his external circumstances. His attitude toward his life, his work, and his wife remain much improved, though there is a certain masochistic quality in it still.

Further Follow-up (2) (11 Yrs. 8 Mos.). The therapist met him by chance and spoke to him briefly. A follow-up under such circumstances is not very reliable, but it appeared that no disasters had happened, and that the above situation had been essentially maintained.

Latest Assessment. Improvement maintained.

Score. 3–4.

PARANOID ENGINEER
(Male, 28, single. 13 sessions. Original score for outcome: 0.)

This man was suffering from a borderline paranoid psychosis, a fact of which he was fully aware himself. His main disturbances were an intense preoccupation with comparing himself with other men, a fear that he was homosexual, and a fear that he would shout this out in the laboratory where he worked. He had had sexual relations with women, but suffered from premature ejaculation.

Latest Follow-up in SBP. Two attempts were made to terminate, the first after session 8, and the second after session 13. It was quite clear, however, that he still badly needed help and the therapist then agreed to see him once every three weeks indefinitely.

Further Therapy. These further sessions varied from being essentially supportive in nature to being intensely interpretative. In session 24, nine months after the second attempted termination, he asked for an emergency session because he had met a girl. This resulted in a great deal of Oedipal material, interpreted mainly in the transference. He eventually became engaged to this girl, though his feelings about her contained a great deal of disturbance. Before the end of treatment he passed his final exams, and he then married his fiancée. After an overall total of fifty-eight sessions spread over two years and seven months, he and his wife emigrated to the United States. He continued to send a Christmas card to his therapist every year for the next three years, but this was not accompanied by any news, and the therapist was careful not to ask for any.

Latest Assessment. Considering the severity of his initial disturbances, his ability both to pass his final exams and to get married was a very considerable achievement. Nevertheless, there was plenty of evidence for severe residual disturbance, and my feeling is that this result should be scored very conservatively.

Score. 1–2.

PILOT'S WIFE
(24, married. 19 sessions. Original score for outcome: 0.)

Initial Disturbances. Her complaint was frigidity. Behind this lay an extreme degree of "masculine protest"; she was extremely resentful against men and jealous of them, and an ardent feminist.

Latest Follow-up in SBP (1 Yr.). Six months after termination she had become extremely upset, feeling that she might be pregnant. In fact, this was a false alarm. At one year after termination she said she was happier and more relaxed, but it was clear that this was because her husband wanted intercourse less often. There were no other changes.

Further Follow-up (1) (4 Yrs. 4 Mos.). She was still determined that she did not want children, but had found a way of sublimating her maternal feelings. There had been very serious marital difficulties, nearly ending in divorce. She and her husband have now decided to try and make a go of it again.

Further Follow-up (2) (7 Yrs. 1 Mo.). She got in touch with her therapist after an extremely traumatic experience (not involving the relation with her husband). She was seen for five sessions to help her through this, and she ended by coping with it in a quite adaptive way and expressing violent and appropriate feelings about it. The situation between her and her husband was now improved again, but her feelings about sex were in no way changed.

Latest Assessment. Essentially unchanged.

Score. 0.

RAILWAY SOLICITOR
(Male, 24, single. 30 sessions. Original score for outcome: 3.)

Initial Disturbances. (1) Symptoms: headaches, feelings of tension (two and a half years); (2) extremely shy with girls; and (3) intense competitiveness with men, and difficulties over achievement.

Latest Follow-up in SBP, Letter from Patient (3 Yrs. 8 Mos.). (1) Symptoms much improved; (2) now married; and (3) good progress in his career, accompanied by a marked increase in confidence.

Further Follow-up (5 Yrs. 2 Mos.). (1) His tension has completely disappeared and his headaches seem no more than "normal." (2) He had to overcome his mother's opposition to his marriage. It is also extremely important that he recognized that his wife suffered from considerable anxieties about sex, and he finally succeeded in overcoming these. The sexual relation now appears to be satisfactory to both partners. (3) Progress in his career is maintained. There was possibly some evidence of minimal residual disturbance in his relation with men.

Latest Assessment. This patient appears to be almost completely recovered.

Score. 4.

STORM LADY
(23, married. 19 sessions. Original score for outcome: 0.).

Initial Disturbances. (1) Severe phobias: She has suffered from a fear of death as long as she can remember. Three years ago this fear became particularly attached to thunderstorms; during a storm she becomes paralyzed with fright, and in between storms she is in constant fear that one will occur. (2) She has never had an orgasm and feels she is not a proper woman. (3) Beneath the phobic symptoms there lie severe depressive fantasies that include the feeling that she could never be a normal mother or give birth to a normal baby.

Latest Follow-up in SBP (3 Mos.). The patient was three months pregnant with her first child when she came to treatment, and she stopped coming just before the birth of the baby. When she was seen three months later her disturbances were quite unchanged, and in addition she was extremely anxious about attending to her baby (girl) and unable to play with her. She was taken on for treatment again at once, being given thirty-four more sessions, a total of fifty-three in all.

Further Follow-up (1) (6 Yrs. 2 Mos. Since First Termination, 5 Yrs. 1 Mo. Since Second Termination). (1) Phobias: She said that people who saw her during an actual storm might think she was no better, but the main change is that she no longer thinks of storms when they are not actually occurring. This is a major improvement, because formerly her whole life was spoiled by the anticipation of a storm. Also, whereas previously her reaction to a storm was of an "all or nothing" kind, she can now assess the severity of a storm, and if it is not a bad one she does not react so violently.

(2) Frigidity: There is some improvement here. She sometimes wants sex because of her own needs, and not only because it is part of a woman's role. She still does not have orgasm, but she said she almost did and was sometimes left feeling dissatisfied.

(3) Depressive feelings: Formerly she felt unable to love her daughter properly because of a fear of losing her. She now feels this fear has gone and she can do all the feminine things that she should for her. On the other hand, she denied to herself the reality of two subsequent pregnancies. She also cannot see the future as real; there is still some feeling of impending disaster. She feels her mother's continual presence in the background and it is absolutely essential—"If she should die my world would crack up." The idea of her mother's death some time in the future has no reality for her. The therapist concluded that she was still keeping a depression at bay; but that her insight was quite impressive and that she was now operating much less on a basis of denial.

Follow-up (2) (7 Yrs. 5 Mos. Since First Termination, 6 Yrs. 4 Mos. Since Second Termination). She has stood up to the death of her father without panic or severe depression. Owing to the highly charged relation with him, this was a very severe test. In other respects the position seems essentially unchanged since the last follow-up.

Latest Assessment. This result is extremely difficult to score. All three of her main disturbances are somewhat relieved, but much pathology still remains.

Provisional Score. 1–2.

STUDENT THIEF
(Female, 20, single. 11 sessions. Original score for outcome: 0.)

Initial Disturbances. (1) She had been sent for treatment because she had been discovered to have stolen money from fellow nurses on two occasions; (2) extremely idealized relation with her fiancé; and (3) conflict with her mother.

Latest Follow-up in SBP (About 1 Yr.). This patient acted out severely over follow-up and eventually refused to come. The relation with her fiancé broke down completely during therapy, and we learned later that she had married a West Indian. In one of her letters she said that she and her mother had had a reconciliation.

Further Follow-up. None. It was not considered appropriate to try and follow this patient up.

STUDENT'S WIFE
(27, married. 9 sessions. Original score for outcome: 0.)

Initial Disturbances. (1) (a) Phobic anxiety: fear of falling and hurting herself (eleven months); (b) obsessional anxiety: feeling that unless she touched something or wore certain clothes, something might happen to her mother; (2) she has been married nine months but is not interested in sex and has not yet had intercourse; and (3) constant restless movements observed at interview.

Latest Follow-up in SBP (3 Yrs. 1 Mo.). This patient and her husband emigrated to the United States and she there sought treatment for essentially the same disturbances as listed above. She then moved to another city and had some further treatment. Finally, three years and one month after the first termination, she wrote to her therapist asking to be referred for further treatment. From her account she seemed symptomatically worse.

Further Follow-up (4 Yrs. 5 Mos.).

(1) She still suffers from a fear of fainting whenever she is alone. She is under the care of a psychiatrist who is giving her tranquilizers.

(2) She has now had one child. She could not remember when it was that she first allowed her husband to have intercourse with her. As far as sex is concerned, she said that neither she nor her husband were "that way inclined."

(3) The restless movements had disappeared by the end of her nine sessions with us, but they returned when she was under treatment in the United States. They have now disappeared again.

(4) There was a considerable increase in insight. She said that she now knew that the trouble was her relation with her mother, and she was able to speak of her mother with open resentment. She also said that she used never to have a mind of her own and took all her opinions from her mother. Since she has been away from her, she can think for herself.

Latest Assessment. The changes are not considered enough to justify a score greater than 0.

Score. 0.

SURGEON'S DAUGHTER
(29, single. 18 sessions. Original score for outcome: 1.)

Initial Disturbances. This girl was in a complicated situation involving an illegitimate pregnancy. The inference was that her main difficulty was an inability to assert her rights, particularly in a triangular situation with a man and another woman, and that she had engineered the pregnancy in order to force her fiancé to marry her without actually having to ask.

Latest Follow-up in SBP (2 Yrs.). Shortly after the end of therapy she had had a terrific row with her fiancé's other girlfriend and had slapped her face. She and her fiancé had later got married, and it seemed that she was able to be a very good mother. At two-year follow-up, however, there seemed to have been an almost exact repetition of the original situation. She had had a second unwanted pregnancy, and the baby died shortly after birth. This pregnancy served the purpose of forcing her husband to get a job and support her. Nevertheless, the relation between the two of them seemed to be a good one. She was given a score of 1 on the grounds that she had been helped to assert herself sufficiently to marry her fiancé and to make a reasonably happy marriage.

Further Follow-up (6 Yrs. 2 Mos.). She now asked for a further appointment. The essence of what happened was that her husband was now again exposing her to triangular situations, in which she was totally incapable of standing up for her rights. She was taken on again for individual treatment with a nonworkshop therapist. There is a record of thirty-six sessions in the notes. This was not the end of the story, since the patient also asked for treatment for her son, who was seen in a joint interview with his parents six years and two months after the original termination. Finally, twelve years and nine months after the original termination, the patient again asked for help, with the news that she and her husband were being divorced.

Latest Assessment. It is quite clear that her original problem of being unable to stand up for her rights was never solved, and in view of the divorce, she cannot score anything for making a satisfactory marriage either.

Score. 0.

TOM
(16, single. 4 sessions. Original score for outcome: 0.)

Initial Disturbances. Somatic symptoms accompanied by severe anxiety (four weeks). These occurred when he was about to get his first job. It was thought that the underlying conflict was about the possibility of leaving his father and going to live with his stepmother, who was living away from her husband.

Latest Follow-up in SBP (3 Yrs. 3 Mos.). Between sessions 3 and 4 he went to live with his stepmother, all his symptoms immediately disappeared, and he then broke off treatment. His symptoms returned in full force one month later. Because of their severity he was admitted to a mental hospital, where he stayed for one year. There was some question of a diagnosis of schizophrenia but this was eventually rejected. When last seen he had been out of the hospital for nearly two years, and was still living with his stepmother. He still suffered from the original symptoms, and in addition from claustrophobia, agoraphobia, and a partial spasm in one leg. Nevertheless, he has managed to work at the same job ever since leaving the hospital.

Further Follow-up (3 Yrs. 9 Mos.). There had been an increase of symptoms. His stepmother reported that when he came home from work he spent hours just doodling. Recently he had had a severe attack in which everything seemed "very far away" and he couldn't concentrate enough to hear what people were saying to him. Nevertheless, he made very good contact at interview and there was no evidence whatsoever for delusions or hallucinations.

Latest Assessment. If anything, worse.

Score. 0.

UNSUCCESSFUL ACCOUNTANT
(Male, 31, married. 7 sessions. Original score for outcome: 1.)

Initial Disturbances. This patient came for "advice" about what sort of job he should get. He was qualified as an accountant, but had been trying unsuccessfully to get personnel work. He had been turned down for about twenty jobs in the past two years. It emerged that he had a severe problem over competitiveness, which prevented him from making a choice of a realistic job on the one hand, and probably made him antagonize interviewing boards on the other.

Latest Follow-up in SBP (2 Yrs.). During therapy he abandoned the idea of personnel work, and was accepted for a job with a commercial firm that made use of his qualifications. He has done reasonably well at this. The conclusion was that because of his anxiety, he had given up competing directly in his own profession. Nevertheless, he had been helped to abandon unrealistic goals, and was therefore given a score of 1 for "valuable false solution."

Further Follow-up (4 Yrs. 9 Mos.). This follow-up, later than the one given in the Assessment and Therapy Form, was described on page

165 of *SBP*. The essence of this was that although he made remarkably good progress in his job, he still clearly suffered from as severe anxieties about competitiveness as before. The evidence for this was: (1) that he failed in an exam in which he had specialized knowledge; (2) when he tried to take the same exam again he walked out because of anxiety; and (3) he suffered from fairly severe thought block at the follow-up interview just as he had in therapy five years before.

Latest Assessment. During therapy he was helped to make a realistic decision about a career, and he has maintained this and done well at it. It is clear that the underlying problems have in no way been solved. His score must be greater than 0, but on the scale used for the second series of patients I doubt if he would score as much as 1.

Score. 0–1.

VIOLET'S MOTHER
(42, married. 15 sessions. Original score for outcome: 0.)

Initial Disturbances. This was a complex family problem with an acute exacerbation. Details are not suitable for publication.

Latest Follow-up in SBP. Following the termination of her individual treatment, she was transferred to group treatment.

Further Follow-up (4 Yrs. 7 Mos. Since Termination of Individual Treatment, 2 Yrs. 4 Mos. Since Termination of Group Treatment). She continued in group treatment over a total of two years one month. When finally interviewed she seemed to have made a very good adaptation to life, but owing to the nature of the circumstances a score for outcome is really impossible.
No score.

DISCUSSION

It is immediately obvious that since the position reported in *SBP* there has been a substantial degree of relapse. Of the nine patients who scored more than zero for outcome, only four (the Neurasthenic's Husband, Falling Social Worker, Railway Solicitor, and Unsuccessful Accountant) have not had their scores reduced by one point or more.

These new follow-ups now bring the total who showed either failure to terminate, or resumption of therapy since the first attempted termination, to ten of the eighteen (56 percent). The same occurred in only nine of the thirty in the later series (30 percent). This difference, though considerable, is not significant ($x^2=2.1$, $p>.1$, two-tailed test).

As might be expected, therefore, the therapeutic results in the second series are very considerably better than in the first, the mean score for outcome being 2.11 in the second series and roughly 1.0 in the first (this difference is significant at the 1 percent level by the t test, two-tailed).

This observation can also be formulated as follows: In the first series the overall tendency was toward *deterioration* after termination; in the second series the tendency was toward *improvement*. Of the sixteen patients of the first series whose latest outcome can be scored, six (37.5 percent) showed deterioration, and only two (11 percent) showed improvement (the rest showing no change). Of the thirty patients in the second series, only four (7.5 percent) showed deterioration and thirteen (43 percent) showed improvement. Moreover, in the first series there was a tendency toward deterioration even in those patients who seemed to have had important experiences in therapy; while in the second series there was a tendency toward improvement even in those patients for whom little of therapeutic importance seemed to have happened.

For all these observations I cannot find any explanation against which there is not a counterargument, and I can only suppose that they are due to chance differences between the patients selected in the two series, which of course emphasizes the overwhelming importance of cross-validation.

Re-examination of the Original Hypotheses in the Light of Later Follow-up. In view of the marked changes in the scores for outcome brought about by later follow-up, it might well be expected that the original hypotheses would no longer hold. Miraculously, this is not so.

I have made an exhaustive examination of the evidence but, for brevity, will only summarize the main features. The following preliminary remarks are necessary:

1. The fact that of four patients who had subsequent individual therapy, two ultimately exceeded forty sessions and both improved introduces a complication. (These were the Storm Lady and Paranoid Engineer, final totals fifty-three and fifty-eight sessions respectively.) There are three different ways of handling this: (a) Both can be regarded as failures of brief therapy; (b) both can be omitted, so that the study

becomes one of patients who actually had brief therapy and nothing else; or (c) both can be regarded as partial successes for longer therapy, so that if they are included, the study becomes one of "psychotherapy."

2. Similarly Violet's Mother, who went on to group treatment, can be regarded as a failure of brief therapy; but her final result is almost impossible to score, and if (individual) "psychotherapy" is being considered she is best omitted.

3. No follow-up was obtained on the Student Thief, and she has been omitted from all correlation studies.

4. The result is: (a) $N=17$ for brief therapy, counting the two longer therapies plus Violet's Mother as failures; (b) $N=14$ if these three are omitted; and (c) $N=16$ if the study is of "psychotherapy."

The important observation is that *it makes little difference to the original hypotheses whichever of these alternatives is chosen.*

Results Concerned with Selection Criteria. *Severity of Psychopathology:* With the hindsight provided by later follow-up, it now looks as if the failures of brief therapy in the Civil Servant, Tom, Storm Lady, Paranoid Engineer, Hypertensive Housewife, and Dog Lady were all at least partly due to severe pathology.

On the other hand, if brief therapy had failed in the Neurasthenic's Husband, Falling Social Worker, and Biologist, this could equally have been attributed to the same factor, so that it seems as if some kinds of severe pathology are not contraindications in themselves. Thus, the evidence on this variable remains confusing.

Recent Onset: The evidence that recent onset had no bearing whatsoever on suitability for brief therapy in these patients is greatly strengthened by later follow-up. The correlation with outcome changes from a small negative value to a very large negative value that is actually significant at the .005 level ($\tau=-0.68$, $p=0.003$, two-tailed test)![1] Inspection shows that this result is largely due to the presence in the sample of a high proportion of *young* people (twenty-four or under) with acute problems that proved exceedingly refractory to treatment. Of these, the Girl with the Dreams, Civil Servant, and Tom all suffered from phobic symptoms, while the Pilot's Wife and Draper's Assistant would probably be diagnosed as hysterical personalities. This evidence thus contradicts a widely held preconception that such patients are highly suitable for psychotherapy; and since all these patients showed poor or doubtful motivation, it suggests once more that this criterion should be considered rather than diagnosis or psychopathology.

---

[1] For a discussion of the statistical methods used in the present work, and the use of one-tailed and two-tailed tests, please see the next chapter.

Motivation: Because motivation in every patient tends to be ambivalent, with a positive and a negative component, and it also fluctuates markedly during the early contacts with the clinical situation, the evidence is both extremely difficult to judge and to present. In *SBP* I overcame this difficulty as best I could by only presenting material on those patients in whom the evidence seemed unequivocal. I did, however, make judgments of motivation and its fluctuations on all patients, and I am therefore able to make use of these in considering the effects of later follow-up. The evidence is as follows:

1. Of the two patients who relapsed from an original score of 3 to a score of 1–2 for outcome, the Lighterman showed unequivocally high motivation and the Biologist showed a marked increase from early low motivation, both of which I would regard as favorable prognostic signs. This of course does weaken the evidence, but since both patients did show moderate improvements at later follow-up, their contribution to the correlation is still positive.

2. The three patients who relapsed to a score of zero from an original score of 1 or 2 for outcome (the Girl with the Dreams, Civil Servant, and Surgeon's Daughter) all showed rather doubtful motivation, and in their case the result of later follow-up is to strengthen the correlation.

3. Of the two patients who went on to longer therapy and gave a final moderate therapeutic result (score 1–2), the Paranoid Engineer showed unequivocally high motivation; and the Storm Lady showed what appears to have been high motivation, though she did cancel the third session for reasons that were not recorded at the time and might have been reality rather than resistance. Both these patients strengthen the correlation for "psychotherapy" but not for "brief psychotherapy."

4. One patient who scored 3 and maintained her improvements (the Falling Social Worker) showed unequivocally high motivation throughout.

5. The other two patients who maintained or increased their improvements from an original score of 3 both present problems concerned with ambivalent and fluctuating motivation, in which, however, there was unquestionably a high positive component. The Neurasthenic's Husband was only taken on for treatment at all on the strength of an impassioned letter that seemed to indicate the strongest possible motivation for insight, and his apparently extremely high motivation was the one and only factor in his favor; but when he actually came to therapy he showed marked resistance to accepting painful interpretations, and in fact he canceled session 3. The Railway Solicitor was judged by his therapist to have an initial high motivation, but he attempted to make a flight into health in session 5.

The overall conclusion is that later follow-up on the whole strengthens the evidence in favor of motivation as the only selection criterion that offers any hope of being of practical value.

The Evidence Concerned with Transference Interpretation. Throughout the following discussion there is one point that needs to be constantly borne in mind. This is that the basic hypotheses being tested are really hypotheses of the *necessary condition*, i.e., that a particular factor—here a particular type of interpretation—is in general a necessary condition to success; no one can expect that it should be a *necessary and sufficient* condition. Thus, therapies in which the factor was *present* but which were *not successful* are to be expected, and they do not contradict the basic hypothesis in the same way as do therapies in which the factor was *not present* but which were nevertheless *successful*.

Now, there is no known statistical way of testing hypotheses of the necessary condition, and one therefore has to fall back on correlation coefficients, which are essentially a way of expressing the degree to which any factor is a *necessary and sufficient* condition. Correlation coefficients thus represent a *highly conservative* way of testing the hypotheses under study. This has obvious scientific advantages, since *false positive* results are less likely to be obtained. On the other hand, *false negative* results may be, and therefore simple inspection may sometimes be a better way of examining the data.

Once this has been said, the effect of further follow-up on the hypotheses concerned with transference interpretation can be summed up in a single sentence: To a large extent *only* the *complete transference therapies* gave good results that stood the test of time (the Neurasthenic's Husband, Falling Social Worker, and Railway Solicitor), though not *all* complete transference therapies did so (the Lighterman relapsed). By a "complete transference therapy" is meant one in which transference arose early and was interpreted throughout, the transference/parent link was repeatedly made, and the negative transference and feelings about termination were thoroughly interpreted (these last two statements were less true of the Railway Solicitor).

The correlations with outcome, all based on my single-handed scores, are given in full in Table 6. The following are some notes and comments:

1. Where quantitative measures are available, I have used these rather than measures based on clinical judgment, because they can be scored objectively and in my opinion offer a far more valid measure of the "importance" of a given kind of interpretation.

2. The "transference ratio," "transference minus transference/

TABLE 6. First Series: Effect of Later Follow-up on the Correlations between Outcome and Various Aspects of Transference

	Original follow-up		Later follow-up					
	Longer therapies scored as failures of brief therapy N=18		Longer therapies scored as failures of brief therapy N=17		Longer therapies omitted. Brief therapy only N=14		Longer therapies included and scored for final outcome. "Psychotherapy." N=16	
Variable correlated with outcome	τ	p (two-tailed)	τ	p (two-tailed)	τ	p (two-tailed)	τ	p (two-tailed)
"Importance" judged clinically								
Early transference	+0.27	0.21	+0.41	0.07	+0.54[a]	0.017[a]	+0.52[a]	0.025[a]
Work on termination	+0.44	0.054	+0.38	0.09	+0.34	0.083	+0.38	0.089
Early transference + work on termination	+0.51[a]	0.019[a]	+0.51	0.019[a]	+0.55[b]	0.010[b]	+0.60[b]	0.0056[b]
Negative transference	+0.28	0.19	+0.23	0.28	+0.12	0.32	+0.15	0.26
Quantitative measures								
Transference (T) ratio	+0.28	0.15	+0.36	0.10	+0.37	0.097	+0.33	0.11
T minus T/P ratio	+0.24	0.21	+0.29	0.14	+0.28	0.22	+0.26	0.20
T/P ratio	+0.55[b]	0.0056[b]	+0.43[a]	0.035[a]	+0.40	0.074	+0.36	0.085

[a]Significant at .05 level (two-tailed test).
[b]Significant at .01 level (two-tailed test).

parent ratio," and "transference/parent ratio" are all taken to the nearest 1 percent. This is the reason for differences from the figures given in *SBP*, where I had less confidence in these variables and used coarser scales. (For definition of these variables see Chapter 11.)

3. The variable that shows both the highest and most consistent correlation with outcome is the composite and artificial variable "early transference + work on termination." This can, however, be given a clear clinical meaning, since it represents a measure of the patient's willingness to become involved both *quickly* and *deeply* in the transference relationship.

4. The *transference ratio* includes *transference/parent* (T/P) interpretations, and therefore a better way of testing whether transference interpretations are important in themselves is to compare the correlations given by (a) the T/P ratio, with (b) the transference ratio from which T/P interpretations have been excluded (T minus T/P ratio). At the first follow-up the difference between the correlations was very striking. At later follow-up the difference is much less striking but still considerable.

5. The variable that showed the highest correlation at the first follow-up—namely, the T/P ratio, i.e., the quantitative measure of the importance of transference/parent interpretations—only correlates at the 10 percent level of significance at later follow-up both (a) when the longer therapies are omitted and (b) when they are included and scored for final outcome. It might be thought that this greatly weakens the evidence in favor of the therapeutic effectiveness of the T/P link, but this is not so. Inspection of Table 7 will show that the three therapies whose original good results stood the test of time rank *first, second,* and *third equal* for this variable. In other words, though the *correlation* is not significant the hypothesis of the *necessary condition* is strongly supported. (These three therapies rank third, fifth, and sixth for T minus T/P ratio.)

The final result is that although the emphasis is slightly altered, the original hypotheses concerned with transference interpretation are little affected by final follow-up.

A Factor in the Therapist. There was one further important observation mentioned in *SBP,* namely, that there seemed to be a tendency for the therapist to be successful with his first case, when presumably his enthusiasm was at its highest. Here it should be noted that both the Neurasthenic's Husband the the Railway Solicitor were first cases. However, in order to make the observation meaningful, I had to include preliminary evidence from the second series, and any final verdict must await definitive evidence from the two series together.

TABLE 7. First Series: Relation Between Outcome at Final Follow-up and Two Transference Variables (for "Psychotherapy," $N=16$)

	Outcome	T–T/P%	Rank number	T/P%	Rank number
Railway solicitor	4	45%	3	15%	2
Neurasthenic's husband	3–4	40%	5	19%	1
Falling social worker	3–4	36%	6	8%	3=
Lighterman	1–2	21%	11	8%	3=
Biologist	1–2	17%	13=	1%	14
Storm lady	1–2	19%	12	2%	11=
Paranoid engineer	1–2	30%	7	4%	8
Unsuccessful accountant	0–1	69%	1	0%	15=
Girl with the dreams	0	22%	9	5%	7
Civil servant	0	22%	9	7%	5=
Surgeon's daughter	0	50%	2	3%	9=
Draper's assistant	0	17%	13=	2%	11=
Tom	0	6%	15=	0%	15=
Pilot's wife	0	43%	4	3%	9=
Articled accountant	0	22%	9	7%	5=
Student's wife	0	6%	15=	2%	11=

A Possible Unifying Factor. Thus, the original results are little changed by further follow-up. In *SBP* I wrote that the factors that seem to accompany successful therapy—motivation, transference in all its aspects, strong feelings about termination, and enthusiasm in the therapist—all contain the factor of *involvement,* on both sides, in the therapeutic relationship. It is thus basically this unifying factor that is under scrutiny in the second series.

8

Failure to Terminate and "Spontaneous Remission"

General Statistical Considerations

In chapter 7 I discussed three possible ways of scoring outcome, brought about by the fact that two patients in the first series went on to longer therapy. In the present series the situation is similar. Of the thirty patients successfully followed up, there were twenty-two whose therapy was terminated permanently within an arbitrary limit of forty sessions. These (Patients "A") are the genuinely brief therapy patients. This leaves eight (Patients "B") who exceeded forty sessions, six of whom gave relatively satisfactory results (≥ 2.0 within one hundred sessions) while two exceeded one hundred sessions and gave poor results at the time of follow-up (the Dress Designer, score 1.25; and the Contralto, score 0.9375). In fact, this situation was altered by later events, since the Contralto went on to complete her analysis, which appears to have been ultimately highly successful, though *the original low score is used in all the statistical studies*. There is thus only one patient, the Dress Designer, who had long-term therapy and gave an unequivocally poor result.

Just as in the first series, the question then arises whether (1) to count these eight long therapies as failures of brief therapy, all scoring 0; (2) to omit them, leaving Patients "A" ($N=22$), who had brief therapy and nothing else; or (3) to add them to Patients A, using the *final* scores in the statistical studies, so that the study becomes one of "psychotherapy" (Patients A + B, $N=30$).

When I came to study the second series, I soon found that scoring these eight longer therapies as failures destroyed all the significant correlations. The reason was simple: Almost all the factors that correlated with favorable outcome were the same, whatever the length of therapy. *This meant that with the method of scoring used in* SBP, *none of the hypotheses were cross-validated.*

On the other hand, if either of the other two alternatives was chosen, several significant correlations reappeared; and since in the first series it essentially did not matter which method of scoring was used, these significant correlations were thus shown to hold in two successive samples. The effect of these changes in procedure on the question of cross-validation will be considered later (see chap. 16). It needs to be emphasized, however, that *any alteration in the method of scoring, deliberately chosen to preserve significant correlations, results in a weakening of evidence.*

THE "FALSE" CASES

As described in chapter 6, there were four patients who had brief therapy but whose ultimate improvements occurred in such a way as to suggest "spontaneous remission" rather than the effects of psychotherapy. These patients tend to obscure trends shown by the other brief therapy patients, and it is therefore sometimes helpful to omit them and to study the remaining eighteen brief therapy patients by themselves. Of these, nine gave "successful" results (≥ 2.0) and nine "unsuccessful" (< 2.0). Sometimes also clear trends can be demonstrated if the whole sample is divided into four categories: (1) short, successful ($N=9$); (2) long ($N=8$); (3) false ($N=4$); and (4) short, unsuccessful ($N=9$), as shown in Table 8.

STATISTICAL METHODS USED

In *SBP* the only correlation coefficient used was Kendall's τ (*tau:* Kendall, 1955), which is based solely on rank orders and thus does not depend on any unjustified assumptions that scores for variables as outcome, motivation, etc., are genuine numbers that can legitimately be subjected to such mathematical operations as addition or multiplication. The main disadvantage of τ in comparison with the product–moment correlation coefficient r is that when there are "ties" in one or other of the two rank orders being correlated, τ often cannot attain unity

TABLE 8. Second Series of Patients Classified According to Length of Therapy and Outcome

Patient	Number of sessions	Score for outcome
Short therapy, favorable outcome (N=9)		
Stationery manufacturer	28	3.75
Indian scientist	12	3.5
Almoner	11	3.25
Maintenance man	30	3.0
Gibson girl	28	2.875
Buyer	18	2.75
Zoologist	32	2.5
Pesticide chemist	14	2.5
Mrs. Morley	9	2.25
Mean	20.2	2.93
Long therapy (N=8)		
Personnel manager	62	3.25
Mrs. Craig	76	2.875
Mrs. Clifford	90	2.75
Car dealer	54	2.25
Playwright	93	2.25
Oil director	46	2.0
Dress designer	>200	1.25
Contralto	>400	0.9375
Mean		2.19
"False" cases (N=4)		
Mrs. Lewis	20	2.83
Au pair girl	9	2.5
Gunner's wife	6	2.125
Representative	3	2.125
Mean	9.5	2.40
Short therapy, unfavorable outcome (N=9)		
Cellist	9	1.875
Receptionist	9	1.875
Bird lady	9	1.375
Military policeman	4	1.375
Sociologist	26	1.25
Company secretary	12	1.0
Mrs. Hopkins	33	0.875
Factory inspector	19	0.83
Mr. Upton	5	−0.625
Mean	14.0	1.31 (omitting Mr. Upton)

(see below for a full discussion). One of the consequences of this is that a given value appears considerably lower than it "really" is. An excellent example is a correlation (T/P%-outcome see chap. 13) for which $\tau=+0.29$, which does not appear very high, whereas the value of r was $+0.41$—both having roughly the same significance level.

The use of τ was essential in all the correlations in *SBP* because of the very coarse 0, 1, 2, 3 scale used for outcome. In the present work, where outcome is judged on what is in effect a 33-point scale (32 points + zero), it is more justified to use r, as long as the variable to be correlated with outcome is itself a genuine number rather than a rank order. This applies especially to the most important of the correlations, that between outcome and the above-mentioned T/P%, the *proportion* of transference/parent interpretations in the case notes; but to be absolutely certain I have calculated τ for this in addition. I have also used r for most of the reliabilities, where significance levels are less important, even where the scale used is coarse and is only a rank order.

The passage from *SBP* in which I explained the nature of τ is reproduced below:

Let us suppose that a series of individuals can be assigned a rank order (without ties) on each of two variables, A and B. It is now possible to select at random any pair of individuals and to record whether or not the member of the pair that is higher in the rank order for A is also the higher in the rank order for B. τ_a represents the proportion of the total possible combinations that lie in the same order for the two variables, minus the proportion that lie in the opposite order. Since, if N is the total number of individuals, the total possible number of pairs is $\frac{1}{2}N(N-1)$, τ_a is given by the formula:

$$\tau_a = \frac{\text{(no. in same order)} - \text{(no. in opposite order)}}{\frac{1}{2}N(N-1)}$$

represented by

$$\frac{S}{\frac{1}{2}N(N-1)}$$

τ_a has the convenient property, shared by certain other correlation coefficients, of varying between $+1$ for perfect positive correlation, through 0 for no correlation, to -1 for perfect negative correlation.

When there are ties, to any extent, in either or both rank orders, τ can still be used, though no score is obtained from pairs of individuals that tie on one or other of the rankings. In this case the correlation coefficient is represented by τ_b and is given by the formula:

$$\tau_b = \frac{S}{\frac{1}{2}\sqrt{(N^2 - \Sigma t_i^2)(N^2 - \Sigma u_i^2)}}$$

where t_i represents the total number of individuals tying at each rank for variable A, and u_i the corresponding value for variable B. (The above formula reduces to that for τ_a when there are no ties, since then all values of t_i and u_i are unity, and $\Sigma t_i^2 = \Sigma u_i^2 = N$.)

As mentioned above, where the extent or the distribution of ties is different in the two rank orders, however, τ_b has the disadvantage of often not being able to attain unity. The result may be that two different but fairly close values of τ_b may not be comparable, the larger not necessarily representing the higher correlation. In these cases only the value of p, the probability of attaining or exceeding this value of τ_b by chance alone, can be used for comparison. This has to be accepted.

From long experience, I also suspect that τ has another disadvantage, namely, that there are circumstances in which it is more sensitive than r to changes in single scores. The result may be that its significance level depends to a most unsatisfactory extent on the exact values of single judgments, especially when the samples are as small as they are in these two studies. Several examples of problems of this kind will be encountered, e.g., in the case of correlations involving focality (chap. 10) and "early transference + termination" (chap. 14). In such cases simple inspection, allied to common sense and clinical judgment, may be a better way of examining the evidence.

Despite all this, τ has definite advantages for the present study:

1. As indicated above, it does not depend on the assumption that there is an underlying continuously varying quantity on which the two rank orders are based (this advantage is not shared by the product–moment correlation coefficient, r).

2. It is applicable to any A X B contingency table, where A and B need not be equal and may have any value from 2 upward.

3. Provided that N is greater than 10, the probability of attaining or exceeding any given value of τ_a or τ_b by chance alone can be calculated with reasonable accuracy. (This advantage is not shared by the Spearman Rank Correlation Coefficient when there is a high proportion of ties in either of the two rank orders.)

Since there are always ties in at least one of each pair of variables studied in the present work, it is always τ_b that is used. This is represented simply by τ in the following pages.

A NOTE ON ONE-TAILED AND TWO-TAILED TESTS OF SIGNIFICANCE

Whenever a correlation coefficient is obtained, it is necessary to calculate the probability, on chance alone, that the value will equal or exceed the value found. However, correlations may be positive or negative. When the study consists of hypothesis-finding, as was that reported in *SBP*, one is looking for large correlations in either direction. In this case it is necessary to use the two-tailed test, which gives the probability that the numerical value of the correlation coefficient will equal or exceed the value found, regardless of sign.

When the study is a replication, as that reported here, or whenever the direction of the correlation has been firmly predicted beforehand, the possibility that the correlation will be of opposite sign to that predicted can (one hopes) be ignored, and the probability is calculated that the numerical value will equal or exceed the value found *in the direction predicted*. This is the one-tailed test. Probabilities in the one-tailed test are half those in the two-tailed test, and therefore in the former a given significance level is easier to achieve. Naturally, research workers tend to look for good reasons why they can use the one-tailed test; and there is a certain temptation, after a given correlation has been discovered, to say that one knew it would be in that direction all along.

I have been advised throughout by Dr. A. R. Jonckheere, whose constant help I once more gratefully acknowledge.

HYPOTHESES OF THE NECESSARY CONDITION

I need to emphasize the point made in chapter 7 that usually it is hypotheses of the necessary condition that are under examination; and that since there is no statistical method of examining these, once more some of the evidence is best examined by simple inspection.

We are now in a position to go on and investigate the relation between various factors on the one hand, and outcome on the other, in the second series of patients.

9

Selection Criteria at Initial Assessment

Written in Collaboration with P. Dreyfus

At the time when *SBP* was written, an examination of both the literature and of the workshop's original views showed that most postulated selection criteria could be derived from two main hypotheses. The first was the "static" (i.e., less dynamic) Hypothesis A: The prognosis is best in *mild illnesses* of *recent onset.* The second was the more dynamic Hypothesis B: The prognosis is best in patients who show evidence from the beginning of a willingness and an ability to work in interpretative therapy.

Hypothesis A was subdivided into five individual selection criteria, all of which can be judged essentially from the patient's history and present state:

1. Mild and circumscribed psychopathology.
2. Sound basic personality.
3. History of satisfactory personal relationships.
4. Recent onset.
5. Propitious moment.

Hypothesis B was subdivided into two criteria, both of which need to be judged mainly from the patient's intelaction with the clinical situation:

6. High motivation for insight.
7. Response to interpretation.

Of these seven criteria, only *motivation* appeared to show any positive correlation with favorable outcome. This correlation was probably shown by *"initial* motivation," here taken as an overall value during consultation and projection test; but the correlation was more striking if fluctuations in motivation during the next four sessions (i.e., during the patient's first six contacts) were also taken into account.

Of the other criteria, the relation between *severity of psychopathology* and outcome was complex, but an important conclusion from the evidence was that patients suitable for brief therapy could be much more severely ill than had originally been supposed. *Recent onset* seemed to bear no relation to outcome whatsoever. As discussed in chapter 7, these tentative conclusions were strengthened by later follow-up.

The remaining four criteria could not be properly examined, mainly because they had already been used in the original selection of these patients, and thus the scores were too heavily concentrated at the upper end of the scales. What evidence there was, however, suggested that within the range covered by the sample these criteria were of little prognostic value.

In addition to these, there were other criteria that emerged as the work proceeded, both from the workshop's later discussions, and from the systematic examination of the evidence reported in *SBP*. Of the former criteria a list had already been drawn up by Dr. T. F. Main from a study of the workshop discussions. Of the latter (discussed on pp. 276–8 of *SBP*) the two most important were both dynamic: (1) Early development of transference; and (2) the early crystallization of a focus.

All these criteria either needed cross-validating or systematic testing on a new sample.

METHODS USED IN THE PRESENT STUDY

In the work reported in *SBP*, ratings of selection criteria had to be made retrospectively and single-handed and were contaminated by prior knowledge of outcome, with all the scientific pitfalls that this entails.

In the present study we were fortunate to have the collaboration of two judges who were entirely uncontaminated: Dr. Peter Dreyfus, a Swiss psychiatrist, and Mr. Ray Shepherd, a third-year clinical psychologist, both now psychoanalysts and at that time in psychoanalytic training. Thus, all the scientific pitfalls could be entirely overcome, i.e., *uncontaminated* ratings could be made of *all* relevant criteria by *two judges independently.*

These judgments were made from the initial assessment material,

TABLE 9.   Selection Criteria for Which Statistical Analysis Was Not
Worthwhile

Static criteria	
Ability to cope with reality.	Good basic personality
Ability to cope with conflict and anxiety.	or "ego-strength."
History of relationships.	
Nature and strength of defenses.	
Real/fantastic quality of patient's world.	
Psychiatrist's and psychologist's reports make	
sense together.	
Stable life situation.	

Dynamic criteria
Early transference.
Interviewer expressed positive feelings for patient.

which consisted of reports on (1) the consultation and (2) the projection test, which was usually given next after the consultation.[1] The reports were written on special forms and included verbal judgments (but not scores), written at the time of initial assessment, on those selection criteria thought to be most relevant to any particular case.

The two judges rated nineteen selection criteria independently, using three-point to five-point scales.

Despite careful definition of each point on the scale, however, over half the criteria either failed to reach a satisfactory reliability ($p<.01$), or else the scores covered too narrow a range to make statistical treatment worthwhile. These criteria are shown in Table 9 and will not be considered further. (For a discussion of motivation, which also failed to reach the 1 percent level of significance, see below.)

The criteria accepted for statistical analysis were those for which the reliability reached $r=+0.45$. Unfortunately the most important criterion, motivation, was also the least reliable ($r=+0.48$; $\tau=+0.34$, $p=0.021$). However, a careful analysis of this is the light of Malan and Rayner's judgments, discussed later in this chapter, shows that a considerably higher reliability than this can be obtained and that it is Shepherd who is the "odd man out." Since the overall correlation with outcome is much the same whether the Dreyfus/Shepherd or Malan/Rayner judgments are used, motivation has been included in the table.

The mean values of the two independent scores for each of these criteria were correlated with outcome both for Patients A (brief psycho-

[1] Sometimes the projection test was given after several therapeutic sessions, which would mean that certain factors had been affected by early events of therapy. This complication cannot be avoided.

therapy, fewer than forty sessions, $N=22$) and Patients A+B ("psycho-therapy," all patients followed up, $N=30$). The scales were so arranged that a higher score for each criterion always indicated a more favorable predicted outcome, so that all correlations would be expected to be positive. The results are shown in Table 10.

It can be seen at once that none of the ten criteria gives a correlation significant at the .05 level. However, there are three results that can be regarded as positive: (1) and (2) The fact that *nature of psychopathology* and *duration of symptoms* do not appear to influence outcome is a confirmation of the same finding in the first series, and indicates the important clinical conclusion that *some severe and chronic conditions can respond to brief therapy.* (3) *Motivation,* predicted as the best criterion from the first series, was in fact the best criterion in the second series. However, before we become too excited about this, we need to remember that, since there were ten criteria being studied in the second series, the fulfillment of this prediction has a probability of one tenth of being due to chance alone.

STUDY OF MOTIVATION BY MALAN AND RAYNER

When variables such as these are being rated, there are two possible approaches. One is to define the variables very carefully and practice until a high degree of agreement is reached; the other is to leave each judge to make his own definition and devise his own method of rating, within a broad directive as to what needs to be measured, and to do no preliminary practice at all. If the second approach results in good agreement, it indicates that what is being measured is not something narrow and esoteric but of more general application, and is thus by far the more convincing.

In fact, it was the second approach that was used here, and to a very marked degree, since the two teams (DS, Dreyfus-Shepherd; and MR, Malan-Rayner) differed in almost every possible respect. First, each used somewhat different definitions of motivation: DS, being blind, could make ratings of motivation from the overall atmosphere of the interview, and thus always give a score; MR had to confine themselves to direct evidence concerned with a wish to come for treatment or to acquire insight, and when such evidence was lacking they gave no score. Second, they used different scales: DS a 4-point scale, (3, 2, 1, 0), MR a basic 5-point scale (5, 4, 3, 2, 1) which could be refined to include half-points when required. Finally they used different methods: DS gave only one overall score for the interview and another for the test

TABLE 10. Correlations between Scores for Selection Criteria (Mean Dreyfus/Shepherd) and Outcome

Selection criteria	τ Patients A (brief psychotherapy, N=22)	p (one-tailed) if <0.10	τ Patients A and B (psychotherapy, N=30)	p (one-tailed) if <.10
		Static criteria		
1. Nature of psychopathology	+0.019		+0.056	
2. Recent onset	+0.10		+0.054	
3. Propitious moment	−0.12		−0.14	
4. Good outside relationship	+0.035		−0.035	
5. Absence of deprivation[a]	−0.12		0	
6. Heterosexual experience	+0.125		+0.092	
		Dynamic criteria		
7. Motivation for insight	+0.235	0.081	+0.215	
8. Manner of cooperation	+0.16		+0.11	0.066
9. Contact or response to interpretation	+0.17		+0.064	
10. Ability to find a focus	+0.015		+0.023	

[a]This is the inverse of a negative criterion, "deprivation."

and took the mean of the two as the final value; MR gave a score at every point at which evidence was available, then made a consensus, and took as the final score the mean of the several consensus scores.

The main inter-rater reliabilities for these judgments are shown in Table 11.

This table makes clear that it was Shepherd's scores that failed to correlate highly with those of the other judges, and that the degree of agreement among the others was reasonably high.

When the Malan-Rayner consensus scores were correlated with outcome, the result was similar to that given by Dreyfus-Shepherd, namely $\tau = +0.25$, $p = 0.063$ for Patients A; and $\tau = +0.16$, $p = 0.12$ for Patients A+B.

The overall conclusion, therefore, is that "initial motivation" (i.e., that measured during consultation and projection test) correlates positively with outcome in these patients at about the 10 percent level of significance.

This very limited scientific result can be somewhat strengthened by the following considerations:

1. This is a replication. Motivation, clearly the best criterion in the *SBP* cases, is the best criterion in the second series.

2. There is another study that gives the same result, namely that described by Courtenay in his book *Sexual Discord in Marriage* (1968). This is a study of the treatment of sexual difficulties by a team of doctors connected with the Family Planning Association. They worked in a seminar led by Michael and Enid Balint, and the principles of both selection and therapy were similar to those used in the present study. The scoring of selection criteria was carried out retrospectively, single-handed, and with knowledge of outcome, but it was based on transcripts of what was said in the seminar before therapy started. The aim of therapy had also been carefully defined and recorded in advance, and Courtenay was therefore able to score outcome on a dichotomous scale as "success" or "failure" according to whether or not this stated aim was achieved. Of the twenty patients who could be scored, there were ten failures and ten successes.

Eight criteria were studied, all of which were included, some under different names, in the present work. When correlated with outcome, none of the four static criteria (level of problem, ego strength, personal relationships, recent onset) reached the 10 percent level of significance; of the four dynamic criteria (focus, motivation, contact, and insight), *focus* reached the 10 percent level and *motivation* the 5 percent level. Summation of the static criteria gave a less accurate prediction than the best of the individual static criteria, namely ego strength. Summation of

TABLE 11. Reliabilities (r) of Judgments of Motivation

	Dreyfus	Shepherd	Dreyfus/ Shepherd mean	Malan	Rayner	Malan/ Rayner consensus
	+0.71	+0.42	+0.61			
					+0.59	
		+0.48				

the dynamic criteria gave $\tau = +0.58$, for which $p = 0.0048$ (one-tailed test).

There are thus now three studies involving Balint's basic approach that give the following results: (1) Static criteria are of little value; (2) dynamic criteria are of more value than static criteria; and (3) of the dynamic criteria, the best is motivation.

If we add to these results the strong *clinical* conclusion of Sifneos (1965, 1968) based on well over five hundred cases, that motivation is the most important selection criterion, then we can perhaps say that this variable is at least worth further investigation.

It is clear in the present study, however, that judgments of initial motivation would have been of very little *practical* value in the actual selection of patients: Too many unsuccessful cases would have been selected and too many successful cases rejected. The question is now whether anything of practical value can be discovered.

10

Selection Criteria at the Initial Stages of Therapy

By D. H. Malan and P. Dreyfus

The search for selection criteria at initial assessment having yielded such modest results, it is natural to turn to the next period of the patient's contact with the clinic, namely, the first few therapeutic sessions. The hope that this might yield something of value is strengthened by the evidence from the *SBP* series, in which it seemed that fluctuations in motivation during the first few contacts might have a considerable bearing on outcome.

In order to study this question, Dreyfus made uncontaminated judgments of motivation during the interview, projection test, and first six therapeutic sessions (i.e., the first eight contacts with the clinic), using a 5, 4, 3, 2, 1 scale. He made his judgments session by session, scoring each before he read the next, and thus simulated judgments made by a member of the workshop as therapy developed. As a check, Malan—by now contaminated by knowledge of outcome but uncontaminated by Dreyfus—made similar judgments over the same period.

As with judgments of motivation made on the initial assessment material, there was no preliminary practice; and the difference in contamination led to a difference in the criteria on which the variable was judged: Dreyfus, being uncontaminated, was free to use his intuition, making use of the overall atmosphere of the sessions, particularly where direct evidence for motivation was absent. For a contaminated judge this was felt to be too dangerous, and Malan therefore gave scores only when there was definite evidence for motivation to *come for treatment* or to *achieve insight*. Where such evidence was lacking, he assumed for each patient that motivation remained the same as before until there was definite evidence that it had changed.

Reliability was satisfactory, the correlation coefficient (r) between the two judges for any particular contact lying between +0.64 and +0.79, with a mean of +0.71.

The correlation (τ) between motivation and final outcome was now studied contact by contact, for Dreyfus's and Malan's judgments separately, and for Patients A (fewer than forty sessions, N=22) and Patients A+B (all patients followed up, N=30). The results are plotted in Figures 1 and 2.

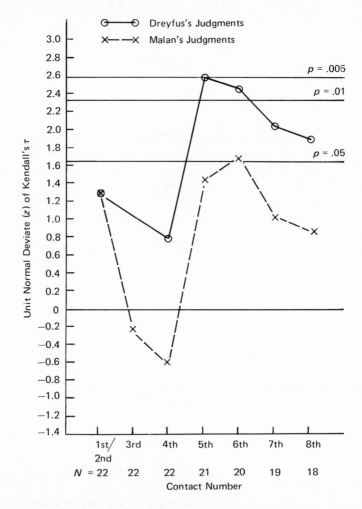

Figure 1. Correlations between ultimate outcome and motivation during the first eight contacts with the clinic (Patients A <40 sessions, N=22).

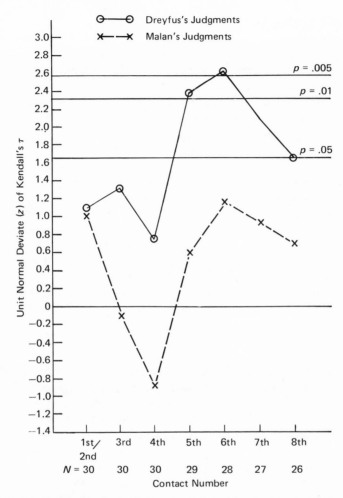

Figure 2. Correlations between ultimate outcome and motivation during the first eight contacts with the clinic (Patients A + B, N=30).

In these graphs z, the "unit normal deviate" of τ, which has to be calculated in order to derive a significance level for τ, is plotted rather than τ itself. The reason for this is arithmetical. The value of z increases as τ increases, but—unlike τ—shows a definite limiting value representing a given significance level even when there are "ties" in the scores, and when—since certain patients withdrew from treatment during the period studied—the total number of judgments correlated (N) varies from one correlation to another. These properties are not shared by τ. We are told that it is statistically improper to use z in this way, but we remain unrepentant. All the essential features of the graphs are reproduced whether τ or z is used, and this is also true if the patients who withdrew before the eighth contact are omitted, so that N remains the same throughout.

These two figures show the following:

1. The overall shape of the graphs given by the two judges is almost identical, showing a decrease in the correlations at contacts 3 and 4, and then a sudden increase at contact 5.

2. Dreyfus's correlations become positive and significant at the 1 percent level (one-tailed test) at contacts 5 and 6 and at the 5 percent level for contacts 7 and 8, for both Patients A and A+B.

3. Malan's graphs, on the other hand, are displaced downward to a considerable degree relative to those of Dreyfus, with the result that the correlations (a) actually become negative at contacts 3 and 4 for both sets of patients, and (b) show only one value significant at even the 5 percent level, namely for contact 6, Patients A.

Thus, the result so far is inconclusive. Further discussion will be postponed until later in this chapter.

FOCALITY

As was described in chapter 9, Dreyfus and Shepherd studied a variable derived from the initial assessment material called "ability to find a focus." Like motivation, it gave a positive correlation with outcome, but one that was far from significant. Dreyfus now defined a focus from the initial assessment material, and went on to score a variable called "focality" (using a 4, 3, 2, 1, 0 scale) during the first eight contacts with the clinic. Focality may be described essentially as the therapist's ability to concentrate on the focus, as originally defined, in his interpretations. In the scoring, evidence about the patient's response to focal interpretations was also taken into account.

Now Dreyfus's figures, when correlated with outcome, gave a pattern strikingly similar to that given by his figures for motivation, and at first we were inclined to accept his result without question. We very quickly saw that this was unacceptable, but by this time Malan had studied Dreyfus's scores and was thus doubly contaminated. There was no other uncontaminated judge available, and the only solution seemed to be for Malan to make the judgments himself, despite the scientific pitfalls involved.

At least we can claim that Malan was not unduly influenced by his high stake in confirming Dreyfus's striking result, since his scores did to those of Dreyfus what his scores for motivation had done, only more so, and went a long way toward spoiling the overall result completely—though not quite, as will be seen.

In fact, mathematically speaking, reliability (r), though smaller than for motivation, was reasonable, the values for each contact varying from +0.54 to +0.74, with a mean of +0.61. Nevertheless, there were some major discrepancies in the individual scores. The results of this will be very clear from Figures 3 and 4, in which the correlations between focality and outcome are plotted, contact by contact, for the two judges and the two groups of patients.

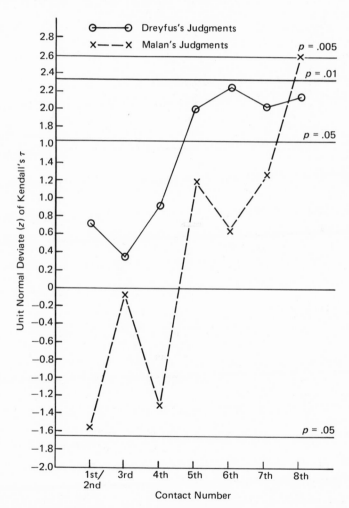

Figure 3. Correlations between ultimate outcome and focality during the first eight contacts with the clinic (Patients A, <40 sessions, $N=22$).

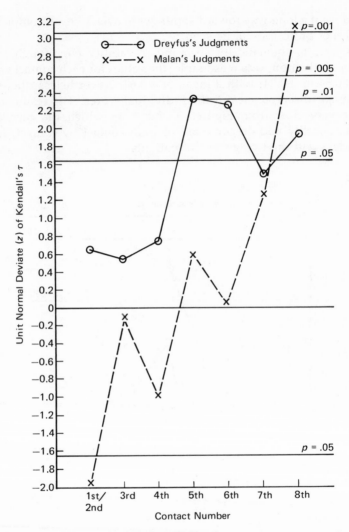

Figure 4. Correlations between ultimate outcome and focality during the first eight contacts with the clinic (Patients A+B, $N=30$).

It will be seen that the shapes of the two graphs bear little relation to one another, that Malan's correlations for contacts 1/2, 3, and 4 are all negative, and that the only significant positive correlations given by Malan are at contact 8.

Yet, the truth is that this unsatisfactory result was really demonstrating both the difficulty of making contaminated judgments and the dangers of taking raw correlations at their face value. There were in fact, hidden in these figures, some patterns of extraordinary interest.

Here we should say at once that having found these patterns, we immediately went on to the next essential step, namely, "back cross-validation", i.e., seeing if the same patterns were present in the first series. The answer was equivocal: The patterns were not identical and few of the distributions were significant. On the other hand, similar trends seemed to be present. In the end we can only say that the results in the second series are worth reporting because of their great interest and apparent clinical meaningfulness, but that cross-validation on a third series is necessary before any conclusions can be reached.

The discussion may be started as follows: It is commonly supposed that contaminated judges are likely to bias their scores in such a way as to make the result more satisfactory to themselves. However, comparison of the scores for outcome given by therapists and nontherapists shows that overcompensation might lead to the opposite effect. As far as focality was concerned, this was true of Malan's judgments on a single patient in particular, the Company Secretary (see Assessment and Therapy Form). Here the therapist had tried to combine two foci into one, against the strongly expressed skepticism of the rest of the workshop at the time. Dreyfus shared the workshop's skepticism even when asked to reconsider; while Malan was in a quandary, being contaminated by later knowledge indicating that the patient had been wrongly assessed and the focus was probably totally inappropriate. Yet, the therapist stuck to his focus within his lights, and Malan therefore gave high scores. If Malan had allowed himself to agree with Dreyfus, not two but five of his eight possible correlations in contacts 5 to 8 (three for Patients A and two for Patients A+B) would have been significant. (This is, of course, an illustration of the main disadvantage of using τ, that is, its extreme sensitiveness to changes in single scores.)

THE PRACTICAL VIEWPOINT

Correlations are of more value theoretically than practically, and if we are concerned with the practical value of these two variables, we need some method by which they can be used to divide patients into those accepted and those rejected.

Obviously this can be done in many ways. The particular method that we have explored is based on the following reasoning: Clinical judgment suggests that for a favorable result in brief therapy the patient needs to have a relatively high motivation, and the therapist needs to use a highly focal technique. We have therefore chosen to give a patient one "rejection score" if motivation or focality falls below the top two points on the scale (i.e., to 3 or below for motivation, and 2 or below for focality) at any given contact with the clinic. Since the two variables appear to be of value only at the four later contacts (5–8) it is these contacts that are considered. The total number of rejection scores is counted for each variable and each judge, and these are then combined in various ways. We regard a patient as a possible candidate for rejection—represented by R in Table 12—if the total of his rejection scores reaches three quarters of the maximum; i.e., three out of four for one judge on one variable, six out of eight for the combination of two judges on one variable or one judge on two variables, and twelve out of sixteen for the combination of both judges on both variables. The results are shown in Table 12.

Let us consider first only the nine short favorable and nine short unfavorable cases. The distributions of acceptance and rejection (or self-rejection) are shown in the 2 × 2 diagrams in Figure 5. Here patients supporting the hypothesis that motivation and focality are prognostic indicators lie in the top right and bottom left-hand corners of each diagram. (It must be emphasized that none of the diagrams have been corrected for Malan's high focality scores in the Company Secretary.)

It is obvious that the trends given by both judges and both variables are remarkably similar; that they are highly suggestive, even when they do not reach significance; and that the two judges together could have predicted outcome in these eighteen cases with considerable accuracy.

If we now refer again to Table 12, it will be clear that the pattern in the *false* cases resembles that in the short, unfavorable cases, thus once more confirming the anomalous position of these four cases. On the other hand, the pattern in the long cases is apparently confused. This latter observation will be considered below.

THE RELATION BETWEEN MOTIVATION AND FOCALITY

The question immediately arises, Are these two variables essentially the same?

Both Dreyfus and Malan are firmly of the opinion that the factors being judged are quite different. Focality is concerned mainly with the therapist, taking account of the theme of his interpretations; motivation is concerned entirely with the patient, taking account of his attitude and behavior.

Arrangement in the 2 X 2 Diagrams	Accept Unfav. / Reject Unfav.	Accept Fav. / Reject Fav.	Significance Level by Fisher Test (One-Tailed)
Dreyfus, Motivation	2 / 7	6 / 3	n.s. (but Highly Suggestive)
Dreyfus, Focality	1 / 8	7 / 2	$p < .01$
Malan, Motivation	1 / 8	6 / 3	$p < .05$
Malan, Focality	3 / 6	6 / 3	n.s. (but Suggestive)
Dreyfus, Motivation and Focality	2 / 7	8 / 1	$p < .01$
Malan, Motivation and Focality	3 / 6	6 / 3	n.s. (but Suggestive)
Dreyfus + Malan, Motivation	1 / 8	6 / 3	$p < .05$
Dreyfus + Malan, Focality	3 / 6	7 / 2	n.s. (but Highly Suggestive; $p < .05$ if Corrected for Company Secretary)
Dreyfus + Malan, Motivation + Focality	2 / 7	8 / 1	$p < .01$

Figure 5. Distribution of acceptance and rejection by two judges on motivation and focality in contacts 5–8 (short favorable and short unfavorable cases only, $N=18$).

The above view that the two variables are quite distinct is confirmed by statistical study. The values of z for the "intra-rater" correlations between the two variables are plotted against contact number in Figure 6. (Once more, z is used for convenience; if τ is used instead the overall shape of the graphs is identical.)

This shows some extremely interesting patterns:

1. Although most of the correlations are positive, those for contact 3, as judged by both Dreyfus and Malan, are negative, the former by a fairly substantial amount.

TABLE 12. Patients Rejected on Motivation and/or Focality in Contacts 5 to 8

	Dreyfus		Malan						
	Rejected on motivation	Rejected on focality	Rejected on motivation	Rejected on focality	Rejected on motivation + focality Dr.	Rejected on motivation + focality Ma.	Rejected on motivation Dr. + Ma.	Rejected on focality Dr. + Ma.	Rejected on motivation + focality Dr. + Ma.
Short favorable									
Stationery manufacturer									
Indian scientist						R			
Almoner			R						
Maintenance man						R			
Gibson girl	R		R	R			R		
Buyer				R					
Zoologist	R	R						R	
Pesticide chemist	R	R	R	R			R		
Mrs. Morley	R	R	R	R	R	R	R	R	R
Long									
Personnel manager		R		R				R	
Mrs. Craig			R			R			
Mrs. Clifford			R		R	R			
Car dealer	R		R		R		R		R

Playwright	R	R	R	R	R	R	R
Oil director	R	R				R	R
Contralto	R	R				R	R
Dress designer							
False							
Mrs. Lewis	R	R	R	R	R	R	R
Au pair girl	R	R					R
Gunner's wife	R	R	R	R	R^a	R^a	R^a
Representative	R^a	R^a	R^a	R^a	R^a	R^a	R^a
Short unfavorable							
Cellist	R	R	R	R	R	R	R
Receptionist	R	R	R	R	R	R	R
Bird lady	R^a	R^a	R^a	R^a	R^a	R^a	R^a
Military policeman	R^a	R^a	R^a	R^a	R^a	R^a	R^a
Sociologist	R	R	R	R	R	R	R
Company secretary	R	R	R	R	R	R	R
Mrs. Hopkins	R	R	R	R	R	R	R
Factory inspector							
Mr. Upton	R^a	R^a	R^a	R^a	R^a	R^a	R^a

[a] These patients withdrew before the eighth contact and are thus "self-rejected." (The Gunner's wife withdrew after the seventh contact and was thus also self-rejected, but her rejection scores are given for the three contacts 5 to 7.)

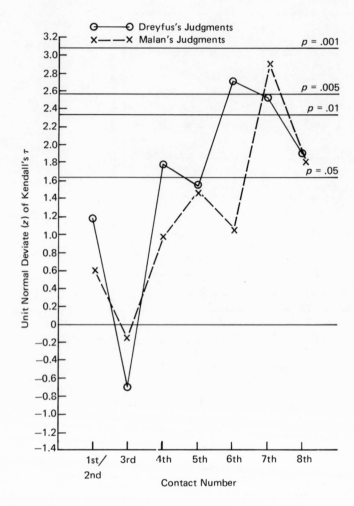

Figure 6. Correlation between motivation and focality during the first eight contacts with the clinic.

2. Of the six correlations for contacts 1/2, 3, and 4, only one is significant (Dreyfus, contact 4).

3. Of the eight correlations for contacts 5 to 8, five are significant, two at better than the .005 level.

The presence of negative correlations in itself strongly suggests a basic difference between the two variables; but the strongest argument is that if the two variables are entirely separate yet are concerned with different aspects of the *interaction* between patient and therapist, then the pattern of correlations actually found is completely intelligible. This argument will be developed in later discussion in the present chapter.

Motivation and Focality in the Four Categories of Patient. When we come to examine these two variables in the series as a whole, a result emerges that is of very great interest and possibly of considerable practical importance. This is best demonstrated in the following way:

1. The mean value of the variable at each contact is calculated, for each of the four categories of patient. Those patients who had withdrawn at the contact considered are omitted.

2. The four categories are arranged, at each contact, in a rank order of their means.

3. An overall rank order is calculated at each contact, for the four categories, from the sum of their rank orders.

The results are shown in Table 13.

From this the following will be noted:

1. The long cases (a) rank almost consistently the highest for motivation; but (b) rank third or fourth overall for focality.

2. The false cases (a) rank almost consistently the lowest for motivation; but (b) rank second overall for focality.

No inferences will be drawn for the false cases, whose number is far too small; but it is worth noting that focality is an exception to the rule that on dynamic factors the false cases tend to rank lowest.

For the other groups, however, the following can be said:

1. The short/favorable cases tend to show high motivation/high focality, and

2. The short/unfavorable cases tend to show low motivation/low focality;

3. On the other hand, the long cases tend to show *high motivation/ low focality*.

These observations immediately make complete clinical sense. If it is true that the success of brief therapy depends on the rapid working through of a particular focus, then:

1. Those cases will tend to be successful who present a focus early and have the motivation to work through it. This will tend to lead to short, successful therapy.

2. Low motivation/low focality will tend to lead to short, unsuccessful therapy, because the therapist's work will fail to increase motivation and the low-motivation patient will withdraw.

3. High motivation/low focality will lead to a long search for a

TABLE 13. Rank Order of the Means for Motivation and Focality for the Four Categories of Patient

Contact number	1/2		3		4		5		6		7		8	
Dreyfus or Malan	D	M	D	M	D	M	D	M	D	M	D	M	D	M
Motivation														
Short favorable	1	2	2	3	2	3	2	2	1	2	2	2	2	1
Long	2	1	1	1	1	1	1	1	2	1	1	1	1	2
False	4	4	4	4	4	4	3	4	4	4	4	4	3	4
Short/unfavorable	3	3	3	2	3	2	4	3	3	3	3	3	4	3
Focality														
Short favorable	1	3	1	2	1	3	2	1=	1	1	1	1	1	1
Long	3	4	4	4	4	4	3	3	2	3	2	2	3	2
False	2	2	3	1	2	1	1	1=	3	4	4	4	2	3
Short/unfavorable	4	1	2	3	3	2	4	4	4	2	3	3	4	4
Overall rank, motivation														
Short favorable	2	2												
Long	1	1												
False	4	4												
Short/unfavorable	3	3												
Overall rank, focality														
Short favorable	1	1												
Long	3	4												
False	2	2												
Short/unfavorable	4	3												
Rank, contacts 5–8, motivation														
Short favorable	2													
Long	1													
False	4													
Short/unfavorable	3													
Rank, contacts 5–8, focality														
Short favorable	1													
Long	2													
False	3													
Short/unfavorable	4													

focus; but, because the high-motivation patient will persist, a focus may eventually be found and therapy will tend to be longer but ultimately successful.

Statistical Relation Between High Motivation/Low Focality and Number of Sessions. Observation 3. above may be confirmed statistically as follows:

1. The measure of high motivation/low focality is chosen logically as the number of times, during contacts 1/2 to 8, that the patient receives *both* an "acceptance score" (i.e., >3) on motivation *and* a

"rejection score" (i.e., ≤2) on focality. Since contacts 1 and 2 are scored together, this gives a whole number score on a scale of 0 to 7 for each patient.

2. The four patients who withdrew before contact 8 (the Gunner's Wife, Representative, Military Policeman, and Mr. Upton), whose scores cannot reach the maximum, are omitted.

3. When the scores given by each judge are correlated with the number of sessions, the results are: Dreyfus: $\tau = +0.44$, $p = 0.0046$; Malan: $\tau = +0.42$, $p = 0.008$ ($N = 26$, one-tailed test).

It is clear that we may have found an early indication that a patient will give a favorable result in long therapy but not in brief therapy.

PRACTICAL CONSIDERATIONS

If we assume that these observations are valid, we may ask whether they can be used practically. The fact that the true prognostic indications do not appear before the fifth to eighth contacts is obviously a considerable disadvantage. Does this really mean that the only way of predicting outcome is to give the patient half a dozen sessions of trial therapy?

The answer is probably both yes and no. First, long subsequent experience has convinced me (DM) that often several exploratory sessions, some of them including projective testing, are needed before a firm opinion can be reached. On the other hand, it must also be remembered that the results presented here are statistical, and that clinical judgment may be far more perceptive than statistics, and may pick up the indications far earlier. For instance, the very high initial motivation shown by such patients as the Indian Scientist and Zoologist could have enabled a clinician to accept these patients unreservedly from the beginning; and equally the poor motivation and lack of focus in such patients as Mrs. Lewis, the Bird Lady, and the Receptionist were present from the beginning and could have served as signs that these patients should be rejected.

However, one of the most cogent arguments in favor of these observations comes from the following considerations: For a long time I had been puzzled by an apparent inconsistency in my own practice: Despite all I have written about the importance of motivation, I was not paying as much attention to this variable in my clinical practice as research results seemed to indicate that I should. At first I thought that this was just yet another example of the split between research and clinical practice. Then it began to dawn on me that the other variables I was taking into consideration, and feeding into the computer of clinical judgment, were (1) the ability to make a therapeutic plan, i.e., to find a focus; and (2) evidence that this plan was acceptable to the patient, as judged particularly by his response to focal interpretations. These are, of course, the main elements that we used in our judgments of focality. Thus, I finally realized that not only was there no split, but there was actually an unconscious convergence between research results and clinical practice. This is an important illustration of the fact that meaningful variables lead to clinically meaningful conclusions, and gives the final justification for presenting these results even though they have not been cross-validated.

THEORETICAL IMPLICATIONS

Motivation and focality are each an aspect of the dynamic interaction between patient and therapist, one from the patient's and the other from the therapist's point of view. As I wrote in a paper summarizing this work (Malan, 1973), all interpretative therapy is a mutual offering. The patient offers his unconscious communications; the therapist offers his interpretations, which are based on his current view of what the patient's communications mean, and, in planned therapy, on a chosen focus. Each is searching for a basic meaning or focus that is acceptable to both of them. Sometimes the patient's high motivation may carry therapy through to the successful discovery of a focus (see, e.g., the Zoologist[1]); sometimes the therapist's convinced adherence to a focus will enable the patient eventually to accept it (see, e.g., the Pesticide Chemist[1]). When therapy is going well, the therapist's focus is acceptable to the patient, and both focality and motivation will tend to increase; when therapy is going badly, the focus is not acceptable, the patient's motivation decreases and the therapist in turn may begin to lose his way, so that focality decreases also. In other words, each of these situations will tend to set up a self-perpetuating cycle; and thus there will develop a marked divergence between those therapies in which motivation and focality are both high, and those in which both are low. Apparently, in the present series, this divergence has begun to crystallize clearly by the fifth contact; and therapies by now will tend to be divided into those in which the mutual offering has been successful and those in which it has been unsuccessful, i.e., into therapies that are clearly "going well" and those that are clearly "going badly."

[1] Not included in the present book. See *The Frontier of Brief Psychotherapy* (Malan, 1976).

Now comes the crucial link in the argument: What bearing has "going well" or "going badly" on outcome? Since the efficacy of psychotherapy is currently much in doubt, the *a priori* answer can only be "not necessarily any." But, in these particular therapies we have just shown that *therapies that are "going well"* tend to be those in which *major improvements are found at follow-up many years later,* and those that are *"going badly"* tend to be those in which there are *no such improvements.* In other words, there is possible evidence for a causal relation between the improvement and the therapy that has preceded them. There are many gaps and uncertainties in the evidence, and no sweeping claims can be made, but—as will be discussed more fully in chapter 16—some new support is given to the possible validity of dynamic psychotherapy.

11

Content Analysis, Preliminary

Written in Collaboration with E. H. Rayner

When the work reported in *SBP* had reached the stage of demonstrating meaningful correlations between outcome and various clinically judged variables, I began to explore a more objective approach. It was a natural step, for instance, to try and substitute for a judgment of "transference orientation" some purely quantitative measure based on the number of transference interpretations recorded in the case notes. This may well be thought to be naïve, a point made by Bergin and Strupp (1972, p. 31; also Strupp and Bergin, 1969, p. 39):

> This approach assumes that the frequency of occurrence of a given communication content is highly correlated with intensity, hence an important index of its importance. The assumption is clearly open to challenge on various grounds.

On the other hand, Truax, in the same publication (p. 325), feels that the approach should at least be explored:

> We discussed the question of how to study the effects of interpretation in content analysis. Truax said that he thought initial inroads into this area could be made quite easily by simply counting the number of interpretations that people make, identifying high and low frequency interpreters, and then watching for short and long term effects.

Here it has to be remembered that these case notes were not transcripts of tape recordings, but were dictated from memory—with widely varying degrees of fullness—by each therapist after the session. Any measure based on these records therefore cannot claim necessarily to represent the emphasis on transference in the *therapy*, but only the emphasis laid by the therapist on transference *in his reporting* of the therapy; and it is hypotheses concerned with the correlation with outcome of the latter rather than the former variable that will be tested. It has to be assumed that there is a fairly high correlation between the two; but, even if there is not, the hypothesis is still clinically meaningful. In a sense, the latter kind of hypothesis may be the more meaningful; it introduces a selection mechanism, based on what the therapist thinks is important, into what otherwise might be a rather blind measure—i.e., one in which interpretations are counted as equal, whatever the therapist's view of their importance, or whatever their impact on the patient.

In choosing the exact means of calculating such a measure, one has to bear in mind that there were large differences both in *length* and in *fullness of recording* among these therapies; and therefore, for instance, that the total *number* of transference interpretations recorded—which is (obviously) highly correlated with both length of therapy and fullness of recording—would be a poor measure to use if one wanted to study transference orientation uncontaminated by other factors. In order to eliminate these two unwanted variables as far as possible, therefore, I divided the number of transference interpretations by the total number of interpretations of all kinds recorded for that particular therapy, obtaining a *ratio* expressed as a percentage. I called this the *transference ratio*. As I later came to realize, this device does not entirely eliminate either of the two other variables, since: (1) If a therapist regards, e.g., transference interpretations as more important than other kinds of interpretation, they will be the last kind of interpretations that he leaves out, and therefore probably the *less* full the recording, the *higher* the proportion of transference interpretations in the records; and (2) certain types of interpretation—probably including transference interpretations of any kind—are more likely to be made in the later stages of therapy, and thus their proportion will tend to increase the longer the therapy lasts. These factors have to be taken into account in interpreting the results.

The obvious clinical objection to this kind of study, clearly implied by Bergin and Strupp in the passage quoted above, may be put forward in a passage adapted from *SBP*. Since for all we know: (1) A single correct and well-timed interpretation may be all that is needed for a successful result (and I wrote this before the direct confirmation of this speculation from our study of one-session patients—see Malan *et al.*,

1975), and since (2) therapists may persist with incorrect or inappropriate interpretations for hours, and since (3) no account whatsoever would be taken of the response to the interpretation, any correlation between outcome and a purely quantitative measure of interpretation might be thought to be clinically meaningless.

Each of these objections can at least be partly answered, in the following way:

1. Although it is apparently true, as our one-session patients indicate, that in certain cases a single interpretation may have important therapeutic effects, it seems to be much commoner that such an interpretation needs to be given on a number of different occasions in different contexts, and thus to be to some extent "worked through," before therapeutic effects can be permanent.

2. As long as therapists can be regarded as both reasonably skilled and constantly guided by the patient's reactions, which was true of all the therapists in the present work, inappropriate interpretations will be quickly abandoned and thus will not figure largely in any quantitative study.

3. Since the patient's response is the only criterion by which a therapist can judge whether or not a given line of interpretation is appropriate, any interpretation that is persisted with is likely to be one that is producing a response, and hence *degree of response* and *quantity* should be positively correlated with one another. This was, in fact, entirely confirmed when the transference/parent link was studied later, since of the four patients in the first series with the highest proportion of transference/parent interpretations, three showed a dramatic response to interpretations of this kind, and the fourth clearly worked with them in a way that showed that they were meaningful to him.

The history of my use of this approach in the *first* series was as follows: I started by marking off every passage in the case notes in which what the therapist said was recorded, and made a judgment, first, of whether or not the passage counted as an *interpretation*. This was defined as a remark in which the therapist indicated, or at least implied, more about the patient's feelings than the latter had already said. Then, if the passage was an interpretation, I judged simply whether or not it included a reference to the transference. The number of transference interpretations was divided by the total number of interpretations in that therapy, giving a percentage that I called the "transference ratio." I used this as a measure of the *transference orientation* of each therapy. The main object of this study of transference was to try and decide between two entirely opposite views about the technique of brief therapy found in the literature: namely, (1) the conservative view that transference interpretations were harmful, and (2) the radical view that they were usually beneficial and indeed often necessary.

When the transference ratio obtained in this way was compared with the clinically judged transference orientation, the result was a high positive correlation, ($\tau = +0.60$, $p = 0.0013^1$). When correlated with outcome—with a single doubtful patient, the Draper's Assistant, omitted—the results were of the same order as those given by transference orientation judged clinically: $\tau = +0.32$, $p = 0.12$ (transference ratio): compared with $\tau = +0.37$, $p = 0.09$ (transference orientation). Since these two correlations were both strongly positive (though not significant by the two-tailed test), they fairly firmly contradicted the conservative view that transference interpretations were harmful.

As I went on studying these therapies I began to realize that a type of interpretation that seemed to be related even more strongly to favorable outcome was the transference/parent link. If the "importance" of this factor was judged on a four-point scale and correlated with outcome the result was $\tau = +0.46$, $p = 0.03$.

Since I had made judgments only of whether or not an interpretation referred to the transference, there was no quantitative information on the transference/parent link; and if I wanted this it meant going through these therapies all over again. After trying to avoid the issue for a long time, I finally did this, rescoring each of the fourteen hundred interpretations according to whether it referred to the patient's feelings about the therapist (i.e., transference), parent, or "nonparent," and whether it made the link between feelings about any one and any other of these three categories.

This considerable labor was fully justified by the results:

1. The transference/parent ratio, when reduced to a four-point scale and correlated with outcome, gave exactly the same figures as did the clinically judged four-point scale.

2. The transference/"nonparent" ratio gave a correlation with outcome close to zero.

3. The transference ratio from which transference/parent interpretations had been subtracted (T−T/P%) gave a weakly positive correlation, far from significant. In other words the transference/parent link seemed to be the most important of all types of interpretation, whether judged clinically or purely quantitatively; and moreover, the quantitative studies numbered 2. and 3. above suggested that this link was important *in itself* and not simply because it was a *link,* nor simply because it was an *aspect of transference.*

---

[1] The p value of .0026 that I gave in *SBP* was for the two-tailed test, which seems unnecessarily conservative of me.

In fact, after long study, I became convinced that not only were the quantitative studies more objective, and not only could they also provide evidence that was difficult to provide by clinical judgment alone, but also they were the most clinically meaningful of all ways of obtaining evidence about therapeutic factors from the material available.

In the first series, almost all this content analysis was carried out single-handed, the only exception being that Rayner scored six of the therapies in a similar way and reached reasonable agreement. I was quite convinced that after careful definition the scoring could be more or less objective. This was important in the design of the second study. Since we knew that the number of trustworthy judges available was limited, not all judgments could be made uncontaminated. Not only this, but the scoring of interpretations was an immense labor, and it could only be done by judges who were fully dedicated. We therefore reserved two of the uncontaminated judges (Bacal and Heath) for the most important variable, namely outcome; and two more (Dreyfus and Shepherd) for selection criteria; and Rayner and I undertook to carry out the content analysis, despite being already contaminated by knowledge of outcome, assuming with confidence that this contamination would negligibly affect the scoring.

The system that Rayner and I devised was basically similar to the one used in *SBP*, but somewhat more complex, and can be described as follows:

1. An *intervention* by the therapist was defined, as before, as any passage, however long, in which what the therapist said was reported, lying between two passages in which what the patient said was reported.

2. An *interpretation* was defined, also as before, as any intervention in which the therapist suggests or implies an emotional content in the patient over and above what the patient has already said.

3. Interventions were thus scored as either an interpretation or a noninterpretative intervention.

4. We then defined three classes of *persons*, toward whom the feelings of the patient were directed in the therapist's interpretation: (a) parent or sibling (P) (references to siblings did not occur very often); (b) therapist (T); and (c) "other" (O): This was defined (somewhat differently from in *SBP*) as *anyone who would appear on a census register* and thus did not include such categories as imaginary characters in dreams, a woman's unborn baby, or general categories of persons such as "men," or "people," or "bosses." If not directed toward any of these three categories or persons, the interpretation was said to be "undirected" (U). This included the patient's feelings directed toward himself.

5. We then defined interpretations that made a link between feelings about any pair of categories or all three. For this purpose the feelings had to be explicitly *compared*.

The following are edited examples of all these categories. Italics have been introduced to make the rationale of scoring clearer. In all these passages the narrator, who uses the first person, is the therapist.

Noninterpretative Interventions

Practical Issues. "I said that I would write to him about September if I did not hear from him."

Answers to Questions. "He then turned to me and said, 'You may think this a rude question, but are you a South African?' I said, no, I wasn't."

Exploratory Questions. "I asked him what he felt about his present girlfriend."

Mechanics of the Session. "I invited her to sit back in her chair instead of perching on the edge."

"Undirected" Interpretations (U)

"I tried to suggest that he was afraid that some fault might be found with his work."

"There has always been the lazy, passive part of him which the other part has pushed out of the picture."

"I was able to show her how she goes some way in a topic and then cuts it short—like her sexual freeze-up."

"I interpreted her feeling that she is a menace to people, her envy of grown-up people, and her feeling that she is not big enough."

Interpretations Scored as "Other" (O)

"He went on to describe to me how it really would be unrealistic and useless to be angry at home because his *wife's* capacity to give to him is limited. I put it to him that what we were really talking about was limitations existing within the *relationship between them*, and that his contribution to this was his fear of his aggressive demands."

"I tried to explore the relation with his *superior officer* and even went as far to suggest that he was angrier with him than he had really been able to admit."

Interpretations Scored as "Parent" or "Sibling" (P)

" . . . it was a really terrible thing to end up by seeing one's *father* crack up."

"I interpreted her own ambivalence to her *mother and father* and her wish to separate them."

"Interpretation: that there is so much rivalry in his cello playing that he cannot stand the triumph of being better than someone else. I likened it to him and his *brother*."

Interpretations Scored as Transference (T)

"He was really making a challenge to *me,* to prove myself."

"She agreed with my interpretation of her disappointment and anger at *me*."

Interpretations Directed to More Than One Category of Person, Without Any Link Being Made between the Two

"I interpreted her jealousy of her *mother's sister* and her wish to excite her *father* but not be excited by him." (O.P)

"We then talked a good deal about his *father's* cruelty, and I made a parallel of it to the patient's cruelty, in particular toward his *wife*." (P.O)

"She had not wanted to come and felt *I* was interfering between her and her *husband*." (T.O)

"I interpreted that she was anxious again in case *I* was cross with her for not being well; and that she wanted to please me, and perhaps felt afraid because of talking to me last week about sex, and her oblique criticism of her *mother*." (T.P)

Link between "Other" and Parent (O/P or P/O)

"I said that when he fought this man in the street it was *as if* he had been fighting his *father,* and since he had been beaten he had felt he had been punished for it and did not want to try again."

" . . . and he says, for the first time, that he thinks his *mother* kept him with her because she felt he would be a wage earner for her. I took up the resentment implicit in *this* (first interpretation, P), /which he confirms/ and suggested that *this* is *also* what he feels about his *wife,* that she married him to be the wage earner." (Second interpretation, P/O).

Link between "Other" and Transference (O/T or T/O)

"I immediately said that surely what was happening was that underneath he envied his *friend* his success, his wife, his nice home, etc., and therefore if he were given things by this man he felt that he was stealing them. I then said that *this reminded me* of something between him and *me*." (O/T).

"I interpret her sexual envy, and eroticized *transference* (first inter-

216

pretation, T). /This leads to anger at me, my methods—what's in it for her?/ I interpret *the same* in relation to her *husband* (second interpretation, T/O). This leads to an outburst against all men."

Link between Transference and Parent (T/P or P/T)

"Very likely what he would want to do would be to spoil the situation even more in order to spite *me, which was* the technique he had employed against his *parents.*" (T/P)

"I interpret his fear of his anger, that if he acknowledges it it may overwhelm him—this in relation to both *father* and *mother* who demanded he be grown up before he was really able, and *also* with *me* who he feels demands things from him that he cannot cope with." (P/T)

"I interpret her fear that *I* will not support her sufficiently—will let her down *as her father* did." (T/P)

"I point out her wish that *I* should behave toward her *as a good mother* who has all the right liberal ideas." (T/P)

"I linked this with her own birth and how she felt her disgrace and that her *mother* hated her for being born, *and* her fear at the beginning of the treatment that *I* hated her and felt she had been forced upon me." (P/T)

"She said that she was not aware of any strong feelings about me, e.g., to do with my lateness. I suggested to her that perhaps she felt with *me as* she did with her *father.*" (T/P)

Complex Interpretations Involving all Three Categories, Two or More of Which May Be Linked

"I said she really had her doubts about her *husband,* did she want him? She really wanted to go down and stay with her *father* and *mother,* but more than this, she wished to be able to rely on *me. . . .*" (O.P.T—not quite O.P/T)

"I interpret her fear that I won't approve [of her pregnancy], her need for my approval, and her sense that she is not being looked after *both* by her *husband and myself . . .* I interpret also her need to get *me* to fight the internal *mother* who doesn't allow her to have babies." (O/T.P)

"I later *linked* the relationship with *me* now as being that in which he gives all his feelings to his *father* and is angry with his *mother,* that is his *wife.*" (T/P. P/O)

"I related her sunbathing to her fears of expressing her sexual feeling toward her *boyfriend,* and suggested she instead brought them to me, *mother,* with whom she felt safe." (O.T/P)

"I said that in contrast to her unwillingness to submit to a man, it is remarkable how readily she submits to her mother. I added that it is as if the man's potency *(her father, her husband, me)* is set up against her mother, and the issue seems to rest on which of us is going to win." (P/O/T)

"I then said that I felt the basic situation in his life was one of disappointment. The original disappointment was with his *parents.* Then *I* faced him with *another* disappointment, which was that I gave him a relationship which did not last as long as he would have wished or give him as much as he would have wished; and now he was facing yet *another* disappointment with his girlfriend." (P/T/O)

"I interpreted here his marked dependence on his *father* in the past *and* on *me* at the present time. This dependence might explain why he so easily accepted a homosexual approach, especially if it came from a man who was his senior or superior: the *porter* or the *older boys* at school *and me.*" (P/T/O)

The following notes are worth making:

1. There are certain differences between the present scoring and that used in *SBP*. The most important of these is that whereas such categories as "men," "people," or an unborn baby were scored as the equivalent "O" in *SBP*, interpretations mentioning only these categories were scored as "undirected" in the present work. A second difference is that a previous therapist was scored as T in *SBP* and as O here. A third is that references to siblings were put in the same category as references to parents.

2. As always with judgments of this kind, we found that there were blurred edges. If we tried to make the judgments entirely objective, so that a particular category must actually be mentioned by name to be scored, then we found that we were involved in the obsessional's difficulty of making the letter more important than the spirit, and scoring in a way that ignored what both therapist and patient clearly understood. On the other hand, if we allowed implications to count, it was very difficult to know where to draw the line. Thus, when feelings in the patient's "marriage" are mentioned, it would seem reasonable to score this not as "undirected" (U) but as referring to the marriage partner (O); if so, what if feelings in "childhood" are mentioned— should this be scored as referring to parents (P)? Similarly links were often *implied,* e.g., by the use of similar words to describe feelings directed toward two categories of person, without the comparison being explicitly made. Differences in our approach to this kind of problem accounted for a number of discrepancies in scoring between the two judges.

An example of this last kind of discrepancy was as follows:

"She said that after their honeymoon her father seemed to be upset at the thought of her sleeping with another man. I tell her that she feels her father's interest to be indecent (P) and she agrees, and describes how she shudders if he kisses her—not quite nice. I then interpret in the transference that she feels me to be a dirty old man, and that this is a projection of her being a dirty young woman, with promiscuous ideas (T). She reddens, enjoys this, laughs flirtatiously, and says it's true and that she disgusts herself with promiscuous thoughts, which include me. *I interpret promiscuous feelings toward her father.*"

Here the transference/parent link is obviously openly implied by the use of the word "promiscuous," and clearly both patient and therapist knew this, but the comparison is not specifically made. In scoring, I laid more emphasis on the spirit of the interpretation and scored P/T, whereas Rayner stuck to the letter and scored simply P.

3. No account was taken of the *direction* in which the link was made; i.e., although we might score one interpretation as P/T (in which feelings about a parent were linked to transference) and another as T/P (in which transference was linked to parent), both counted as transference/parent interpretations in calculating the T/P ratio. (This also is different from the principle used in *SBP*, but we felt it was more meaningful clinically.)

Because we regarded this content analysis as the central part of the whole study, we carried it out with the greatest care possible in the circumstances. We first of all needed cases for practice. The obvious records to use were those of the first series, but here we were hampered because at that time the sessions had been reported verbally, so that only the therapist's copy of each session was available, and these had already been marked by me with the scoring that was used in *SBP*. Since our secretary's time was limited, we felt unable to get more than one case copied, and we started practice on this. We then went on to practice on seven of the second series, discussing our scoring after each case, until we had agreed as far as possible on the principles.

We had thus contaminated each other on these seven cases, but we dealt with this situation by rescoring them independently, and leaving this rescoring until we had completed the scoring of all the others.

We did our best to score in random order, both of therapists and outcome, although we realized too late that we had weighted the practice cases in favor of those with successful outcome. We scored the cases that had failed follow-up as well as those that had been followed up successfully, making a total of thirty-nine. There were nearly three thousand interpretations and the process took about six months.

Before studying the inter-rater reliability I carried out a study of my own intra-rater reliability, rescoring a total of 752 interpretations from twenty cases. Here I first studied the overall agreement; and, since I had dated the original scorings, I also plotted out the *percentage agreement* against *chronological order of scoring,* to see if there was any trend.

If the criteria of scoring had changed with time, one would expect that the percent agreement between scoring and rescoring would decrease as the time gap between the two scorings increased. In fact, the distribution was clearly random, the percent agreement, in chronological order of blocks of five therapies, being 85 percent, 79 percent, 84 percent, and 81 percent respectively.

The inter-rater reliability between Rayner and myself was arithmetically considerably smaller than my own intra-rater reliability. For the total of 2914 interpretations the overall agreement was 67.8 percent. This was made up of 68.2 percent for the contaminated practice cases referred to above and 67.7 percent for uncontaminated nonpractice cases. It is therefore clear that the effect of contamination was negligible.

The question is whether this degree of agreement is satisfactory or not. The answer can only come both from a comparison of the important *ratios,* e.g., the transference and transference/parent ratios; and, above all, of the correlations of these ratios with outcome, given by the two judges. Here it must be remembered that our method of calculating the percent agreement gives a highly conservative, minimum value, since many of the discrepancies are trivial and some do not even lead to differences in the ratios. In fact, all the work reported in the next sections makes clear that the agreement is entirely satisfactory.

12

Number of Sessions, Passage of Time, and the Validity of Psychotherapy

Before we consider the apparent influence on outcome of various factors in technique, we need to study the influence of certain nonspecific variables, the most important of which is *number of sessions*. Obviously, as the number of sessions increases, the total quantity of supposedly "specific" factors such as interpretations will increase, but so will the quantity of nonspecific factors such as support or warmth.

The correlations between outcome and number of sessions that are found for various combinations of categories of patient are shown in Table 14.

It is worth noting that: (1) all correlations are positive; (2) the correlation approaches significance for the twenty-two patients with fewer than forty sessions; (3) the correlation does reach significance for the twenty-eight patients with fewer than one hundred sessions; but (4) if the two really long (and relatively unsuccessful) therapies are included, the correlation is no longer significant.[1]

In other words, there is a definite tendency for the longer therapies, up to a point, to be the more successful.

[1] If the score for the Contralto is changed from 0.9375 (outcome at the time of follow-up) to an estimated value of 3.5 (outcome when her analysis was finally completed), then the correlation with *number of sessions* for the whole sample ($N=30$) becomes significant once more ($p=0.04$).

TABLE 14. Second Series: Correlations between Outcome and
Number of Sessions in Four Different Combinations of Categories
of Patient

Patients	N	τ	p (one-tailed)
Short favorable + short unfavorable (excluding "false")	18	+0.21	0.12
Fewer than 40 sessions (patients A)	22	+0.23	0.069
Fewer than 100 sessions	28	+0.25[a]	0.035[a]
All patients (patients A + B)	30	+0.12	0.19

[a] p <0.05.

THE CORRELATION BETWEEN OUTCOME AND PASSAGE OF TIME

Before the clinical meaning of the above result is discussed, it is necessary to consider the following question: Might it be possible that what is responsible for the improvements in these patients is not psychotherapy at all, but factors quite independent of therapy such as "life experience" or "maturation," a rough but simple measure of which will probably be found in *passage of time?*

In fact, *passage of time* gives much the same correlation with outcome in the whole sample as does *number of sessions,* namely, $\tau = +0.11$, $p = 0.2$ (one-tailed test). One might expect therefore that *passage of time* and *number of sessions* would be positively correlated, but this is not so: They are not merely strongly negatively correlated but actually significantly so ($\tau = -0.26$, $p = 0.05$, two-tailed test), a result that I can only suggest must be due to chance.

There is another extraordinary result given when *passage of time* is plotted against *outcome,* namely, an almost empty lower right-hand quadrant of the diagram, there being only one patient who scored more than 2.5 for outcome and for whom passage of time was less than six years (whereas the other three quadrants are well filled).

The significance of this observation will be considered below.

NUMBER OF SESSIONS AND PASSAGE OF TIME IN THE FIRST SERIES

If we now examine the first series we find that *number of sessions* and *passage of time* give identical, appreciable, but not significant

TABLE 15. First Series: Correlations Involving Number of Sessions and
Passage of Time ("Psychotherapy," $N=16$)

Variable 1	Variable 2	τ	p (one-tailed)
Number of sessions	Outcome	+0.23	0.13
Passage of time	Outcome	+0.23	0.13
Number of sessions	Passage of time	+0.067	0.5 approximately

TABLE 16. Correlation between Outcome and Passage of Time
(Consultation to Follow-up), Range 2–15 Years, in Four Series of Patients

Series	N	τ	p (one-tailed)
First brief therapy series	16	+0.23	0.13
Second brief therapy series	30	+0.11	0.20
One-session series	45	+0.05	0.5 approximately
Group series	40	+0.11	0.17

positive correlations with outcome; and this despite the fact that between the first and second follow-ups the tendency was toward deterioration. On the other hand, the negative correlation found in the second series between the two variables themselves is not reproduced, reinforcing the view that in the second series this correlation was due to chance. The figures are summarized in Table 15.

PASSAGE OF TIME AND OUTCOME IN OTHER SERIES

In fact, we also have available two more series in which the relation between outcome and *passage of time* can be studied: (1) forty-five one-session patients (range of passage of time two to ten years, median two years ten months—see Malan *et al.,* 1968 and 1975) and (2) a series of forty randomly selected patients given group treatment at the Tavistock Clinic (range seven to fifteen years, median nine years six months—see Malan *et al.,* 1976).[2]

For this correlation the one-session series gives $\tau=+0.05$ (obviously negligible) and the group series $\tau=+0.11$, $p=0.17$.

It is thus very interesting that the correlation between outcome and passage of time *is positive in all four series* (see Table 16).

It has to be remembered that nothing can be said about the influence of values of passage of time of less than two years, which are entirely excluded from these studies.

---

[2] Two patients who were not actually interviewed have been omitted. To include them makes no appreciable difference to the figures.

What tentative conclusions can be reached? In my view all the evidence suggests that there are two genuine and quite separate trends: Improvement tends to increase both with increasing *number of sessions* and, quite independently, with increasing *passage of time,* though rather weakly in both cases.

IS A CERTAIN MINIMUM NUMBER OF SESSIONS NECESSARY FOR A GOOD THERAPEUTIC RESULT?

In Fig. 7 outcome (for "psychotherapy" rather than brief psychotherapy) is plotted against *number of sessions* for the two series combined. As might be expected, with the larger sample of $N=46$, the positive correlation is now nearly significant ($\tau=+0.16$, $p=0.06$), and it is quite significant if the two longest therapies are omitted ($\tau=+0.22$, $p=0.02$, one-tailed test in each case). However, there is a much more interesting observation than this, namely, that the bottom right-hand corner of the diagram is empty, there being *no patient who had fewer than ten sessions and scored more than 2.5 for outcome.* In other words, the distribution supports the hypothesis *that a certain minimum number of sessions is a necessary condition to a really satisfactory outcome.*

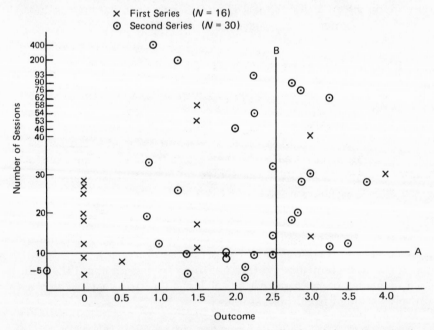

Figure 7. Outcome—number of sessions (nonparametrically plotted above 40 sessions).

Now, it will be remembered that the scatter diagram of *passage of time* against outcome showed a similar feature, apparently supporting the hypothesis that a passage of time of at least six years was a similar necessary condition. But further consideration suggests that this is absurd, since most of the changes had already occurred long before six years; and it looks as if this observation is in fact due to chance. A similar argument does not apply to *number of sessions*, since many changes occurred after therapy was over. Thus, the above hypothesis seems to stand.

However, we know from our study of "untreated" patients (Malan *et al.*, 1968 and 1975) that this hypothesis is not true in any absolute sense; there were at least three patients in our sample of forty-five who had *only one session* and would have scored more than 2.5 for outcome. Nevertheless, the evidence from the two brief therapy series suggests that the hypothesis is statistically true. This is one of many pieces of circumstantial evidence in the present work in favor of the validity of psychotherapy.

THE INFLUENCE OF NUMBER OF SESSIONS ON CORRELATIONS INVOLVING OUTCOME AND PROPORTIONS OF VARIOUS TYPES OF INTERPRETATION

This section has an important bearing on the interpretation of the results to be presented in the next chapter.

As described in chapter 11, the quantitative measure of such variables as *transference orientation* that we have used involves measuring the *proportion* rather than the absolute number of transference interpretations recorded in the case notes. This was an attempt to eliminate factors concerned with *fullness of recording* or *length of therapy*. But these proportions will increase with *length of therapy* for any types of interpretation that tend to occur more often in the later stages of therapy, which may well apply to transference interpretations of any kind. We have now detected a clear trend toward greater improvement in the longer therapies. We therefore need to be very careful in interpreting the results of the quantitative studies, as we may simply be measuring the positive correlation with *length of therapy* in another way.

However, we meet here a further complication. Although the twenty-two "brief" therapies were all fully recorded (with the exception of very few isolated sessions that the therapist did not have time to dictate), all of the eight longer therapies were only partially recorded. For the content analysis it is therefore the *number of sessions recorded* rather than the actual number of sessions that is the relevant variable. The figures are shown for these eight patients in Table 17.

Thus, in the six therapies with fewer than one hundred sessions one third to one half of therapy was recorded; in one of the two very long therapies this was less than one fifth, and in the other less than one twentieth.

Therefore, if we find significant correlations involving the proportion of a given kind of interpretation in the case records, the following two conditions apply:

1. If the sample consists of the fully recorded "brief" therapies (Patients A, $N=22$), we can legitimately speak of the correlations involving (roughly) the proportion of this kind of interpretation in the *therapy*.

2. If, however, the sample consists of all patients (Patients A+B, $N=30$), then we either (a) must assume that the observed proportion roughly holds for the rest of the (unrecorded) sessions, or else (b) we must say that for these eight patients we are concerned not so much with actual *therapeutic* factors, as with *prognostic* factors derived from the earlier stages of therapy. In other words, the type of hypothesis being tested is that a high proportion of a given kind of interpretation *in the earlier stages of therapy* will tend to lead to favorable outcome. As with motivation and focality, this type of hypothesis is still highly meaningful.

It is also a fortunate fact that the two very long therapies, in which these proportions of interpretations might be expected to deviate most from their true values over the whole of therapy, tend to be "exceptions" in the important correlations, so that if they were omitted the correlations would be increased.

In the previous part of this chapter we studied the correlation between *outcome* and *number of sessions*. In order to check on fallacies

TABLE 17. Number of Sessions Actually Recorded in the Longer Therapies

Patient	Actual number of sessions	Number of sessions recorded	Proportion recorded
Personnel manager	62	32	0.52
Mrs. Craig	76	37	0.49
Mrs. Clifford	90	40	0.44
Car dealer	54	18	0.33
Playwright	93	41	0.44
Oil director	46	26	0.57
Dress designer	>200	37	<0.18
Contralto	>400	18	<0.04

concerned with the higher proportion of types of interpretation in the later stages of therapy, we need to study the correlation between outcome and *number of sessions recorded*. For Patients A ($N=22$), as already described, the figures are identical. For the whole sample, Patients A+B ($N=30$), the correlation is: $\tau=+0.19$, $p=0.074$. This is greater than the correlation given by the actual number of sessions ($\tau=+0.12$, $p=0.12$). The reason is, of course, mainly that with *number of sessions recorded*, the two very long therapies are brought far more into line with the trend in all the others.

This result implies that we need to be doubly careful in interpreting significant correlations between outcome and proportions of various types of interpretation.

Finally, we need to study the correlation between outcome and *fullness of recording*. As was discussed in *SBP*, one might expect that those therapies in which the therapist showed his high enthusiasm by full recording might be the more successful. In fact, no such trend was observable in *SBP*, neither among *different therapists* nor among the *individual patients of a given therapist*. This observation is fully confirmed in the present series. The overall correlation between *outcome* and *number of interpretations recorded per session* is slightly negative, $\tau=-0.05$ for Patients A ($N=22$) and -0.04 for the whole sample ($N=30$). There is also no clear trend among the patients of an individual therapist.

These observations have two consequences:

1. There is little evidence from this particular sample to support the therapeutic effectiveness of the therapist's enthusiasm (but see the tendency toward success with the therapist's first case, chap. 14).

2. Fullness of recording does not seem likely to be a contaminating factor affecting the correlations studied in the next chapter.

13

The Transference/Parent Link

Written in Collaboration with E. H. Rayner

We now come to what I always regarded as the central issue, the relation to outcome of interpretation of the transference/parent link, around which the whole study was designed.

There were several reasons for this. First, the clinical evidence pointed unequivocally to the hypothesis that the transference/parent link was the most important single factor in the technique of this type of therapy. Second, the importance of the T/P link could be judged easily and convincingly in a purely quantitative and essentially objective way. And, third, this link is the specific therapeutic factor emphasized time and again in the theory of psychoanalytic technique. If its importance could be cross-validated, the consequences would extend far beyond parochial issues to do with a particular kind of brief psychotherapy. This is given special point by the accumulating *contrary* research evidence, emphasized by Strupp and Bergin and discussed in chapter 1, tending toward the conclusion that therapeutic effects are due to elements common to all the verbal psychotherapies, and that specific therapeutic factors simply do not exist.

It is perhaps worthwhile to summarize once more the evidence from the first series:

1. At the first follow-up (that is, the follow-up published in *SBP*) both the clinically judged "importance" and the quantitative measure of the T/P link gave a positive correlation with outcome significant by the two-tailed test ($\tau=+0.46$, $p=0.03$; and $\tau=+0.55$, $p=0.006$; respectively).

2. Later follow-up weakened the formal statistical evidence in the sense that the quantitative measure of the T/P link (which I regard as more accurate than clinical judgment) gave correlations—according to the sample considered—that were no longer significant by the two-tailed test, though they remained significant by the one-tailed test: For brief psychotherapy, i.e., patients who had forty sessions or fewer ($N = 14$), $\tau = +0.38$, $p = 0.094$ (two-tailed), $p = 0.047$ (one-tailed); for "psychotherapy" (including the two patients who had more than fifty sessions, $N = 16$), $\tau = +0.36$, $p = 0.085$ (two-tailed), $p = 0.042$ (one-tailed).

3. On the other hand, simple inspection if anything strengthened the evidence, since the three therapies in which major improvements stood the test of time ranked first, second, and third equal respectively for T/P ratio.

The quantitative study on the second series was designed, of course, before the second follow-up on the first series became available, and it was really built around an examination of the T/P link, the aim being to calculate the proportion of T/P interpretations together with a number of other proportions whose purpose was simply to act as controls. If T/P% correlated significantly with outcome, it would be important to be able to show that this property was not shared by *transference* interpretations, *parent* interpretations, or *linking* interpretations, in general; nor was it shared by other types of interpretations with which the T/P link had nothing in common.

For this purpose I calculated all the basic proportions: U%, O%, P%, T%, T_{term}% (interpretations to do with termination), O/P%, O/T%, and T/P% (see Table 19 for a key to the notation). It is important to remember that these proportions are not logically independent of one another, and therefore their sum adds up to considerably more than 100%. For instance, P% includes all interpretations containing a reference to parent and thus includes O/P and T/P interpretations. It is this lack of logical independence that accounts for the fact that the majority of the correlations are positive. In order to increase the independence, therefore, I also calculated various artificial proportions, which included especially "transference interpretations excluding those making the T/P link" (T–T/P%), "all linking interpretations excluding those making the T/P link" (Links–T/P%), and "transference interpretations excluding those making links of any kind" (non-linked T%).

For these calculations I had the assistance of a number of postgraduate students at University College, London, whose invaluable work I should here like to acknowledge. The work was greatly facilitated by the fact that Mr. Rawles and Mr. Owen had access to a computer.

RELIABILITY

The inter-rater reliability (r) was calculated for the fifteen ratios on the thirty patients. These ranged from +0.83 to +0.97, with a mean of +0.91. This, however, is not the best way of demonstrating reliability; the values of r *should* be high for such relatively objective judgments, and indeed there would be something seriously wrong if they were not. The true test of reliability comes from a comparison of the correlations with outcome given by the two raters. All should be of the same order of magnitude, and where that given by one judge is significant, that given by the other should be also.

The values of T/P% given by the two judges are shown in Table 18. The reliability is +0.91.

CORRELATIONS WITH OUTCOME

Each of the fifteen ratios was correlated with outcome for each rater for both "psychotherapy" (Patients A+B, $N=30$) and brief psychotherapy (Patients A, $N=22$). This was carried out by Mr. Owen on a computer, using both r and τ. The result was eight sets of fifteen correlations, resulting from the fact that there were two judges, two sets of patients, and two correlation coefficients.

Strictly speaking, the use of r is not quite justified, since the basic scores for outcome were given by each rater on a scale whose relation to a strictly numerical scale is questionable. Nevertheless r has definite advantages over τ in that it can always attain unity, and therefore a greater value of r does always represent a greater correlation. Neither of these statements is true of τ. Moreover, as mentioned before, τ is more sensitive to large "exceptions" in individuals, which sometimes obscure a clear trend shown by the others. The result is that a *rank order* of correlations has far more meaning for r than it has for τ. On the other hand, *significance values* have more meaning for τ than for r. The figures are shown in Tables 20 to 23. The key to the notation used is given in Table 19.

From these tables three observations will stand out immediately:

1. T/P% heads the rank order by a substantial margin for all eight combinations.

2. The correlations given by T/P% are significant for six of the combinations and approach significance for the other two (both of the latter being for Patients A as judged by EHR).

TABLE 18.   Values of T/P%, to the Nearest 1%, Given by the Two Judges

Patient	Outcome	T/P% (DHM)	T/P% (EHR)
Stationery manufacturer	3.75	3%	3%
Indian scientist	3.5	0%	0%
Almoner	3.25	16%	15%
Maintenance man	3.0	9%	7%
Gibson girl	2.875	15%	14%
Buyer	2.75	4%	4%
Zoologist	2.5	8%	6%
Pesticide chemist	2.5	12%	12%
Mrs. Morley	2.25	0%	0%
Personnel manager	3.25	10%	13%
Mrs. Craig	2.875	9%	9%
Mrs. Clifford	2.75	18%	19%
Car dealer	2.25	8%	6%
Playwright	2.25	5%	6%
Oil director	2.0	7%	7%
Dress designer	1.25	9%	8%
Contralto	0.9375	5%	2%
Mrs. Lewis	2.833	4%[a]	0%[a]
Au pair girl	2.5	2%	0%
Gunner's wife	2.125	10%	10%
Representative	2.125	0%	0%
Cellist	1.875	10%	8%
Receptionist	1.875	9%[a]	0%[a]
Bird lady	1.375	5%	5%
Military policeman	1.375	0%	0%
Sociologist	1.25	4%	3%
Company secretary	1.0	4%	3%
Mrs. Hopkins	0.875	0%	0%
Factory inspector	0.833	1%	2%
Mr. Upton	⁾−0.625	0%	0%
		Reliability: $r = +0.91$	

[a]Major discrepancy between the two judges.

3. T/P is the *only* type of interpretation that gives significant positive correlations.

It needs to be remembered once more that many of these ratios are not logically independent of one another, e.g., P% and T% and Links% include all T/P interpretations. Inspection of the tables will then show another important observation: When T/P interpretations are diluted by (1) other interpretations referring to parents, as in P%, (2) other interpretations referring to transference, as in T%, and (3) other interpretations making links, as in Links%, the correlations—though positive—

TABLE 19. Key to Notation Used in Tables 20 to 23

U	Undirected interpretations, i.e., interpretations not referring to any specific person.
O	Interpretations referring to "other", i.e., anyone excluding parents, siblings, or the transference.
P	Interpretations referring to parent or sibling.
T	Transference interpretations.
T_{term}	Interpretations concerning grief or anger about termination.
O/P	Interpretations linking "other" with parent or sibling.
O/T	Interpretations linking "other" with transference.
T/P	Interpretations linking transference with parent or sibling.
Links	Any interpretations making the links O/P, O/T, or T/P.
P–T/P	Parent or sibling interpretations excluding those making the transference/parent link.
T–T/P	Transference interpretations excluding those making the transference/parent link.
Links–T/P	Linking interpretations excluding those making the transference/parent link.
Nonlinked O	Interpretations referring to "other" but not making the link with either of the two other categories of person.
Nonlinked P	Interpretations referring to parent or sibling but not making the link with either of the two other categories of person.
Nonlinked T	Transference interpretations not making the link with either of the two other categories of person.

TABLE 20. Correlations (r) between Outcome and Proportions of Various Kinds of Interpretation (Patients A, $N=22$)

DHM			EHR		
T/P%	+.404[a]	$p=.03$[a]	T/P%	+.348	$p=.059$
P%	+.331	$p=.07$	Nonlinked T%	+.241	$p=.14$
T_{term}%	+.219	$p=.16$	P%	+.229	$p=.15$
P–T/P%	+.217		T%	+.218	
T%	+.201		T–T/P%	+.138	
Links%	+.193		Nonlinked P%	+.126	
Nonlinked P%	+.191		Links%	+.101	
O/P%	+.156		P–T/P%	+.097	
Nonlinked T%	+.147		T_{term}%	+.097	
T–T/P%	+.089		O/P%	+.093	
O%	+.019		O/T%	−.044	
Nonlinked O%	+.010		O%	−.106	
Links–T/P%	−.031		U%	−.154	$p=.25$
O/T%	−.062		Links–T/P%	−.156	
U%	−.333	$p=.06$	Nonlinked O%	−.309	

[a] $p<.05$ (one-tailed test).
Reliability of correlations: $r=+.79$.

TABLE 21. Correlations (τ) between Outcome and Proportions of Various Kinds of Interpretation (Patients A, $N=22$)

DHM			EHR		
T/P%	+.313[a]	$p=.025$[a]	T/P%	+.254	$p=.059$
P%	+.213	$p=.087$	Nonlinked T%	+.177	$p=.13$
T_{term}%	+.191	$p=.125$	P%	+.168	$p=.14$
O/P%	+.161		Links%	+.149	
P–T/P%	+.159		O/P%	+.139	
T%	+.138		T%	+.138	
Links%	+.130		O/T%	+.121	
Nonlinked P%	+.124		Nonlinked P%	+.107	
Nonlinked T%	+.088		T–T/P%	+.098	
Links–T/P%	+.086		T_{term}%	+.096	
T–T/P%	+.071		P–T/P%	+.079	
O/T%	+.032		Links–T/P%	−.018	
O%	−.018		U%	−.098	
Nonlinked O%	−.080		Nonlinked O%	−.159	
U%	−.284[a]	$p=.037$[a]	O%	−.167	

[a]$p < .05$ (one-tailed test).
Reliability of correlations: $r = +.78$.

TABLE 22. Correlations (r) between Outcome and Proportions of Various Kinds of Interpretation (Patients A + B, $N=30$)

DHM			EHR		
T/P%	+.405[a]	$p=.013$[a]	T/P%	+.403[a]	$p=.014$[a]
P%	+.249	$p=.09$	P%	+.240	$p=.10$
T%	+.232	$p=.11$	T%	+.230	$p=.11$
Links%	+.229		Nonlinked T%	+.198	
T_{term}%	+.216		Links%	+.190	
Nonlinked T%	+.149		T_{term}%	+.178	
O/P%	+.144		T–T/P%	+.128	
T–T/P%	+.134		O/P%	+.128	
P–T/P%	+.117		Nonlinked P%	+.099	
Nonlinked P%	+.086		P–T/P%	+.073	
O%	+.050		O/T%	+.023	
Links–T/P%	+.039		O%	−.030	
O/T%	+.029		Nonlinked O%	−.050	
Nonlinked O%	+.020		Links–T/P%	−.081	
U%	−.303	$p=.052$	U%	−.184	$p=.17$

[a]$p < .05$ (one-tailed test).
Reliability of correlations: $r = +.93$.

TABLE 23. Correlations (τ) between Outcome and Proportions of Various
Kinds of Interpretation (Patients A + B, $N=30$)

DHM			EHR		
T/P%	$+.290^a$	$p=.015^a$	T/P%	$+.293^a$	$p=.015^a$
T%	$+.168$	$p=.10$	P%	$+.210$	$p=.056$
T_{term}%	$+.154$	$p=.13$	Links%	$+.183$	$p=.084$
Links–T/P%	$+.150$		T%	$+.176$	
Links%	$+.149$		O/T%	$+.167$	
O/P%	$+.138$		O/P%	$+.154$	
P%	$+.123$		T_{term}%	$+.142$	
O/T%	$+.112$		Nonlinked T%	$+.108$	
P–T/P%	$+.078$		Nonlinked P%	$+.106$	
T–T/P%	$+.078$		P–T/P%	$+.071$	
Nonlinked T%	$+.059$		T–T/P%	$+.062$	
Nonlinked P%	$+.047$		Links–T/P%	$+.014$	
O%	$+.021$		Nonlinked O%	$-.054$	
Nonlinked O%	$-.005^a$		O%	$-.057$	
U%	$-.205^a$	$p=.037^a$	U%	$-.132$	$p=.27$

$^a p<.05$ (one-tailed test).
Reliability of correlations: $r=+.86$.

become much smaller and no longer significant. If T/P interpretations
are *excluded* from these ratios, and artifical ratios are calculated (P-T/P%,
T-T/P%, and Links-T/P%), representing "all interpretations referring to
parents excluding those making the T/P link," etc., then in general the
correlations become even smaller.

Clinically speaking, these observations mean that transference/
parent interpretations apparently have an importance of their own, and
do not simply have an importance by virtue of the fact that they refer to
parents or to *transference,* or that they *make links.*

Examination of the actual scatter diagrams given by T/P% against
outcome reveals further features of considerable interest. T/P% (DHM)
against outcome for Patients A+B, which gives the highest correlation,
is shown in Figure 8 and T/P% (EHR) against outcome for Patients A,
which gives the lowest correlation, is shown in Figure 9. It will be seen
that in each diagram nearly half the patients lie close to a straight line
AA, along which outcome and T/P% are roughly proportional to one
another; whereas there is another group of patients lying along the
whole length of the line BB, along which T/P% is zero. This suggests the
following: that (1) there is a certain class of patient with whom greater
emphasis on T/P interpretations is associated with greater improvement; but (2) there is also a certain class of patient with whom improvement occurs when this type of interpretation is absent.

Even if Fig. 9 were the only figure that we had, therefore, it would suggest a clinical importance to this type of interpretation, despite the fact that the correlation does not reach significance.

There is also another feature of great interest. In the two figures the four "false" cases have been marked with their pseudonyms. It will be seen that three of them (the Representative, Au Pair Girl, and Mrs. Lewis) lie well below the line AA, which means that they come into the category of good outcome with an unexpectedly small proportion of T/P interpretations. This is what would be expected if T/P interpretations were usually the main therapeutic factor but these patients were actually cases of spontaneous remission. Moreover, in the fourth case, the Gunner's Wife, there were only two T/P interpretations recorded, and the *proportion* is high simply because this was a short therapy of only six sessions. In fact, if these four cases are removed from Figure 9, EHR's correlation becomes unequivocally significant ($\tau = +0.37$, $p = 0.02$). Thus, once more the anomalous position of these four cases is demonstrated.

"UNDIRECTED" INTERPRETATIONS

There is a further observation that also is important, namely, that the proportion of "undirected" interpretations (U%), i.e., interpretations that do not refer to feelings about any actual person, correlates

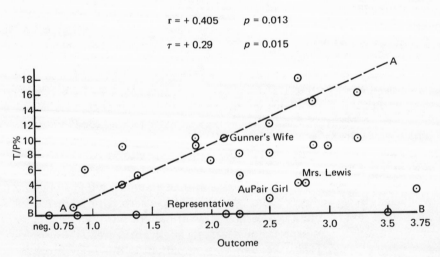

Figure 8. T/P% (DHM)—outcome Patients A+B, $N=30$.

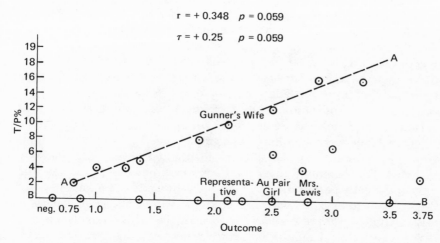

Figure 9. T/P% (EHR)—outcome Patients A, N=22.

negatively with outcome for all eight combinations and that the values of r as judged by DHM (not those by EHR) *approach* significance, while those of τ *achieve* significance.

This observation is given more weight by "back cross-validation" on the first series. Here, though neither value is significant, the correlations given by the brief therapy and the psychotherapy patients are both negative, $\tau = -0.30$ ($p = 0.09$, one-tailed) and $\tau = -0.12$ respectively.

The corollary is, of course, that *directed* interpretations, i.e., those that do refer to actual people, give strong *positive* correlations with outcome. This obviously fits in with clinical common sense: Since outcome is largely judged on the basis of changes in human relations, it is not surprising that those therapies concerned more with interpretations about human relations should be the more successful. Here is yet another piece of circumstantial evidence supporting the validity of psychotherapy.

DISCUSSION

Before drawing any final conclusions, however, we need to examine a possible fallacy. As has already been shown, *number of sessions* correlates positively with outcome both for Patients A and A + B, though not significantly so in either case (for Patients A, $\tau = +0.23$,

$p=0.069$; for Patients A+B, $\tau=+0.12$, $p=0.12$). Now the proportion of any interpretation that tends to be made more frequently after the initial stages of therapy will tend to increase, up to a point, the longer therapy lasts. If *length of therapy* itself correlates positively with outcome, then the proportion of such a type of interpretation will also tend to do so. Therefore, the fallacy may be that T/P% is correlating significantly with outcome not because of any direct causal relation, but because it tends to increase as the length of therapy increases.

The danger of overlooking this is underlined by a further consideration. For Patients A, as already mentioned, every session was recorded. For Patients B (over forty sessions), however, this was true only of the early part of therapy. The relevant variable for Patients A + B that needs to be correlated with outcome is thus not *actual number of sessions* but *number of sessions recorded*. In fact this variable gives a higher, and almost significant, correlation with outcome ($\tau=+0.19$, $p=0.07$). The main reason for this is that the two very long and relatively unsuccessful therapies are by this means greatly reduced in number of sessions, and thus make a much smaller negative contribution to the correlation.

Now a study of the distribution of T/P interpretations over all these therapies reveals that in fact their relative frequency does increase, up to a point, as therapy progresses. Table 24 shows that the proportion in the first five sessions is relatively low (4.35% of all interpretations recorded for the thirty patients), and that it progressively increases in each block of five sessions, up to 9.27% in sessions 15–20, only beginning to fall thereafter. The cumulative total shows a similar increase.

As would be expected from these figures, the correlation between

TABLE 24.   Distribution of T/P Interpretations (DHM) Averaged over All 30 Therapies, in Blocks of 5 Sessions

Session numbers	Number of interpretations recorded	% T/P interpretations	Cumulative % T/P interpretations
1–5	689	4.35%	4.35%
6–10	526	7.61%	5.76%
11–15	365	7.95%	6.27%
16–20	259	9.27%	6.88%
21–25	170	5.29%	6.57%
26–30	119	5.05%	6.49%
31–35	62	8.07%	6.53%
36–40	29	0.00%	6.44%

TABLE 25.   Correlations between Proportions of Various
Types of Interpretation (DHM) and Number of Sessions
Recorded

Variable (as judged by DHM unless otherwise stated)	τ	p (one-tailed)
$T_{term}\%$	+0.61	0.0000071
O/T%	+0.52	0.000067
T–T/P%	+0.38	0.0021
T/P% (EHR)	+0.33	0.0073
Nonlinked T%	+0.28	0.016
T/P% (DHM)	+0.26	0.026
O/P%	+0.21	0.058
O%	+0.21	0.059
Nonlinked O%	+0.045	0.37
P⊥T/P%	−0.14	
Nonlinked P%	−0.19	

T/P% and *number of sessions recorded* is positive and significant ($\tau = +0.26$, $p = 0.026$ for DHM; $\tau = +0.33$, $p = 0.007$ for EHR).

In view of this result, I asked Mr. Rawles to calculate the corresponding correlations with *number of sessions recorded* given by some of the other ratios as judged by DHM. These are ranked and shown in Table 25.

Leaving aside for the time being some of the astonishingly high correlations obtained, one can see from this table that T/P% is by no means the variable showing the highest correlation with *number of sessions recorded*. The high correlation given by *interpretations about termination* ($T_{term}\%$) would of course be expected; but apart from this, it is clear that *all* transference interpretations tend to be given more frequently the longer therapy lasts; but, as already shown, all transference interpretations do not correlate significantly with favorable outcome. Therefore, the figures imply that there is some property of T/P interpretations leading to a high correlation with favorable outcome quite apart from their increasing frequency as therapy progresses.

This inference is strengthened when some of the corresponding figures are examined for the first series of patients. Here, if "psychotherapy" is considered ($N = 16$) the correlation between *outcome* and *number of sessions recorded* is very slightly negative ($\tau = -0.05$). The fact that T/P% shows a small positive correlation with *number of sessions recorded* ($\tau = +0.14$, $p = 0.25$) is therefore neither here nor there. (For the correlations with *actual number of sessions*, *outcome* gives $\tau = +0.23$,

$p = 0.13$—i.e., positive but far from significant; while T/P% gives $\tau = +0.32$, $p = 0.052$—i.e., almost significant, but in view of the nonsignificant correlation between actual number of sessions and outcome, this also is neither here nor there. Exactly similar results are given for brief psychotherapy ($N = 14$).) To sum up, in the first series, the fallacy to do with increasing frequency as therapy progresses simply does not apply.

SIGNIFICANCE OF THIS OBSERVATION

My own view is that this result is of incalculable importance. It is worthwhile recapitulating the steps by which it was reached. First, in *SBP*, the quantitative *emphasis laid by the therapist on T/P interpretations* was measured by myself single-handed but in a relatively objective way, and correlated with outcome previously judged single-handed. If further follow-up was taken into account, the correlation obtained was significant by the one-tailed test; while simple inspection indicated a far more striking relationship.

The obvious scientific pitfalls in this were now eliminated one by one. First, for outcome, it was shown that two teams of two judges working independently, one of which was entirely blind, could achieve a reliability of over +0.8. Second, for the proportion of T/P interpretations, it was shown that two independent judges could achieve a reliability of over +0.9. Third, the correlation with outcome was repeated on a second sample. Not only was the result significant for three of the four possible combinations of judge and sample of patient; but, in all four combinations, this proportion headed by a substantial margin the rank order given by fifteen different variables.

There are three remaining possible objections to accepting this result as a fairly securely based scientific conclusion. The first is that in the second study the judges of T/P interpretations had both taken part in scoring outcome. Because of the relative objectivity of these judgments, I do not regard this objection as of any account. The second is that since for the longer therapies later sessions were not recorded, in them we are concerned with direct evidence about T/P interpretations not as *therapeutic* but as *prognostic* factors. Here it must be said (1) that this is still a highly meaningful hypothesis; (2) that almost certainly the high proportion of T/P interpretations was continued in later therapy so that in fact we *are* concerned with therapeutic factors; and (3) that we are definitely concerned with therapeutic factors in the short therapies where all sessions were recorded and T/P interpretations still headed the rank order.

The third objection is that in order to obtain this agreement between the two studies, I had to change the method of scoring. Instead of counting longer therapies as failures of brief psychotherapy, scoring zero, I had either to omit them or to take the score for the final improvements, whatever the length of therapy.

This must be admitted, and it seems to me to be the only ground on which the present study could be refused the status of a cross-validation. But even here the result makes clinical sense if it is simply concluded that many of the principles of brief psychotherapy are essentially the same as those of all psychotherapy, and, as far as T/P interpretations are concerned, are the same as those of analysis itself.

It has been accepted for several decades that the most important single therapeutic factor in psychoanalysis is the working through of the transference relationship and the link between this relationship and childhood feelings. It must be realized that practically all the T/P interpretations in the therapies considered here did—at least by implication—refer to the past, many of them to early childhood. Thus, the emphasis on T/P interpretations means, essentially, emphasis on linking the transference relation with childhood. It is now worth requoting two passages given in *SBP* about the importance of this link. The first is concerned with the technique of psychoanalysis, and comes from Edward Glover's book on the subject (Glover, 1955, pp. 132–3):

> . . . we are never finished with a transference interpretation until it is finally brought home to roost. To establish the existence of a transference-fantasy is only half our work; it must be detached once more and brought into direct association with infantile life.

The second is from Alexander, on the technique of psychotherapy (1957, p. 68):

> Interpretations which connect the *actual life situation* with *past experience* and with the *transference situation*—since the latter is always the axis around which such connections can best be made—are called *total interpretations*. The more that interpretations approximate this principle of totality the more they fulfil their double purpose; they accelerate the assimilation of new material by the ego and mobilize further unconscious material.

The above passage describes in different language what Karl Menninger (1958) has called the triangle of insight, which he also emphasizes as an important principle of psychoanalysis and psychotherapy. In our notation, an interpretation that completes the triangle of insight is scored as T/O/P. Examples are quoted in chapter 11. Finally, I think T/P interpretations are essentially what Strachey (1969) means by *mutative* interpretations, which—in one of the best known papers ever written on psychoanalytic technique—he argues are the essential therapeutic factor in psychoanalysis.

Thus, what has apparently been achieved in the present study is a scientific validation of a fundamental principle long held on clinical grounds for dynamic psychotherapy and psychoanalysis. This offers some hope to those psychotherapists who have despaired of ever demonstrating anything convincingly about their work; and some counterargument to those who have doubted the existence of specific factors in any form of psychotherapy, or the effectiveness of dynamic psychotherapy, or the validity of theories based on psychoanalysis.

14

Other Correlations

This is a chapter of miscellaneous items, but it contains some interesting observations, two pieces of light relief, and a final important section concerned with the quality of the evidence in this whole study.

EARLY TRANSFERENCE AND WORK ON TERMINATION

Reference to Table 6 will show that of all the transference variables studied on the first series, the highest correlation after further follow-up was given by the sum of the scores for the clinically judged "importance" of (1) *early transference* and (2) work on *termination* (for "psychotherapy," $\tau = +0.60$, $p = 0.006$, two-tailed test). This is an artificial variable, but it does give a measure of the patient's willingness to become involved (1) quickly, and (2) deeply in the relationship with the therapist. In the final summing-up in *SBP* it therefore played a considerable part in the unfiying hypothesis that *involvement* is a fundamental factor leading toward favorable outcome.

Nevertheless, I never set very much store by this variable, as is shown by the fact that I published only a table in which its relation to outcome could be judged by inspection, and apparently did not even calculate the correlation. Moreover, in the design for the present study, I did not arrange to have it rated blind by independent judges. It is interesting that if the results of further follow-up had been available at the time when this study was designed, I would have been forced to pay more attention to it, and might have taken less trouble over judging the transference/parent link, with a marked effect on the balance of the study as a whole.

In previous publications (Malan, 1973b and 1975) I have written that though in the second series neither of the two individual variables correlated significantly with outcome by itself, and though the sum of the two did not do so for brief psychotherapy, the sum almost did so for "psychotherapy" ($\tau = +0.22$, $p = 0.056$). Since then I have discovered a passage that I had overlooked in the therapy of one of the unsuccessful cases (Mrs. Hopkins), which clearly implies a single important moment of work on termination. This reduces the correlation well below significance (another example, I am afraid, of the sensitiveness of τ to changes in single scores). One of the important reasons for the relatively low correlations is that in four of the short successful cases (the Stationery Manufacturer, the Almoner, the Buyer, and Mrs. Morley) neither individual variable was important, and it is therefore clear that the kind of very rapid and deep involvement in the transference relationship that is measured by the two variables is not even approximately a necessary condition to successful outcome.

The data are shown in Table 26, and although the correlations are not significant, there are several features of interest:

1. The trend is fairly strongly in the expected direction.

2. The long cases score most highly on both of these two variables (this is, of course, not surprising for work on termination).

3. The false cases score very highly for early transference, but all four score zero for termination.

4. As always, the Dress Designer, who was wrongly assessed initially, stands out as a major exception, with maximum scores for both variables and a relatively poor outcome. If she is omitted, the correlation for the sum of the two variables for Patients A+B (N now being 29) is in fact significant.

In the end, especially since this is an artificial variable and since the judgments were made by myself single-handed, I have concluded that it is best to say that the original hypothesis has not been cross-validated. As will be discussed below, this means that the evidence in favor of the hypothesis about *involvement* is considerably weakened.

NEGATIVE TRANSFERENCE

As was described in chapter 11 of *SBP*, the clinically judged "importance" of negative transference, when compared with outcome, gave a distribution that suggested the hypothesis of the necessary condition; but when later therapy and outcome were both taken into account, this result was completely obscured.

TABLE 26. Scores on 3, 2, 1, 0 Scale for Importance of (a) Early Transference and (b) Work on Termination

Patient	Early transference max. 3	Work on termination max. 3	Early + termination max. 6
Short favorable			
Stationery manufacturer	0	0	0
Indian scientist	2	0	2
Almoner	0	1	1
Maintenance man	3	3	6
Gibson girl	3	1	4
Buyer	0	1	1
Zoologist	3	3	6
Pesticide chemist	3	0	3
Mrs. Morley	0	0	0
Mean	1.56	1.0	2.56
Long			
Personnel manager	3	3	6
Mrs. Craig	3	3	6
Mrs. Clifford	2	2	4
Car dealer	2	0	2
Playwright	0	2	2
Oil director	0	3	3
Dress designer[a]	3	3	6
Contralto	3	0	3
Mean	2.00	2.00	4.00
Omitting Dress designer "	1.85	1.85	3.71
False			
Mrs. Lewis	2	0	2
Au pair girl	3	0	3
Gunner's wife	3	0	3
Representative	0	0	0
Mean	2.00	0	1.00
Short unfavorable			
Cellist	1	0	1
Receptionist	1	1	2
Bird lady	2	0	2
Military policeman	1	0	1
Sociologist	3	3	6
Company secretary	1	0	1
Mrs. Hopkins	2	0	2
Factory inspector	0	1	1
Mr. Upton	0	0	0
Mean	1.22	0.56	1.78

[a] The only case definitely in the category of long, unfavorable, since the result of a protracted analysis in the Contralto was clearly highly favorable.

In *SBP* I did not feel equal to judging single-handed exactly which interpretations referred to "negative" transference and which did not, and therefore did not carry out the corresponding quantitative study; but, with greater experience, I did not see why this should not be done. On the second series, therefore, I carried out a content analysis of transference interpretations, defining any interpretation as "negative" that contained various aggressive words, ranging from such milder expressions as wanting to be "impolite," or to "rebel," or to "do things against authority," right up to "rage" or "fury" or "wish to kill." These were counted and, as always, divided by the total number of interpretations recorded, and then correlated with outcome.

The results can be dismissed quickly. Correlations for Patients A and A+B were positive but not significant; and since there were a number of successful therapies with a low emphasis on negative transference, the distribution did not even suggest the hypothesis of the necessary condition.

THE THERAPIST'S INVOLVEMENT

In *SBP* some emphasis was laid on the therapist's enthusiasm as a possible factor leading to success; although, of the two possible measures of this, the first gave a null result. If a number of *sessions of a particular therapy* are considered, there is little doubt that those with which the therapist is most satisfied tend to be the most fully recorded. It might therefore seem reasonable to suppose that if a number of *different therapies of a single therapist* are considered, those into which the therapist put most enthusiasm would be the most fully recorded; and, provided that differences between *individual therapists* averaged out over the whole sample, it might be expected that *fullness of recording* would correlate significantly with favorable outcome.

This expectation is not fulfilled. If *number of interpretations per session* is used as the measure of fullness of recording, then no such trend is discernible in the original series, neither in the overall sample, nor in the individual therapies of a given therapist. The result is the same in the second series.

The second measure of a therapist's enthusiasm comes from the chronological order of patients treated by a given therapist. There seemed considerable evidence from provisional data that each therapist showed a tendency to be successful on his first case, when his enthusiasm would be expected to be highest. The definitive data may now be studied in the two series combined. For this purpose I divided therapies into (1) eleven first cases, and (2) all other cases, and compared outcome in the two classes. What correlation was found was in favor of first cases, but it was very small ($\tau = +0.079$).

However, in studying the figures in detail I came upon a startling observation. Of the eleven therapists, six came from the Tavistock Clinic, and five from the Cassel Hospital. The scores for the eleven first cases are shown in Table 27. No prizes are offered for rediscovering my observation within five seconds.

This observation is best illustrated by means of a 2×2 diagram as in Figure 10.

This distribution is significant at the 1 percent level (Fisher test, two-tailed) whether the figure in the bottom left-hand corner is taken as 5 or 6.

What can this mean? Have we at last revealed a truth, presumably long regarded as self-evident in the Cassel Hospital, that, compared with Tavistock therapists, Cassel therapists have an overwhelming superiority?

Before reaching any such conclusion, however, we need to compare the results for the two groups of therapists omitting the first cases. This is still in favor of the Cassel but is now far from significant ($\tau = +0.22$, $p = 0.17$). In other words, the difference seems to be a special property of first cases. The Tavistock can breathe again.

It seems to me that this result has two possible explanations. The first is simply that it is due to chance and should be ignored. The second is as follows: The original team as founded in 1955 consisted entirely of Tavistock members. Between 1956 and 1959 the five Cassel members joined in ones and twos. These new members may well have felt that entering an already constituted group at another institution

TABLE 27. Outcome in First Case Treated by Each Therapist, Tavistock and Cassel Therapists Compared

Tavistock therapists	Cassel therapists
0	3.5[a]
1.5[a]	4
0	2.875
0	3.25
1.5[a]	2.833
(The 6th case failed follow-up after showing little improvement at termination)	

[a] I have given scores for the first series halfway between the upper and lower limits in order to make them easier to grasp.

Cassel	0	5
Tavistock	5 (or 6)	0
	< 2	> 2.5

Outcome

Figure 10. Outcome in first case treated by each therapist, Tavistock and Cassel therapists compared on 2 × 2 diagram.

was a major challenge, and thus may have been stimulated to put more into their first cases than members working on their home ground. If this is so, then we may possibly have still detected a favorable effect to do with therapeutic enthusiasm; but, of course, such a tentative speculation can be given very little weight.

THE RELATION BETWEEN WORKING THROUGH OF THE TRANSFERENCE AND BEHAVIOR OVER FOLLOW-UP

On p. 265 of *SBP* I published a table showing that optimum behavior in relation to the therapist after termination, which means *minimal dependence* accompanied by *willingness to return for follow-up*, was shown only by those patients with whom the therapist had laid most emphasis on interpreting the transference, i.e., those with high values of T percent in the content analysis. The figures were in fact so striking that I was convinced that this must be a valid observation. Of course, it is in full accord with what clinicians have always emphasized, namely, the importance of resolving transference before terminating.

In *SBP* the follow-up period was relatively short. Over the longer follow-up period in the second series, it has not been so easy to make judgments of gradations of behavior, and I have therefore simply judged whether behavior was optimal or not; the latter includes inability to terminate, and various degrees of acting out after termination, increasing to a maximum of refusal of follow-up altogether. In whatever way these factors are judged, however, no appreciable relation to T percent can be discovered.

It has to be remembered that conditions were different in the second study. The workshop disbanded in 1961, and therefore little systematic attempt was made to follow many of these patients up within the first few months and years after termination. When follow-up was finally attempted, usually more than five years after termination, problems of unresolved transference may well have been softened by the passage of time.

This conjecture is strengthened by our study of patients given group treatment at the Tavistock Clinic (Malan *et al.*, 1976). Here follow-up was very long indeed (range two to thirteen years, median seven years five months, since termination); and here many patients came back willingly for follow-up despite the fact that their feelings about their treatment were almost uniformly negative.

Apart from this consideration, therefore, one can only say that the original result has not been confirmed.

THE TRANSFERENCE/"OTHER" LINK AND LENGTH OF THERAPY

In chapter 21 I examined the relation between the *transference/ parent link* and *number of sessions recorded,* and, while examining the *transference/"other" link* as a control, inadvertently discovered that the latter gave a correlation that was enormously higher ($\tau = +0.52$, $p = 0.00007$, one-tailed.) The correlation with *actual number of sessions* is smaller but still very striking ($\tau = +0.43$, $p = 0.0007$). Now, whereas the transference/parent link refers largely to childhood, the transference/ other link refers largely to people in the patient's current life; but it is certainly not obvious why this link and length of therapy should be positively related.

In fact, the explanation becomes very clear when the individual figures are examined. The ten patients heading the rank order for T/O percent are shown in Table 28.

This table shows that, first of all, eight of the ten therapies were longer than the median; and, second, that of the ten patients involved: (1) all but one were married (the one living with a man is counted as married); (2) six were married women; (3) five of the married women were frigid (including Mrs. Lewis, who had been unable to allow consummation); while one of the three married men was impotent; and (4) the sixth married woman, Mrs. Clifford, clearly had severe problems in relation to her partner; as did the three married men.

In summary, nine of the ten patients had *marital problems;* and thus each of these nine therapies represents an attempt at dealing with a marital problem in *brief psychotherapy without treating the partner.* The high values of T/O percent are observed because, in each of these therapies, the therapist concentrated on making the link between the transference and the relation to the partner.

We may return here to problems of applying statistics to self-selected samples.

TABLE 28. Patients with the Highest Values of T/O%

Patient	Sex	Marital status	Complaint and other disturbances	T/O%	Number of sessions	Outcome
Mrs. Hopkins	F	Married	Frigidity.	19%	33	0.875
Mrs. Craig	F	Married	Frigidity.	17%	76	2.875
Mrs. Clifford	F	Single, living with a man	Quarrels with her "husband."	15%	90	2.75
Dress designer	F	Married	Panic attacks (frigidity).	15%	>200	1.25
Sociologist	F	Married	Spots on her neck, frigidity.	14%	26	1.25
Pesticide chemist	M	Married	Outburst of rage against his wife.	12%	14	2.5
Company secretary	M	Married	Indigestion, impotence.	8%	12	1.0
Mrs. Lewis	F	Married	Unconsummated marriage.	8%	20	2.833
Maintenance man	M	Married	Panic attacks (unable to handle his wife).	8%	30	3.0
Personnel manager	F	Single	Car phobia.	8%	62	3.25

Median number of sessions for Patients A + B = 19.5.

In a fully controlled study, where some variable A is deliberately manipulated in a random manner among a particular sample, if a correlation is found with some subsequent variable B, one may legitimately conclude that probably A influences B. Where the values of both A and B are the result of what may be called natural processes, a relation between them may be found not only for this reason, but also because B influences A, or because both A and B are influenced by C. Thus, when the relation between *T/P percent* and *number of sessions* is considered, it is probable that *number of sessions* influences *T/P percent;* when that between *T/O percent* and *number of sessions* is considered, probably *T/O percent* and *number of sessions* are both influenced by a third factor. This may be put in clinical terms as follows: When a therapist deals with a marital problem, he will tend to relate transference to the marital relationship; and he will also find, especially if he does not bring the partner into therapy, that the work will tend to be relatively long drawn out. It should be noted here that these therapies were undertaken at a time in the history of the clinic when conjoint marital therapy did not automatically come to mind in problems of this kind.

I give the above as a tentative clinical conclusion because the evidence is so striking; but it must be noted that there are definite exceptions. Thus, the Pesticide Chemist had only fourteen sessions, and the result was relatively successful, although the marital problem itself was less influenced than problems at work. Also, in the *SBP* series, the Neurasthenic's Husband gave a strikingly successful result in fourteen sessions, despite having a very severe marital problem.

THE PATIENTS WHO FAILED FOLLOW-UP

In almost all clinical research projects a certain proportion of patients become lost in one way or another, and most authors go through the ceremony of publishing statistics showing that there is no significant difference between these patients and those who remained, with the inference that the latter can be regarded as representative of the sample as a whole. It always seems to me that this is something of a wasted effort, because it ignores the fact that lost patients inevitably differ from the rest on crucial dynamic variables simply by virtue of the fact that they were lost. For instance, it is obvious that patients who drop out of treatment must have a lower motivation than those who stay, and those who accept follow-up must have a more positive attitude to their experiences in therapy than those who refuse. Even patients who cannot be traced will obviously contain a higher proportion who have not wished to remain in contact with their therapist after termination, the implications of which can be either positive (e.g., greater independence) or negative (e.g., unexpressed resentment).

In the present work, in addition to the thirty patients used in the statistical studies, there were the following: (1) One patient (Mrs. Curtis) who was followed up but was clearly not telling the truth and for whom no outcome score was considered possible, (2) seven who failed to answer letters or refused follow-up, and (3) one (the Manicurist) who could not be traced—in all, two women and seven men.

I have compared these nine patients with the thirty used in the statistical studies, using either τ or χ^2, on the following variables: motivation, focality, early transference + work on termination, T/P percent, number of sessions, age, sex, marital status, and "unsatisfactory termination."

Of these the only variable that shows a significant difference is *number of sessions*, which tended to be much smaller than in the patients followed up ($p = .02$, one-tailed). The essential factor in this result appears to be the fact that all the eight longer-term patients accepted follow-up. This is perhaps not surprising, since most of these patients were at least intermittently in touch with their therapists over a number of years, and one of course (the Contralto) was still in treatment. Therefore, this result may really give more information about the long-term patients than about those who failed follow-up.

It may be remembered (see the last section but one) that if failed follow-up is taken as one aspect of unsatisfactory behavior over follow-up, then no relation could be found with T percent, i.e., *emphasis on transference interpretations during therapy.*

The end result is that comparison of these nine patients with the thirty used in the statistical studies provides hardly any information of value.

MORE LIGHT RELIEF

In Figure 11 a mysterious but genuine variable X is plotted against outcome for Patients A+B, giving a striking positive correlation ($\tau = +0.31$, $p = 0.01$, one-tailed). This needs to be "back cross-validated" on the first series; but the result is a positive correlation that is far from significant. Nevertheless, examination of the scatter diagram reveals that a single patient, clearly badly selected for this particular variable, makes a major negative contribution to the correlation. When this patient is omitted, τ becomes $+0.32$, $p = 0.07$ for $N = 15$, i.e., nearly

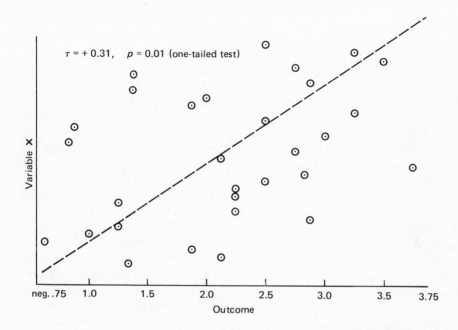

Figure 11. Variable X—outcome second series, Patients A+B ($N=30$).

significant. It seems unlikely that such a result can be without clinical meaning, and in fact I think this can be found.

Freud once said that being his mother's favorite son had given him a start in life that could never be annulled by subsequent events, and which he implied had carried him through many of the difficulties that he subsequently met. The patients who score highly on X are those who, in many situations, would be expected to be given priority over their less fortunate fellows; and it seems likely that this has given them a self-confidence that has helped to carry them through the difficulties and vicissitudes of therapy to an ultimately successful outcome. This justifies the use of the one-tailed test above. Moreover, a clear-cut reason quickly comes to mind for the negative contribution of the one patient in the first series; this patient was discovered by accident, during the follow-up period, to have been adopted, so that his "natural" name, so to speak, was not the name by which he was known. It is clear that he must have always unconsciously known that the priority given to him was falsely based.

This is an important result, as it gives an easy and entirely objective criterion for selecting patients for brief psychotherapy. Indeed, it could be used even before the patient arrived at the clinic, thus saving hours of tedious clinical assessment.

The variable? Alphabetical order.

A NOTE ON CORRELATIONS AND CHANCE

The above piece of self-parody in fact has intensely serious implications. During the course of the previous chapters I have mentioned the following striking observations that I believe to be—possibly or probably—due to chance:

1. The much more satisfactory therapeutic results in the second series (significant at the 1 percent level by the t test, two-tailed).

2. The fact that only one patient with a *passage of time* (consultation to follow-up) of less than six years scored more than 2.5 for outcome.

3. The fact that in the first series at later follow-up *recent onset* correlated significantly *negatively* with outcome ($p < .01$, two-tailed test).

4. The fact that Cassel therapists did significantly better than Tavistock therapists on their first cases.

5. Finally, the extraordinarily high correlation between outcome and *alphabetical order*.

In any research project involving correlations, as Goldstein, Heller, and Sechrest (1966) point out, the total number of correlations calculated ought to be published so that the reader can judge the probability of obtaining a number of "significant" correlations by chance alone. Obviously, if a hundred correlations are calculated, it is probable that about five will be obtained that are significant at the 5 percent level, including one that is significant at the 1 percent level.

In the present work I have calculated *several hundred* correlation coefficients. This means that drawing conclusions from correlations that are significant, but have not been cross-validated, is very hazardous, however strongly they may fit in with clinical reasoning. Here we only need to mention the relation between *transference orientation* and *behavior after termination* in the first series, which was both so striking and made such complete clinical sense that I could not believe that it was not genuine. I think I still believe this result, but I cannot justify such a view, since the relation was not cross-validated in the second series.

This leads at once to the original unifying hypothesis that emerged from the first series, according to which the major favorable prognostic factor was *involvement* in the therapeutic process on the part of both therapist and patient. This relied on the fact that favorable prognostic factors in the patient were: motivation, early transference, feelings about termination, and the transference/parent link; while therapists appeared to do best on their first cases, when presumably their enthusiasm was highest. One of the features that convinced me that what I was observing in the first study did not simply consist of random patterns made meaningful by retrospective reasoning was the fact that all the significant correlations appeared to fit in with this basic hypothesis that made such complete clinical sense. It now begins to wear a bit thin: Motivation and the transference/parent link seem to remain important, but the hypotheses about early transference, termination, and "first cases" have not been cross-validated. When we come to consider, in the next chapter, the unifying factor underlying the evidence as it stands at present, we need to temper enthusiasm by remembering both the partial failure to cross-validate the hypothesis about involvement, and the fascinating result on alphabetical order.

It is therefore quite clear that only those hypotheses that have been cross-validated can be regarded as conclusions; the rest are, I am afraid, "interesting, possibly chance observations" (Sullivan *et al.*, 1958) that need to be tested out on a third series.

15

The Evidence and Its Implications

We are now in a position to review the whole evidence and to examine its practical and theoretical implications.

The main favorable prognostic factors have been found in aspects of the following: (1) motivation, (2) focality, and (3) the emphasis on the transference/parent link. This evidence needs to be summarized in an easily digested form.

Motivation and focality present a problem. The significant correlations with outcome occur in contacts 5 to 8, and therefore a reasonable measure of these variables would be the sum of the scores given by both judges during these four contacts. However, four patients withdrew before contact 8 and therefore cannot attain maximum scores. I therefore decided to use the scores over the whole period, contacts 1 to 8, for all thirty patients; and, with the four patients who withdrew, to increase their scores proportionately as if they had stayed for the full eight contacts. These are highly conservative operations, both having the effect of *reducing* the correlations with outcome.

It is now possible to assign a rank number to each of the thirty patients on each of the three prognostic factors; and then, by summing the rank numbers, to obtain an overall rank order for the combination of all three factors.

There is, of course, nothing startling in the fact that the correlation of this overall rank order with outcome is highly significant; if one combines three significant correlations, one is likely to obtain a further significant correlation. However, close study yields several extremely interesting observations, which have surprisingly deep implications about selection criteria, mechanisms of improvement, and the question of specific versus nonspecific factors in psychotherapy. In Table 29 the overall rank is shown in relation to *length of therapy* and *outcome,* while in Table 30 the patients have been rearranged into the four categories and the rank order has been reduced to a 3, 2, 1, 0 scale (with 3 implying high-ranking and 0 low-ranking) in order to make it easier to grasp.

THE LONG CASES

These two tables show some striking features concerning the long cases: (1) Of the nine patients ranking highest for the sum of the three factors, four are short favorable and five are long. (2) The mean rank of the long cases is higher than that of the short favorable cases. (3) The Dress Designer, whose rank number for outcome is twenty-fourth out of thirty, ranks highest of all on the prognostic factors.

This immediately reveals a negative result of great practical and theoretical significance: that these prognostic factors do not distinguish between those patients who give favorable results in brief therapy and those who will need longer therapy. The practical implication is that *these prognostic factors cannot be used in selection to eliminate the long cases;* the theoretical implication is that *therapeutic mechanisms are the same whatever the length of therapy.*

Now, as far as the practical issue of selection is concerned, it may be remembered that in chapter 10 I reported the observation that the longer cases tended to show high-motivation/low-focality; but in fact this is essentially a statistical result, and it only applies clearly to two of the long cases individually, the Personnel Manager and the Contralto. If criteria are to be found to predict the long cases, then they must be found outside the factors being considered here.

In fact, such criteria are not hard to find, and come from (1) psychopathology and (2) life situation. The data are shown in Table 31.

Thus, seven of the eight long cases showed deep-seated pathology and/or were tied in a disturbed relationship to another person, only the Oil Director being excluded. Although some of the short favorable cases also showed one or other of these features (notably the very severe pathology in the Stationery Manufacturer and Mrs. Morley), it is quite clear that when such features are found, they must serve as a warning that therapy, though it may be successful, will probably not be brief.

THE FALSE CASES

Reference to Table 30 will show that the false cases obviously rank at least as low as the short unfavorable cases in terms of the sum of these

TABLE 29. Overall Rank Order for Motivation + Focality + T/P%

Patient	Length of therapy	Outcome	Patient	Length of therapy	Outcome
Dress designer	Long	Unfavorable	Zoologist	Short	Favorable
Mrs. Clifford	Long	Favorable	Gunner's wife	Short	False
Maintenance man	Short	Favorable	Buyer	Short	Favorable
Almoner	Short	Favorable	Au pair girl	Short	False
Mrs. Craig	Long	Favorable	Company secretary	Short	Unfavorable
Pesticide chemist	Short	Favorable	Car dealer	Long	Favorable
Oil director	Long	Favorable	Playwright	Long	Favorable
Indian scientist	Short	Favorable	Mrs. Morley	Short	Favorable
Personnel manager	Long	Favorable	Mrs. Lewis	Short	False
Factory inspector	Short	Unfavorable	Receptionist	Short	Unfavorable
Stationery manufacturer	Short	Favorable	Mrs. Hopkins	Short	Unfavorable
Gibson girl	Short	Favorable	Military policeman	Short	Unfavorable
Cellist	Short	Unfavorable	Bird lady	Short	Unfavorable
Contralto	Long	Unfavorable	Sociologist	Short	Unfavorable
Mr. Upton	Short	Unfavorable	Representative	Short	False

Mean rank numbers

Short favorable ($N=9$)	11.2
Long favorable ($N=6$)	8.25
Long unfavorable ($N=2$)	7.5
False ($N=4$)	22.5
Short unfavorable ($N=9$)	21.4

TABLE 30. Motivation + Focality + T/P% (Reduced to a 3, 2, 1, 0 Scale) in the Four Categories of Patient

	Mot + foc + T/P% (3, 2, 1, 0 scale)		Mot + foc + T/P% (3, 2, 1, 0 scale)
Short favorable		**Long unfavorable**	
Stationery manufacturer	2	Contralto	2
Indian scientist	3	Dress designer	3
Almoner	3	**False**	
Maintenance man	3	Mrs. Lewis	0
Gibson girl	2	Au pair girl	1
Buyer	1	Gunner's wife	1
Pesticide chemist	3	Representative	0
Zoologist	1	**Short unfavorable**	
Mrs. Morley	0	Cellist	2
Long favorable		Receptionist	0
Personnel manager	2	Bird lady	0
Mrs. Craig	3	Military policeman	0
Mrs. Clifford	3	Sociologist	0
Car dealer	1	Company secretary	1
Playwright	1	Mrs. Hopkins	0
Oil director	3	Factory inspector	2
		Mr. Upton	2

TABLE 31. Factors in Long Cases

Patient	Factors in psychopathology	Factors in life situation
Personnel manager	Deeply depressive problem presenting as a simple phobia.	Living in an extremely tense situation with her mother, who was completely dependent on her.
Mrs. Craig	Depressive, frigid.	Inadequate husband.
Mrs. Clifford		Severe marital problems.
Car dealer		Severe marital problems.
Playwright	Very deep-seated character disorder.	
Oil director		
Contralto	Deep-seated inability to form real relationships, relieved only by a prolonged analysis.	
Dress designer	Extremely deep-seated pathology involving problems of identity, presenting as an apparently simple phobic state.	Frigid, marital problems.

prognostic factors. This can be illustrated even more strikingly by calculating the mean value of each of the individual factors for each category of patient. The details are shown in Table 32.

Although, since the numbers are so small, this table can only be suggestive, the following features stand out: (1) the long cases rank *higher* than the short favorable cases on motivation and T/P percent, thus confirming that these prognostic factors do not distinguish patients who will need longer therapy. (2) The false cases rank *lower* than the short unfavorable cases on motivation, and come closer to these cases on all three factors, thus confirming that they resemble the short unfavorable rather than the short favorable cases despite their relatively high scores for outcome.

It is also worthwhile bringing in some marginal evidence about the false cases from two sources. The first consists of the "dynamic" selection criteria judged by Dreyfus and Shepherd, blind, on the consultation and projection test only, usually the first two contacts. These factors can be said to represent various aspects of the patient's initial willingness to work in interpretative therapy. Of these, initial motivation gave a correlation with outcome of $\tau = +0.21$, $p = 0.07$; and the sum of all four dynamic criteria gave $\tau = +0.20$, $p = 0.07$ (one-tailed test in both cases). The mean values in the four categories of patient are shown in Table 33.

This table shows that the false cases rank lowest (or lowest equal) on all four of these dynamic criteria.

The second source of evidence concerns the twin factors *early transference* and *work on termination*. It may be remembered that in the first series the sum of the scores for these two factors correlated most highly with outcome of all factors studied; while in the second series the correlation was positive but not significant. These factors represent a measure of the patient's willingness to involve himself (1) quickly and (2) deeply in the transference relationship. It is now found that the false cases rank highest equal (with the long cases) for *early transference*, but lowest of all four categories (all four individual patients in fact scoring zero) for *work on termination*.

Now all these factors can be arranged in chronological order. The *initial selection criteria* were judged (usually) from the *first two contacts*; early transference was judged from the *first four contacts* (excluding the projection test); *motivation* and *focality* from the *first eight contacts*; *T/P percent* from the *whole therapy* (or all that was recorded in the long cases); and *work on termination* mostly from the *end of therapy*. We can now make the following statements, on average, about the false cases:

That they started by showing the least willingness to work in

TABLE 32. Mean Values of the Scores for the Three Prognostic Factors in Four
Categories of Patient

Category	Motivation (max. 10)	Focality (max. 8)	T/P%
Short favorable	6.64	5.39	8.14%
Long	7.10	4.26	10.6%
False	4.15	4.13	3.76%
Short unfavorable	5.28	3.51	3.14%
Long nearer to:	Favorable	Unfavorable	Favorable
False nearer to:	Unfavorable	Unfavorable	Unfavorable

Rank orders				Sum of rank numbers	Overall rank
Short favorable	2	1	2	5	2
Long	1	2	1	4	1
False	4	3	3	10	3
Short unfavorable	3	4	4	11	4
Long nearer to:			Favorable		
False nearer to:			Unfavorable		

TABLE 33.   Mean Values of Initial "Dynamic" Selection Criteria as Judged by Dreyfus and Shepherd

Category	Initial motivation max. 3	Manner of cooperation max. 3	Contact, response to interpretation max. 4	Ability to find a focus max. 2	Sum max. 12
Short favorable	2.11	1.83	3.0	1.11	8.05
Long	2.19	1.37	2.56	1.00	7.12
False	1.37	1.00	2.25	1.00	5.62
Short unfavorable	1.83	1.22	2.56	1.11	6.72
Long nearer to:	Favorable	Unfavorable	Unfavorable	Favorable	Unfavorable
False nearer to:	Unfavorable	Unfavorable	Unfavorable	Unfavorable	Unfavorable
Rank orders					
Short favorable	2	1	1	1=	1
Long	1	2	2=	3=	2
False	4	4	4	3=	4
Short unfavorable	3	3	2=	1=	3

interpretative therapy; nevertheless, there was some tendency for two positive features to be shown, namely, that the therapist was able to discover a focus early, and the patients showed a fair response to focal transference interpretations in the initial stages; but that these factors failed to lead to an increase in motivation or to much involvement with therapy; that there was no true working through of the transference/ parent link; and, finally, that a feeling of loss at termination was never an important issue. The above statements are true individually of Mrs. Lewis, the Au Pair Girl, and the Gunner's Wife; while the Representative did not show even the two positive features shown by the others (early focus and early transference) and broke off treatment prematurely, as did the Au Pair Girl and Gunner's Wife.

Now, it may be remembered that the first time these four cases were singled out from the others was in chapter 6, when events leading to improvement were being considered. Mrs. Lewis and the Gunner's Wife both showed minimal improvement at termination, and the final improvement only occurred at about six and seven years later respectively; the Au Pair Girl showed symptomatic improvement at termination, but a severe relapse about two years later, leading to a situation worse than when she came for therapy, and she only improved three or four years after termination. In each of these cases, the final improvement could be attributed to some factor in the patient's life experience. Finally the Representative broke off treatment after three sessions, unequivocally making a flight into health. Nevertheless, he did receive an important piece of insight that apparently enabled him to break the vicious circle of his social and sexual anxieties. This purely clinical evidence, taken by itself, suggested strongly that in these patients there was little justification for attributing the improvements shown to any true working through of their problems.

To this can now be added the statistical evidence: It is now possible to show that in the majority of this sample of thirty patients there is a clear trend, in which certain prognostic factors tend to lead to more favorable outcome; and that these four patients, already picked out on clinical grounds, show these factors to a very limited degree, and clearly stand out from the other patients as anomalous. Even without clinical considerations, therefore, the evidence is quite strong that in these four patients some different kind of therapeutic mechanism is involved; and now when the clinical evidence is brought in, it points strongly to the likelihood that in three patients at any rate this mechanism involves mainly *maturation through life experience*. In other words, we have probably identified at least three cases showing what is more loosely called *spontaneous remission*.

"EXCEPTIONAL" CASES

When I plotted the rank order for the sum of the three main prognostic factors against outcome for the whole sample, I came upon a further important observation. This was that there were other patients who stood out as anomalous, in addition to the false cases, and that *most of these patients could be seen clearly to be also exceptional on purely clinical grounds.* Further investigation showed that this observation could be seen even more clearly if the overall rank order for motivation + T/P percent (i.e., omitting focality) was used. This variable is plotted against outcome in Figure 12.

In the scatter diagram two arbitrary lines have been drawn. The patients outside these lines stand out as anomalous. In the six who lie to the right of the lower line, outcome is *more* favorable than the prognostic factors would predict. Three (Mrs. Lewis, the Au Pair Girl, and the Representative) are false cases and have already been fully discussed. One (the Indian Scientist) was suffering from an Oedipal problem and was not exceptional in any way. However, both of the other two (the

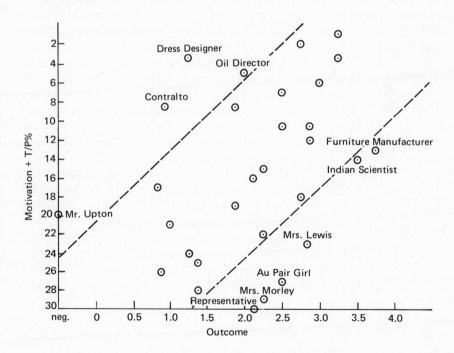

Figure 12. Motivation + T/P% ranked—outcome.

Stationery Manufacturer and Mrs. Morley) were regarded as severely disturbed, and with both a carefully superficial technique was used with success. The Stationery Manufacturer was potentially psychotic; while Mrs. Morley was a woman in her sixties judged to be in danger of a severe depressive breakdown, for which the word "psychotic" was also used. Thus, both were clearly exceptional on clinical grounds alone.

With patients to the left of the upper line, outcome was *less* favorable than the prognostic factors would predict. Again there is one patient (the Oil Director) who was not exceptional in any way. However, all three of the others were incorrectly assessed at the beginning and were suffering from far more deep-seated disturbances than was originally realized: the Contralto, for whom the original plan was simply to work through her identification with her father, was eventually found to be suffering from an inability to form real relationships of any kind and was taken into a prolonged analysis; the Dress Designer, who presented as a simple phobia, was found to be suffering from an extremely deep-seated disturbance involving fears of loss of identity; and Mr. Upton, who presented as a simple problem of growing up, was found at follow-up to be showing bisexual, manic-depressive, and possibly borderline features. (The graph of *all three* factors plotted against outcome shows exactly similar features, but since the overall correlation is higher, there are fewer anomalous patients. Again, however, the Stationery Manufacturer, Mrs. Lewis, and the Representative appear to the right of the lower line; and the Dress Designer, the Contralto, and Mr. Upton to the left of the upper line; while the only patient to appear who is not exceptional on clinical grounds is the Factory Inspector, where a highly dynamic therapy failed to lead to a satisfactory result.)

The meaning of these observations can be formulated as follows:

The three factors, motivation, focality, and the transference/parent link, can be regarded as examples of a number of possible measures of "dynamic interaction." It now appears that in the majority of therapies in this sample—e.g., those lying between the two lines in Figure 12—*outcome* and *dynamic interaction* are roughly proportional to one another. On the other hand, there are a number of patients who give results that fail to conform, in one direction or the other, to the trend shown by the remainder. Most of these are patients who can be seen clearly on clinical grounds to be different from the majority of patients in the sample. Thus, the entire body of data provided by these thirty cases can be shown to make clinical sense.

There is a further consequence that is of even greater importance, which may be introduced as follows:

The variable *motivation* was specifically defined as *motivation for insight based on psychodynamic understanding; focality* is a measure of the therapist's ability to make use of a therapeutic plan or focus *based on psychodynamic understanding*, and included the patient's response to this focus; and the working through of the *transference/parent link* is the *specific* therapeutic factor emphasized above all by many writers on the technique of psychoanalysis and psychoanalytic therapy.

From these two series we thus seem to have come upon something for which the world of psychoanalysis has been waiting ever since Freud's original discoveries, namely, *strong research evidence for therapeutic factors specific to psychoanalytic therapy.*

OVERALL VIEW OF THERAPEUTIC MECHANISMS; SPECIFIC AND NONSPECIFIC FACTORS

It will be remembered that in at least three of the four false cases we appear to have identified therapeutic mechanisms that come under the heading of "spontaneous remission." In a previous research project (Malan *et al.*, 1975) we have attempted to study this phenomenon more systematically. We originally started with the hypothesis that untreated patients would never show the quality of improvements that we would wish for in patients who had been given dynamic psychotherapy. This hypothesis received a rude shock. Of forty-five patients who had been assessed at the Tavistock Clinic but had never received treatment, we found *eleven* who would score 2.0 or more for outcome on the scale used for the present study, and two who would probably score at least 3.5. We then came upon a totally unexpected observation: that in nine of these eleven patients clear evidence could be found for *therapeutic effects arising from the single diagnostic interview.* We had thus rediscovered the existence of one-session psychotherapy.

Intensive study of these nine one-session patients enabled us to make a very clear formulation of some of the therapeutic factors at work. The part played by the single diagnostic interview appeared to show a complete spectrum: from being a minor contributory factor in the improvement, to being the turning point in the patient's whole life. In many cases there was clear evidence for features that would be classed as "spontaneous remission" as well. But the essential point relevant to the present discussion is that in one case only had there been any evidence for transference interpretations (and this patient showed the least improvement), and the transference/parent link was almost certainly never mentioned at all in any of these cases. Moreover, since the majority of these patients *rejected offers of therapy*, their motivation can be said to be zero. In other words, in these cases there appear to be entirely different kinds of therapeutic mechanisms at work, which do not involve the same dynamic interaction as seems to have been the main factor operating in the two brief therapy series.

We thus seem to have reached very important evidence on the controversy between specific and nonspecific factors in psychotherapy. First we have observed the one-session series, in which the important factors seem to have been, for instance: (1) normal maturation, (2) finding a satisfactory marital partner (both of which may be called "spontaneous remission"), (3) the patient's realization that he must take responsibility for his own life (which can be either a mechanism in spontaneous remission or a "nonspecific" effect of psychotherapy), and (4) insight of an entirely nontransference kind (a more "specific" factor in dynamic psychotherapy, but still not *the* specific factor). Now, in the brief therapy series, we continue the spectrum, which can be seen to overlap with the one-session series: (1) maturation in response to life events (the Au Pair Girl and Gunner's Wife), (2) the patient's taking responsibility for his own life (shown in fact by the Cellist), (3) nontransference insight (the Representative, Mrs. Morley), (4) the transference/parent link without any measure of dependence on the therapist (the Almoner and Pesticide Chemist), and finally (5) the deep working through of the transference/parent link, including a strong measure of dependence (the Personnel Manager).

The evidence suggests that all these factors can be therapeutic, and that their relative importance in any given sample of patients will depend on methods of selection and often purely upon chance. It so happened that in the first brief therapy series (1) there were apparently *no* cases of powerful nonspecific factors at work, and (2) the only patients who showed major improvements were those who had undergone *complete transference therapies*, including much work on the transference/parent link and usually involving dependence and the working through of feelings about termination. In the second brief therapy series the situation was different and a far wider spectrum of therapeutic mechanisms appeared. However, (1) the operation of "spontaneous remission" was not sufficiently important to swamp the evidence on specific therapeutic factors; (2) the operation of *insight of all kinds* appeared in the statistics through the factors of *motivation* (for insight) and *focality* (the giving of insight on a particular theme); (3) *dependence*, such a powerful factor in the first series, was not sufficiently wide-spread in the second series to appear significantly in the statistics; and finally (4) the *transference/parent link* is apparently of such crucial importance in this type of therapy that it was able to over-ride all the other factors and appear strongly in the statistics of both samples. These observations illustrate, incidentally, both the complexity of the problems that we encounter when we undertake psychotherapy research, and the extent to which research projects are at the mercy of random and unforeseeable factors in the samples under investigation.

The evidence therefore finally suggests a very clear position on the controversy about specific versus nonspecific factors in psychotherapy. There is no question but that psychoanalysts have to abandon their belief—shared by myself ten years ago—that a patient can *only* "get well" through deep insight, or the working through of his conflicts in the transference relationship. There is now conclusive evidence—from behavior therapy, from assertive training and social retraining, from our own study of one-session patients, and from the present series—that all-pervading changes can follow from the direct attack on symptoms, or from life events. However, from these two brief therapy series, there is now almost conclusive evidence that the element that psychoanalysts have always regarded as the cornerstone of their technique, and of their theory about technique, in fact operates as a very powerful therapeutic factor as well. It could be said, perhaps, that one of the best ways of resolving controversies is to show that both sides are right.

16

The Question of the Validity of Psychotherapy

It remains to try and draw together the overall implications of this pair of studies.

The framework within which *SBP* was written was the investigation of evidence about the *conservative* and *radical* views of selection criteria, technique, and outcome in brief psychotherapy. Shades of opinion covering a wide spectrum, many of them in complete contradiction to one another, could be found scattered everywhere throughout the literature. On the one hand, it was said that only the least ill patients could be helped; the technique should be superficial and should contain no reference to the transference; and results were only palliative. On the other hand, it was claimed that severe psychopathology could be substantially modified by a technique using transference freely, and containing most of the essential elements of psychoanalysis itself.

In *SBP* I examined these mutually incompatible views systematically as they applied to our own patients. The result was that not only on all three major headings, but on every subheading also, the radical view was overwhelmingly supported:

For selection critieria, neither severity of pathology nor chronicity of symptoms seemed to be contraindications in themselves, and the only criterion that seemed to be of value was motivation for insight. For technique, not only could transference be used freely, but the best results were obtained when the transference was linked to feelings derived from childhood. For outcome, the results could be long-lasting and apparently deep-seated.

In the present study, these results have been entirely confirmed. Insofar as psychopathology is concerned, the following can be said: that once those patients have been eliminated for whom inevitable dangers are forecast, there appears to be no statistical relation between outcome and severity of pathology; and moreover, the patient in the second series with probably the most severe pathology gave what appears to be the best therapeutic result. It is quite clear that with careful selection and skilled technique, severe pathology is in itself no bar to brief therapy. Insofar as duration of symptoms is concerned: In the first series, after further follow-up, the statistical relation with outcome lies in the opposite direction to that predicted by the conservative view; and though in the second series it lies in the expected direction, it is far from significant; and again motivation for insight seems to be the main relevant factor. Insofar as outcome is concerned, there is no doubt that many of the results are long-lasting; and, insofar as quality is concerned, they appear to be indistinguishable from what would be expected if neurotic conflicts were truly resolved.

It surely is therefore not too much to say that *the conservative view of brief therapy has been disproved.* Opinions based on this view should really disappear from the literature from now on, never to return; but it is probably too much to hope that they will.

At a similar point in my previous book I gave a summary of the factors that seemed to lead to favorable outcome, which may be put as follows: (1) High motivation in the patient; (2) high enthusiasm in the therapist; (3) early transference; (4) the transference/parent link; and (5) work on termination.

I saw in this the crystallization of a single unifying factor, which can be reformulated as *intense involvement, on both sides,* in the therapeutic relationship.

In the second study, all these factors have been examined, and where new factors or patterns have been found, they have been examined retrospectively on the first series. We now need to consider the status of all these factors in the two studies taken together. The answer varies in an interesting way from one factor to another:

1. *Motivation* comes near to being cross-validated (see below for a full discussion of this).

2. The evidence in favor of *high enthusiasm in the therapist* has become doubtful (but see chapter 14) and this factor is best abandoned.

3. and 5. In the first series the composite variable *early transference + work on termination* correlated most highly with outcome of all factors studied; but in the second series the correlation, though strongly posi-

tive for the whole sample, was not significant. The importance of these two aspects of involvement has therefore not been entirely confirmed.

4. On the other hand, the importance of the *transference/parent link* appears to have been fully confirmed.

6. Finally a new factor, *focality*, appears to be both highly related to outcome in the second series, and also related to motivation in a highly meaningful way. However, study of the same variable in the first series does not entirely confirm these observations, and further study on other series is clearly indicated.

Now, motivation and the transference/parent link certainly imply *involvement* on the part of the patient; but the evidence on motivation and focality presented in chapter 10 suggests the importance of a somewhat different factor, namely, *successful dynamic interaction* between patient and therapist, a factor that is also certainly contained in the transference/parent link. It is therefore this factor that now brings all the evidence together.

The meaning of this term "successful dynamic interaction" is best approached from a purely clinical and subjective point of view, by stating what it is that a therapist would most like to find when he works with any particular patient in any form of psychoanalytic therapy, including full-scale analysis. This can be put as follows: He wants a patient who has a wish to understand himself and who quickly establishes a therapeutic alliance. This is precisely what we mean by motivation. He wants to see clear and understandable themes in the patient's material, to be able to put his understanding to the patient in the form of interpretations, and to see the patient genuinely confirm these interpretations and work with them further, thus cementing the therapeutic alliance. This is precisely what we mean both by focality and by the interaction between focality and motivation. Finally, he wants to see the patient develop transference feelings, and to be able to demonstrate by interpretation that these feelings repeat a pattern derived from the past. This is precisely what we mean by the transference/parent link.

It now seems from the present study that all these factors are associated with improvements found at follow-up many years later. In other words, the whole evidence converges toward suggesting both the validity of some of the fundamentals of psychoanalytic or psychodynamic theory and the effectiveness of dynamic psychotherapy.

What about the scientific status of this conclusion? What are the reservations, and the possible fallacies and pitfalls?

First, it must be said that, in order to obtain the significant correlations in *both* series, it was necessary to count the results of medium-term therapy (forty to one hundred sessions) as they stood, and not to regard them as failures of brief therapy. This was an alteration in the method of scoring, and there is no question that every time such an alteration is made the evidence is weakened. In fact, the result of this may be that one is no longer justified in using the word "cross-validation." Nevertheless, it does make complete clinical sense to score in this way, as it suggests that the longer brief therapies, medium-term therapies, and long-term psychoanalytic therapies all form a continuum in which the same fundamental psychoanalytic principles apply. The discontinuity apparently occurs only when we reach the ultra-brief (e.g., one-session) therapies, where principles such as the importance of transference interpretation no longer hold true.

Something more can be said about the question of cross-validation. This work provides some fascinating examples of the interaction between statistical evidence and clinical judgment; one could say, of the principle that statistics, the blind servant, should be treated as such and not regarded as a master. The first example concerns motivation, about which, because of its complexity, I could in the first series only make an overall intuitive judgment, taking into account especially its fluctuations in the first few therapeutic sessions. These intuitive judgments appeared to show a strong relation to outcome. In the second series motivation could be judged in a far more formal and objective way. Again it was found to show a significant correlation, though only in the fifth to eighth contacts. This would seem to have confirmed the original finding. However, when the same formal method was then used on the original sample, the correlation found in the second sample essentially failed to be confirmed. Yet, the fact remained that an intuitive judgment in the first sample was confirmed by formal methods in the second. All this adds up to a strange kind of incomplete cross-validation, the scientific status of which may well be a matter for disagreement.

Another example both of incomplete cross-validation and of the interaction between clinical judgment and statistical evidence occurred in connection with the transference/parent link. At the time when *SBP* was written the correlation between T/P percent and outcome in the first series was significant by the two-tailed test. When the results of later follow-up became available, the correlation was no longer significant by the two-tailed test, though it remained significant by the one-tailed test. Yet, strictly speaking, it was necessary to use the two-tailed test, because the original study was carried out as an attempt to distinguish between (1) the conservative view that transference interpretations were harmful, and (2) the radical view that they were an important element in therapeutic technique—i.e., no prediction had been made beforehand of whether the correlation would be positive or negative. I was then threatened with getting involved in some of the niceties of statistical philosophy: Since by now it has become so clear that the conservative view is utterly mistaken, surely it might be justified to use the one-tailed test in both samples? But this would be a retrospective judgment only reached when the results on the first sample became available . . . and so it goes on. In fact, I was saved from this because the hypothesis of the *necessary condition* was supported by the figures, the three therapies ranking highest for T/P percent also ranking highest for outcome. Yet, in the second series the *correlation* was significant, while the hypothesis of the necessary condition became much more doubtful, since of the two therapies that ranked highest for outcome, one showed a low value for T/P percent (3 percent) and the other showed a value of *zero*. Thus, the final result is that the patterns in the two series are not the same, the hypothesis of the *necessary condition* being supported in the first series, and the *correlation* in the second. Again, perhaps it is not justified to use the term cross-validation, but I hardly think this matters. What does emerge is that T/P interpretations appear to have a *powerful association with favorable outcome in both series*.

The interaction between clinical judgment and statistical evidence came about as follows: Clinical judgment convinced me that the transference/parent link was the crucial factor in technique in the first series, and much of the replication was therefore designed around a study of this variable. Yet, in fact the composite variable "early transference + work on termination" correlated more highly with outcome; but I was naturally suspicious of this artificial variable and never even calculated its correlation at the time. If I had had the results of later follow-up I would have been forced to pay attention to it, since the effect of later follow-up was to increase further the correlation shown by "early + termination" and to decrease that shown by the T/P link. Yet, when these variables were studied in the second series, it was only the T/P link whose importance was confirmed, so that clinical judgment was entirely vindicated. All this indicates the crucial part that clinical judgment can play in research, sometimes justifiably over-riding the formal statistical evidence.

Returning to reservations and fallacies, the second main objection to this pair of studies is that they were "naturalistic" and not truly controlled or "experimental." There was obviously no possibility, for instance, of allocating patients at random to two different forms of therapy, in only one of which was the transference/parent link allowed to be interpreted. When a variable under study is the result of self-selection, as it was here, various possible fallacies are allowed to creep in. Critics often point out to me a fact of which I am only too well aware, and about which I have written many times, namely, that the interpretation of correlations in terms of cause and effect is a hazardous occupation, beset with pitfalls. In the present example, could it be not that *dynamic interaction* causes *favorable outcome*—the most obvious explanation of the correlations—but either that *favorable outcome* in some way causes *dynamic interaction*, or simply that both are associated with some unknown third factor? Such critics have too often failed to think the situation through. What one needs to say to them is that in face of the overwhelming support derived from clinical experience for the obvious explanation, combined with the justification for this view embodied in years of psychoanalytic theory, they must offer not simply an *alternative* explanation but a *more plausible* explanation. Let us take the two main alternative types of explanation in turn. I do not see any plausible means by which favorable outcome should cause greater dynamic interaction; improvements in all cases *followed* dynamic interaction, they did not precede it. On the other hand, a theoretical justification can be found for the possibility that both improvement and dynamic interaction are associated with a third factor. The most likely explanation of this type is that the interaction with the therapist is an example of the patient's *general capacity for interaction*, and that it is interaction in his relationships *outside* therapy, rather than *within* therapy, that is responsible for the improvements. But this argument ends up as a boomerang that threatens to come back and strike the thrower, because if it is correct, why should interaction *with the therapist* not be responsible for part of the improvements also? In fact, what this explanation suggests is that some of the mechanisms of psychotherapy and of "spontaneous remission" are essentially the same, a view which I would wholeheartedly subscribe to.

There is one final argument that needs to be mentioned. In many controlled studies of psychotherapy, differences found at termination between treated patients and controls have disappeared at follow-up. The most likely explanation for this is that the effects of therapy have been swamped by those of life experience. In the present study the median number of sessions was 19.5, while the median length of follow-up lay between five and six years. Obviously, the number of experiences available to the patient outside therapy was incomparably greater than within therapy. If therapy has no effect, why should any correlations be found at all? Indeed this argument suggests that therapeutic factors in this kind of therapy are *extremely powerful* and themselves swamp the effects of life experience for many years after termination.

So we come to the end of this prolonged and intensive labor. Surely it can hardly be denied that the result has been strong circumstantial evidence for the validity of dynamic psychotherapy. Here it needs to be said once more that circumstantial evidence is not to be despised; that certainty in science is rarer than is commonly supposed, and the compulsive search for it may be self-defeating; and that important advances are not necessarily made by crucial experiments alone.

References

ALEXANDER, F. (1957). *Psychoanalysis and psychotherapy*. London: George Allen and Unwin.

BENE, E. (1965). On the genesis of male homosexuality: An attempt at clarifying the role of the parents. *Brit. J. Psychiat.* **111,** 803.

BERGIN, A. E. and STRUPP, H. H. (1972). *Changing frontiers in the science of psychotherapy*. Chicago: Aldine.

BIEBER, I. (1962). *Homosexuality*. New York: Basic Books.

BROWNE, S. E. (1964). Short psychotherapy with passive patients. *Brit. J. Psychiat.* **110,** 233.

CAMPBELL, J. (1973). We have ways of making you behave. *London Evening Standard,* 6th June.

COURTENAY, M. J. F. (1968). *Sexual discord in marriage*. London: Tavistock.

GELDER, M. G., BANCROFT, J. H. J., GATH, D. H., JOHNSTON, D. W., MATHEWS, A. M., and SHAW, P. M. (1973). Specific and non-specific factors in behaviour therapy. *Brit. J. Psychiat.* **123,** 445.

GLOVER, E. (1955). *The technique of psycho-analysis*. London: Baillière, Tindall and Cox.

GOLDSTEIN, A. P., HELLER, K., and SECHREST, L. B. (1966). *Psychotherapy and the psychology of behavior change*. New York: Wiley.

KENDALL, M. G. (1955). *Rank correlation methods*. London: Charles Griffin.

KERNBERG, O. F., BURSTEIN, E. D., COYNE, L., APPELBAUM, A., HORWITZ, L., and VOTH, H. (1972). Psychotherapy and psychoanalysis. Final report of the Menninger Foundation's Psychotherapy Research Project. *Bull. Menninger Clinic* **36,** 3.

LUBORSKY, L. (1962). Clinicians' judgments of mental health. *Arch. Gen. Psychiat.* **7,** 407.

LUBORSKY, L., SINGER, B., AND LUBORSKY, L. (1975). Comparative studies of psychotherapies: Is it true that "Everybody has won and all must have prizes"? *Arch. Gen. Psychiat.* **32,** 995.

MALAN, D. H. (1959). On assessing the results of psychotherapy. *Brit. J. Med. Psychol.* **32,** 86.

MALAN, D. H. (1963). *A study of brief psychotherapy*. London: Tavistock. Philadelphia, Lippincott. Republished by Plenum Press, New York 1975. Referred to in the text by the initials *SBP*.

MALAN, D. H. (1973a). The outcome problem in psychotherapy research: A historical review. *Arch. Gen. Psychiat.* **29,** 719.

MALAN, D. H. (1973b). Therapeutic factors in analytically oriented brief psychotherapy. In: *Support, innovation, and autonomy* (ed. R. H. Gosling). London, Tavistock.

MALAN, D. H. (1975). Psychoanalytic brief psychotherapy and scientific method. In: *Issues and approaches in the psychological therapies* (ed. D. Bannister). London: Wiley.

MALAN, D. H. (1976). *The frontier of brief psychotherapy*. New York: Plenum Press.

MALAN, D. H., BACAL, H. A., HEATH, E. S., and BALFOUR, F. H. G. (1968). A study of psychodynamic changes in untreated neurotic patients. I. Improvements that are questionable on dynamic criteria. *Brit. J. Psychiat.* **114**, 525.

MALAN, D. H., BALFOUR, F. H. G., HOOD, V. G., and SHOOTER, A. M. N. (1976). A long-term follow-up study of group psychotherapy. *Arch. Gen. Psychiat.* **33**, (in press).

MALAN, D. H., HEATH, E. S., BACAL, H. A., and BALFOUR, F. H. G. (1975). Psychodynamic changes in untreated neurotic patients. II. Apparently genuine improvements. *Arch. Gen. Psychiat.* **32**, 110.

MENNINGER, K. (1958). *Theory of psychoanalytic technique*. New York: Basic Books.

PHILLIPSON, H. (1955). *The object relations technique*. London: Tavistock; Glencoe, Illinois: The Free Press.

RACHMAN, S. (1971). *The effects of psychotherapy*. Oxford: Pergamon.

SIFNEOS, P. E. (1965). Seven years' experience with short-term dynamic psychotherapy. In: *Selected lectures, 6th International Congress of Psychotherapy, London, 1964*. New York: S. Karger.

SIFNEOS, P. E. (1968). The motivational process: A selection and prognostic criterion for psychotherapy of short duration. *Psychiat. Quart.* **42**, 271.

STRACHEY, J. (1969). The nature of the therapeutic action of psycho-analysis. *Int. J. Psychoanal.* **50**, 275.

STRUPP, H. H. (1974). Toward a reformulation of the psychotherapeutic influence. *Int. J. Psychiat.* **11**, 263.

STRUPP, H. H. and BERGIN, A. E. (1969). Some empirical and conceptual bases for coordinated research in psychotherapy. *Int. J. Psychiat.* **7**, 18.

SULLIVAN, P. L., MILLER, C., and SMELSER, W. (1958). Factors in length of stay and progress in psychotherapy. *J. Cons. Psychol.* **22**, 1.

WOLPE, J. (1958). Psychotherapy by reciprocal inhibition. Stanford: Stanford University Press.

Index